THE NEW WINTER SOLDIERS

A volume in the series
PERSPECTIVES ON THE SIXTIES
Edited by Barbara L. Tischler

The New Winter Soldiers

GI AND VETERAN DISSENT DURING THE VIETNAM ERA

Richard R. Moser

 RUTGERS UNIVERSITY PRESS

New Brunswick, New Jersey

Library of Congress Cataloging-in-Publication Data
Moser, Richard R., 1952–
    The new winter soldiers : GI and veteran dissent during the
Vietnam era / Richard R. Moser.
       p.   cm.—(Perspectives in the sixties)
    Includes bibliographical references and index.
    ISBN 0-8135-2241-2 (cloth : alk. paper)—ISBN
0-8135-2242-0 (pbk. : alk. paper)
    1. Vietnamese Conflict, 1961–1975—Protest movements—United
States.   2. United States—Armed forces—Political activity.
3. Soldiers—United States.   4. Vietnamese Conflict, 1961–1975—
Veterans—United States.   5. Veterans—United States.   I. Title.
II. Series.
DS559.62.U6M67 1996
959.704'373—dc20   95-4631
                                                   CIP

British Cataloging-in-Publication information available

Dedicated to the memory of

John Beaudin
Mark Bradley
Joe Burke
Clarence Fitch
Bob Mihalko
Harold Poor
Elroy Schultz

Contents

Acknowledgments

In the course of writing this book I have acquired many debts. I must first acknowledge the friends and teachers who introduced me to this topic a long time ago. I often think of Mr. Richard Connelly, a Vietnam veteran who came to New Jersey to teach at Neptune High School in 1969. His Volkswagen van sported a large peace sign, and he gently told us that the war in Vietnam was not such a good idea. Mr. Connelly's long hair, tinted glasses, and controversial ideas lost him his job, but made some of us think. As the years passed, I heard more stories from Steve Shuey, Guy Osmer, and other veterans, that convinced me that a rich history of soldier and veteran dissent existed.

It was not until 1985, when confronted with a master's thesis at Montclair State College, that I first began systematic research on soldier and veteran war resistance. Joseph Moore ably guided my work as I started what would become a ten-year project.

When I returned to Rutgers University the following year, I found a community of friends, activists, and scholars who believed that ideas really mattered and could maybe even change the world. Although too numerous to mention by name, the people who created New Brunswick's thriving political and cultural life gave me a chance to experiment with ideas and actions. Special thanks go to the Court Tavern and its fine staff. The Court became a cultural center in the great tradition of working-class taverns where people were free to talk and think, and to celebrate life. I spent many a night in its warm refuge.

This book began as a doctoral dissertation, and I hope it does justice to the efforts of the Rutgers history department. I would especially like to thank Paul Clemens, John Gillis, David Oshinsky, Mary Ann Holtsclaw, Dee Garrison, Michael Adas, Muriel Clawans, Norman Markowitz, Richard McCormick, and Lloyd Gardner for their support and instruction. I am also indebted to the Center for the Critical Analysis of Contemporary Culture, also at Rutgers, for lively weekly seminars and a generous fellowship during 1989–90. My training at Rutgers entirely reshaped my thinking, and I am grateful for those years of discussion and inquiry.

In particular, I would like to thank John W. Chambers for his detailed commentary on every phase of my dissertation. Dr. Chambers lead me through the new military history and forced me to refine and refocus my direction. Cynthia Enloe offered a number of insightful criticisms that helped me navigate some difficult issues, including those of war and gender. Allen Howard taught me the enormous scholarly potential of oral history. Philip Greven's teaching and writing repeatedly raised the question of continuity and change in ways that deeply touched my own thinking. I was also privileged to learn from Jackson Lears and

Jim Livingston. Their conversation and conflicts about history inspired and educated me. From his personal knowledge of military dissent, Lears encouraged me to reclaim the liberating potential of patriotism and military culture. Livingston wisely guided me through both the very practical and sublime obstacles I encountered in writing this book. He helped me face perhaps the most pressing question of politics and history: How can we, given the very disfigurement of our fallen condition, still find sources of freedom, redemption, and dignity? I hope the story of the soldier and veteran peace movements can offer some small beginning.

I would also like to thank my colleagues at Middle Tennessee State University for their support. Research funds and release time generously granted from both the history department and University Faculty Research Committee allowed me the time necessary to complete my research and prepare the manuscript for publication. Philip Stankiewicz and Jonathan Beach helped with the daunting tasks of checking citations and proofreading.

The archivists at Fisk University, the Tamiment Library at New York University, the State Historical Society of Wisconsin, and Indiana University, Bloomington, were models of efficiency and cooperation. Alyson Wiecek was an industrious and capable research assistant. I would like to thank Marlie Wasserman, Barbara Tischler, and Leslie Mitchner at Rutgers University Press for their enthusiasm, support, and recommendations, helping me plot the course for turning a dissertation into a book.

My deepest appreciation goes to the veterans themselves. They are wise and patient teachers. I am particularly grateful to Dave Cline for his strong support of this project, willing cooperation with many phases of the research, and inspiring political vision. Gerry Gioglio helped with thorough comments on an early version of the manuscript. In our many conversations Ed Sowders offered much good advice and prodded me to get beyond the formal GI movement. Without the assistance of Annie Luginbill and Jess Jesperson some of my best research would not have been done. Barry Romo, Charles Shaughnessy, and Jan Barry also helped me with critical phases of the work. W. D. Ehrhart read the entire manuscript and offered much-needed criticism and comments. And, of course, I am indebted to all past and present members of the Vietnam Veterans against the War, Veterans for Peace, and Vietnam Veterans of America who contributed to this project. Without their words this book could not have been written.

I also need to thank a special group of veterans who do not appear in this book but helped me in ways I am sure they are unaware of. As I traveled around the country, I invariably met veterans who verified for me the pervasiveness of military discontent. For their hospitality and help I would like to thank Kip Price from West Virginia (thanks too for the great fishing on the New River); Zeke Smith, probably still commuting between Arizona and Montana; Black Bart from around Fairplay, Colorado; Mr. Hill from outside of Arcata, California, who offered his home to me and other participants in Redwood Summer; and the pilot from White Rock, New Mexico, who quietly told me over breakfast about the tragic consequences of his massive firepower.

For advice and other help I also thank Albert Valeri, Don Eastwood, Wendell and Laura Etienne, Judith Choamsky, Gabrielle Wilders, Jim Robinson, Peter Irons, Chuck Winants, Dennis Greely, Robert Glover, and Pershing Anderson. I would like to give special thanks to David and Paula Antebi, who have long inspired me by their example.

Through all the years of study, research, and writing my family has been there. My father and mother, Robert and Jean Moser, helped me as much as they possibly could and more than anyone could ever ask or repay. In addition to her editorial work on the entire manuscript, her patience, and moral support, I am forever grateful to my wife and partner Mary Luceri for the way her powerful love and joy for living always inspires my own.

I hope this book can be accepted as payment for such risky investments from so many people. Otherwise I am afraid I find myself with debts no honest man can pay.

Nashville, Tennessee
July 1995

Introduction

Historically, veterans have always been used to convince the next generation to fight in the next war. . . . Vietnam is when all that history changed. Now they're trying to rewrite that!
—DAVE CLINE, VIETNAM VETERAN

THE HISTORY of the modern United States turns on the history of war: the Spanish–American War, the Philippine Insurrection, World War I, the Central American campaigns, World War II, the Cold War, the Korean conflict, and the war in Vietnam. All these wars changed people and history, but the Vietnam era changed the way wars change us.

The most divisive event of recent American history, the Vietnam War threatened to dissolve the political and social bonds that held American society together. In that great upheaval millions of Americans created political movements that attempted to recast American society in a new light. At the center of the Vietnam crisis stood a powerful figure generating social change and cultural transformation: the antiwar soldier and veteran. This book is about the soldier and veteran movements for peace and justice and the cultural changes that are the legacy of those movements. It tells a story of how antiwar soldiers and veterans created dissident political movements and what these unique struggles for peace mean within the larger contours of American history and culture.

To tell this story I need to go well beyond a conventional recounting of the collapse of the American war effort. Journalists, historians, political analysts, social critics, and retired military officers have all documented the failure, decline, collapse, or fragmentation of the American effort, or the political will, or the cultural world that created the war. In these accounts, soldier dissent is conventionally thought of in terms of defeat and declining morale.[1] Understandably, almost all the historical scholarship on Vietnam has an overwhelmingly critical thrust, focusing on what went wrong.

Instead, *The New Winter Soldiers* seeks to understand how thousands of American soldiers and veterans created something good from what was one of the worst experiences of their lives. I am interested in how the Vietnam experience prompted the reconstruction and transformation of American political beliefs and cultural traditions. The primary thesis of this book is that antiwar soldiers and veterans, inspired by the social and cultural upheavals that created the war's context, produced a new cultural form of immense historical importance—the figure of the new winter soldier. The new winter soldier came to life as dissident soldiers and veterans collectively reconstructed and transformed the heroic tradition of the American citizen–soldier into a new model of citizen activism for peace, empowerment, and justice.

This transformation of military culture offers a viable and constructive alternative to both the existing order and to existing strategies for social change. As such, the military antiwar movement and the creation of the new winter soldier ranks among the most significant recent developments of the American political tradition.

I propose then to tell a story about social action, collective consciousness, and the historical consequences of this war against war. This book is about ideas-in-action; in it I assume that all people are philosophers: "A spontaneous philosophy which is proper to everybody," is contained in language, common sense, and religious beliefs—indeed in all the assumptions, prejudices, feelings, and ideas that guide society.[2] In every human act ideas weigh in. I have set before myself the task of discovering the philosophy of soldiers—as soldiers—and how the ideological and cultural crisis of the Vietnam War was shaped by and influenced their changing conceptions of self and society.

The history of the soldier and veteran movements also challenges our collective memories about Vietnam. Trauma shapes memory in curious ways, and Vietnam was a national trauma of immense proportions. For many, Vietnam seemed so jarring, so outside of the expected patterns of American history, that as soon as the fighting finished, a decade-long amnesia ensued. When the clouds cleared in the early 1980s, Vietnam was increasingly remembered as a noble cause, lost only because we fought with one hand tied behind our back. This new memory recalled the Vietnam War as America's other wars had been remembered, justified and moral with the sole important question being how to achieve victory. The story of the soldier and veteran peace movements were forgotten, however—lost in the period of amnesia.[3]

The New Winter Soldiers is about those lost memories and forgotten voices. It is based on the recollections and words of people who fought two wars; first the war in Vietnam, then, as veteran William Crandell claims, "a second tour as citizen–soldiers in an effort to end an unjust war and bring their brothers and sisters home."[4] The memories of the antiwar soldiers offer us vitally important lessons about war. Steve Tice saw combat in the 101st Airborne Division and now works as a veterans' counselor. He gives voice to the memory of the antiwar veteran.

> It is increasingly popular now for government officials, media, and the public, and Vietnam vets themselves, to say the lesson of Vietnam is: never again shall we fight a war without going all out. We already knew that about war. That's not the lesson. . . . The lesson of war is very simple—the lesson of war is no more war. . . .
>
> It is time to care for and nurture each other and our planet. It is time to search for and find peace within ourselves.[5]

For Tice and the many other soldiers and veterans we will hear from in this book, the battlefields have shifted. The struggle now is to "nurture each other and our planet," and to turn from the fear of enemies beyond our borders to the "search for . . . peace within ourselves."

The contest over the memory of Vietnam is such a highly charged and compelling debate because in its outcome lies the way we view war, peace, and America itself. The stakes are high. Although the United States has already fought a war to kick the Vietnam syndrome, the military antiwar movement suggests that it is not the memory of Vietnam we need to abolish but rather unjust war and its causes.[6]

Unlike other wars, Vietnam issued a serious challenge to the existing cultural strategies for making war and glorifying military ideals. Significantly, the challenge came from the very heart of the military culture and the traditions that moved it. With unprecedented scope and consequences, approximately 20 percent of Vietnam-era soldiers and veterans actively resisted the conflict in which they fought. Along with other social movements of the day, the military peace movement helped to create political and cultural alternatives to war and empire. The overriding purpose of this book is to articulate those alternatives as they existed in the actions and ideas of the soldier and veteran movements.

The Vietnam War and the military resistance to it were of historic proportions in the usual sense of influencing other events and changing the course of history. But it is even more important to understand that events of the Vietnam era radically remade the idea of American history itself. We have been trained to remember American wars in relation to the three most formative struggles of the country's military and national past. The most influential conflicts in American history were the many wars of the frontier. That centuries-long process of conquest and expansion exerts a truly mythic power by setting the cultural standards to which all other wars are compared and understood. In the context of the frontier myth, America fought a special mission to civilize wayward people, make barren lands productive, and ensure the tranquility of home and hearth.

Although the Vietnam War was largely conceived of as the latest battle for a "New Frontier," a significant minority of soldiers and veterans began to act in the tradition of America's other primal struggles: the American Revolution and the Civil War.[7] Remembered by dissident veterans for their promise of freedom and ideals of equality rather than their military exploits, the American Revolution and Civil War became potent sources of criticism and models for alternatives to the war in Vietnam.

> The whole world is rising up following the same ideas that we put forward in 1776, and from the French Revolution. The Democratic revolution initiated a period of revolution. Those ideas are heard in the Third World as well as in Europe.[8]

Those ideals were first articulated in the Declaration of Independence, and the Constitution—particularly the Bill of Rights—then recast in the Gettysburg Address. This story of revolution claims that freedom, equality, justice, democracy, and the right to revolution are the universal values that guarantee the right of every nation to self-determination. The upheavals of the Revolution and Civil War also created a powerful cultural figure, the citizen–soldier. Part history, part myth, that figure embodied the aspiration for freedom in the actions and ideals of the common people. Citizen–soldiers fought freedom's battle for the nation, and won liberty and political power for themselves and their communities. The political ideals of freedom and the military ideal of the citizen–soldier were the raw materials from which Vietnam-era soldiers and veterans would fashion a new kind of peace movement.

When antiwar soldiers used the ideals of the American revolutionary tradition to contest the legitimacy of the war in Vietnam, they necessarily transformed their understanding of the past and their vision of the future. And, because our view of history is so central to how we perceive ourselves, we might say that the changes embodied by the military peace movement represent a leap, a sea change, that recast the most fundamental assumptions from which American national identity was structured.

In the 1960s and 1970s this changing sense of history and identity was acted out most powerfully through the struggles of the new social movements. Conflicts over issues of class, race, age, gender, and sexuality opened up many pathways to an antiwar and anti-imperial consciousness. For working-class soldiers issues of economic justice, such as war profiteering, cued dissent. Racial consciousness catalyzed the opposition of African American, Latino, Asian, and Indian antiwar soldiers against another war targeting people of color. For women and gay soldiers the macho mentality of the military first sounded the alarm against war. Teenagers sent to war condemned an illegitimate authority that exploited the young and powerless. Although the relationships between the military antiwar movement and other social movements were sometimes strained and contentious, these movements provided both critical insights and organizing principles for the military peace movement.

It may surprise some readers that radical organizations and left-wing political parties play a minor role in this account of military dissent. This book is about changes in popular consciousness and the way in which American historical traditions both shaped and were transformed by the soldier and veteran revolt. The political character of the military resistance had little to do with any existing leftist organization or strategy. Although many veterans came to consider themselves leftists, radicals, or revolutionaries, and several leftist organizations did attempt to influence soldiers and veterans, the Left failed to recognize the emerging revolutionary perspectives that the veterans themselves were creating. Whether because of ideological rigidity or organizational priorities, leftist groups practiced their politics in ways that rendered much of their activity with veterans or soldiers marginal in the long run.

It is my argument that the American citizen–soldier ideal was the most important ideological reference for antiwar soldiers. Socialism, feminism, black nationalism, the youth movement, and pacifism, as represented by social movements and communities, were critically important as available examples of the ideals of freedom and equality.

The crisis of Vietnam revealed to the antiwar soldiers that the ideals they so deeply believed in were made tangible only by the movements for peace and justice. The social movements began to represent the good of the nation to the antiwar soldiers. The military antiwar movement fused the ideals of the American Revolution, embodied in the citizen–soldier, with the peace and justice movements of the period. This fusion between cultural materials central to American identity and the social movements suggests that the developments of the 1960s represented a rebirth of American culture and the universal values it claims to represent.

Today, the cultural changes that were both cause and effect of soldier resistance continue to reshape our understanding of American history, military traditions, and the consequences of modern warfare. The military has remained an important indicator of social change. African Americans, women, and gays have all made claims for equality within the armed forces. Antiwar veterans and the peace movement generally continue to be outspoken voices against unconstitutional and unjust military adventures. The legacy of the Vietnam War and the 1960s remains one of the most powerful influences shaping contemporary culture.

The aftershocks of the Vietnam era continue to polarize America, if not always in sharp political showdowns, then as a slow, simmering cultural civil war. The history of the GI and veteran movements enables us to understand how that cultural crisis started, why its conflicts have been so enduring, and, most important, what political and cultural alternatives exist for Americans as we approach the twenty-first century.

Two recent events bear on the history presented in this book. The first is Robert McNamara's belated admission that the war in Vietnam had been ill conceived and tragically wrong. One certainly wishes that McNamara had acted as the new winter soldiers had: protesting the war while there were still lives to save in Vietnam. Yet McNamara has added new historical evidence and reinvigorated an important debate that may yet shape policy and prevent future military misadventures. He is the only high-ranking official to publicly apologize and hold himself accountable for America's war in Vietnam. Whatever our misgivings about McNamara's actions, then or now, we must welcome every opportunity to collectively confront the past.

The second event is the terrorist bombing of the federal building in Oklahoma City and the subsequent political debut of the right-wing militia movement. We need to reckon with the militia movement's claim that they are the inheritors of the citizen–soldier legacy.[9] *The New Winter Soldiers* presents the history of a vastly different development in American soldier traditions—one that turned paranoia, hate, and the glorification of weapons and war into citizen activism for social justice and peace. There are other variations of the soldier ideal present in the contemporary United States, but the right-wing militia and the new winter soldiers stake out opposing positions in the cultural war over the meanings and possibilities that remain within American military traditions.

Our story begins in the present. Chapter One describes a new Veterans' Day celebration that veterans in Wisconsin have held for over a decade. Based on personal observations, oral history accounts, audio recordings, photographs, and newspaper articles, the story I tell is a composite account drawn from selected years since the ceremony first began in 1983. This ceremony, which honors the warrior but not the war, embodies the newborn traditions still being nurtured by the veterans' antiwar movement.

Chapter Two introduces the cultural history of the military peace movement. It is important to understand the interaction between the historical events of the Vietnam experience and the transformations in worldview that military resistance created. I organize these changes in consciousness by referring to the notion of a "soldier ideal." The soldier ideal is a powerful cultural construction that in many historical forms has stirred people to action. I argue that the American soldier ideal exists in the tension between two opposing visions: a dominant vision of a fighter rooted in the experience and culture of the frontier and empire, and an alternative, yet equally compelling, figure of the citizen– soldier produced by the great upheavals of the American Revolution and Civil War. By investigating military sociology, basic training, film, and oral history, I try to reconstruct the soldier ideal as it was embraced by the young people who would later go to Vietnam.

The next four chapters present the history of the soldier and veteran resistance against the war in Vietnam. This military peace movement was a key feature of the collapse of American armed forces in Vietnam. The abundance of examples and events in these chapters, while only a fraction of the historical record, are a necessary reply to the forms of collective memory and amnesia that influence our understanding of the Vietnam era.

Chapter Three takes us to Vietnam and the GI resistance to war. The dozen major incidents of combat refusal mentioned in this chapter were only the more dramatic expressions of the pervasive failure to obey orders to engage the enemy. Explosive prison rebellions shook the already-eroding foundations of military discipline. Fragging—attempts to wound or kill officers—occurred over a thousand times. These desperate acts only suggest the degree to which the command structure failed to function. The soldier antiwar resistance also hampered war operations through a widespread, unorganized, and spontaneous pattern of quiet resistance. Perhaps most important, soldier identity and action were being transformed by antiracist, anti-authoritarian, and antiwar sentiments shaped by the dramatic political and cultural developments of the period.

Chapter Four presents the GI movement beyond the theater of war. In the United States, Germany, Japan, and on the sea lanes, the GIs responded to the war with a rich repertoire of protest and resistance, giving voice to their own concerns and demonstrating solidarity with the civilian antiwar movement.

Over 250 underground newspapers and dozens of dissident soldier organizations articulated the democratic movement of resistance that touched tens of thousands of soldiers.

Chapter Five discusses the veteran antiwar movement. The Vietnam Veterans Against the War (VVAW) was the first organization of Vietnam veterans and became the primary force of the veterans' movement. Free from military restraints, the veterans articulated a broad and mature vision of peace and social justice.

Chapter Six provides a summary and evaluation of soldier and veteran dissent as social movements. Approximately 20 percent of all Vietnam-era service members took some part in the movements for peace and justice. Their activism influenced and represented the political climate of America's working-class and minority communities.

Chapter Seven concludes the book by looking at the ways American military culture was fragmented and transformed as a result of the Vietnam experience. Under the historical conditions of the Vietnam War the soldier ideal of popular consciousness was fundamentally altered. This transformation in consciousness represented elements of both continuity and change. For the antiwar soldier, the values of the fighter were destroyed or discredited, while the core ideals of the citizen–soldier struggled to find a new life. Combat in Vietnam destroyed any recognizable or compelling image of warrior heroism and so demanded a revolution of values. The struggle for peace became the "moral equivalent of war." This multifaceted soldier ideal served, then, both as incentive for young Americans to fight in Vietnam and as a new model of antiwar heroism. In Vietnam-era America, the new winter soldier became the only historically available enactment of the classic American citizen–soldier. I will also suggest that this new soldier figure transcends the old soldier ideal because it implies new universal forms of heroic action in the civil struggles for peace, power, and a whole earth. Taken together, these transformations were the emerging moves of an alternative yet characteristically American culture.

The best-known and most important work that this book takes as its point of departure is Robert J. Lifton's *Home from the War*, published in 1973. Lifton employed a psychohistorical analysis inspired by participation in "rap groups" organized by the VVAW. Based in part on the soldier ideal, Lifton explored the psychological struggles of Vietnam veterans. *The New Winter Soldiers* complements Lifton's work by moving through the more American, historical, cultural, and political aspects of soldier consciousness, toward the archetypal categories that also concern Lifton.

The collection of oral histories by active-duty conscientious objectors in *Days of Decision* by Gerald Gioglio exemplifies the changes I am trying to explain in historical and cultural terms. An indispensable resource, the work also suggests some of the themes concerning patriotism and heroism that I have found compelling. I am also deeply indebted to David Cortright's *Soldiers in Revolt*, published in 1973. As participant–observer, Cortright documented the breadth and scope of military resistance, providing an important point of departure for the history of the military antiwar movement. Important recent work on GI resistance has been published by *Vietnam Generation*, including Harry W. Haines's insightful introduction, Barbara L. Tischler's ground-breaking research on GI newspapers, and Skip Delano's helpful bibliography. Several good short studies, including one by veteran activist William F. Crandell, were recently published in *Give Peace a Chance*, edited by Melvin Small and William D. Hoover.

Although I have utilized none of the near mountain of evidence presented by fictional rendering of the Vietnam War, I hope my argument has absorbed some of the insights offered by writers and critics. When antiwar veterans created 1st Casualty Press in 1972 and published *Winning Hearts and Minds: War Poems by Vietnam Veterans*, they helped to initiate one of the most remarkable developments in recent American literature. W. D. Ehrhart, Lamont Steptoe, Tim O'Brien, and many, many others have created an enduring body of poems and stories that convey the complex human dimensions of the Vietnam experience. Thomas Myers, John Hellman, Lloyd Lewis, and others have applied social criticism and literary theory to stories told about Vietnam.[10] They analyze the powerful forces of fragmentation and dissolution that Vietnam writers have crafted into their remarkable reworking of existing poetic and literary forms. Philip D. Beidler's *Re-Writing America* comes closest to capturing the transformative changes I also seek to explore.

I also hope to join the debates presented in the growing literature on the protest movements of the 1960s and 1970s. I find of particular interest the works of Charles DeBenedetti and Charles Chatfield on the antiwar movement; Sara Evans on the women's movement; Clayborne Carson on civil rights; and Wini Breines, Todd Gitlin, and Ron Grele on the student New Left. These writers have created a body of exemplary histories that both appreciate the complexities of social movements and extend the political vision of their historical subjects.[11]

Another trend is important to my analysis of Vietnam-era history. Beginning in the late 1970s, so-called revisionist accounts of the war began to appear. The works of Norman Podhoretz and Guenther Lewy typify this type of historical writing on Vietnam.[12] These works are the formal historical expression of a powerful new memory that recalls the war as a noble cause, consistent with an understanding of America as a nation destined to deliver a unique moral righteousness to the world. This historiography became widely accepted and harmonized well with the political ethos of the Reagan and Bush administrations. However, these stories have generally omitted or marginalized soldier and veteran dissent, and I hope my work will challenge the conclusions of these historical accounts.[13]

My primary goal is to articulate an alternative history represented by antiwar veterans. I use the words of some of the seventy-five people I have interviewed, and the scores of veterans who have left their stories in oral history archives, underground newspapers, books, and magazines. It is with this historical material that I hope to contribute to a philosophical project begun by William James.

In "The Moral Equivalent of War," James struggled to give peaceful and productive form to the enduring human fascination with war. James's wisdom rings true to our time. Real peace, if we are ever to achieve it, must be wrested from war; it must be created from the disintegration and transformation of the war culture itself.

Happy Veterans' Day

1

We gather together to share the healing energy which is generated by this ceremony. To call forth the spirits of the dead and to resurrect the hopes and the dreams of the living. To feel the support of our community around us and to help us assure that the lessons so painfully learned by these veterans shall never be forgotten or repeated. The veterans here tonight span three generations of men and women who were asked to sacrifice their lives for you and the ideals of freedom.
—SUKIE WACHTENDONK, AGENT ORANGE ACTIVIST

SINCE THE EARLY 1970s, Veterans' Day has been a focus of activity for dissident Vietnam veterans. Today, the Vietnam Veterans Against the War (VVAW) and the Veterans for Peace (VFP) continue this twenty-year tradition of making Veterans' Day a day to honor the warrior but not the war. The Veterans' Day ceremony held by the VVAW chapter in Madison, Wisconsin, is perhaps the most striking example of this new tradition. For more than a decade the people of Wisconsin have gathered together in solidarity using song and words to create a powerful ceremony that mends the wounds of war but does not ignore its costs.

The ceremony takes place on Madison's high ground. Built on an ancient Indian council site, the Wisconsin state capitol building dominates the landscape and provides a dramatic setting for Veterans' Day. The rotunda of this grand and stately Greco-Roman monument has the same wondrous feel as the national capitol building—it creates a sweeping, elevated space with crystal-clear acoustics. In four huge glass mosaics, colossal figures representing Government, Legislation, Justice, and Liberty preside over the scene from above.

As dusk becomes night, a large crowd fills the rotunda. Hundreds have come from around the state to pay their respects and to participate. Pastor, World War II veteran, and former POW Wells Grogan opens the ceremony. Grogan evokes the original meaning of Veterans' Day, with its long-overdue promises. Originally called Armistice Day, November 11, 1918, marked the end of World War I—an end to the war to end all wars and to make the world safe for democracy. Like the first Armistice Day, this Veterans' Day ceremony also commemorates war with the hope for peace in a democratic world.

Grogan intones the traditional introduction, "In the eleventh hour of the eleventh day of the eleventh month in 1918, the bullets stopped. The guns were laid down, and the war to end all wars was finished." Beside him a tall, thick, white candle on a wooden stand lends a sacramental touch. As Vietnam veteran John Zutz approaches the candle, the sound of distant church bells, rung for the ceremony, filters into the rotunda. As Zutz begins to speak, the audience rises.

As we remember all of our nation's veterans we especially remember those who . . . lost their lives, or pieces of their minds or bodies. . . . We remember especially the thirty-seven Wisconsin men who are still missing in action in Vietnam along with the thousands of MIAs of our nation who served during World War I, World War II, and Korea.

I shall light the candle . . . to symbolize the hope . . . that not another family will ever . . . suffer through the ordeal of knowing that a loved one is missing in action or a prisoner of war. And to symbolize the hope that the day may come when there will be no veterans anywhere in the world because there are no more wars.[1]

Zutz lights the candle, its solitary flame offering atonement and hope. He continues:

Let us not forget that every war claims lives on all sides, including the lives of countless civilians, whether they be men, women, or children. No one detests war and has a stronger desire for peace than those who have served and survived our nations' wars. Peace sometimes seems like an elusive dream. We are here tonight because we believe that peace is possible. We believe that wars should become obsolete. This dream will only happen when each of us makes or renews a commitment to work for peace. We can each do that tonight for ourselves and most importantly for our children and the children of the world.[2]

As the audience sits, the rotunda fills with the sounds of singing and drumming. Every year a group of Indian musicians comes to sing, dance, and offer their help for Veterans' Day. They bring with them their own traditions for honoring warriors and healing wounds.[3] Over the years people from many different tribes have come to play: the Chippewa, Menominee, Oneida, Stockbridge–Munsee, and Winnebago. Tonight, Percey Miner, Nathan Decoreh, and the Thundercloud brothers, all from the Winnebago Nation, have brought their voices and drums to sing the "honor song." Morgan Whiteagle, a Winnebago elder, looks on as they perform.

Circles of sound rise and fall in the rotunda's open space: voices, drumbeats, and echoes merge in the dome above. Over and over the voices chant and the drummers pound out their rhythmic thunder. It is mesmerizing—we are drawn out of our ordinary rounds of time and activity. We are made ready for something extraordinary. The honor song cleanses the area, the musicians say, making it a kind of sacred space. Slowly the drums fade; now the silence seems heavy and pregnant.

Then Murial Hogan and Vietnam veteran Jim Wachtendonk perform a haunting old World War I song called "The Fields of Flanders." Its story is told by a woman who addresses the tombstone of Willie McBride. She laments the "sorrow, the suffering, the glory, the pain," of the Great War. In a chilling Celtic wail, Hogan mourns dead McBride and condemns the failed promise of a new world without war, because "it all happened again, and again, and again."

Next, Gloria Hayes stands before her hammer dulcimer—an old American folk instrument big enough to bear the spirit of this Veterans' Day. Calling on a populist patriotism, she begins playing "America the Beautiful," celebrating once more the "amber waves of grain." Smoothly, subtly, Hayes surprises the audience by transforming the tune into the famous civil rights anthem "We Shall Overcome." The well-worn melody of that old African American spiritual fills the audience with its message of redemption and determination. As the two traditional songs mix again, the memory of martyrs and marches lingers on. "America the Beautiful" returns but is now heard with new ears.

The ceremony shifts from music to words. A series of readings by veterans tell of the inglorious history of modern war. Chief Joseph's "I will fight no more forever" recalls the final days of the Indian wars on the American frontier. The poems of Wilfred Owen speak of the despondency of English soldiers during World War I. A letter from a common German soldier at Stalingrad questions the grand designs of his war. Little Shaka Smart, a third grader, comes forward to read Susuma Mitsuda's childhood remembrance of the bombing of Hiroshima.

Finally, the ceremony turns to the Vietnam War, and the veterans can recall their own transformation from warriors to peacemakers. Tracey Suprise, Vietnam veteran and nurse, reads a Christmastime letter written by another nurse, Lynda Van Devanter, during her service in Vietnam. Exhausted and disgusted by her months of "death, destruction, and misery," Van Devanter and Suprise spoke for those nurses who struggled to say: "I'm beginning to feel like it was all a mistake."[4]

Vietnam veteran Marv Freedman steps forward to read and reaches back to 1971, when several thousand Vietnam veterans marched on Washington, lobbied Congress, and returned their medals on the steps of the Capitol. Freedman reads from The New Soldier, a book of photographs and words documenting the event. He has chosen the book's epilogue by John Kerry, now a U.S. senator from Massachusetts. According to Kerry, a different type of veteran returned from Vietnam in the early 1970s—a "new soldier" that "does not accept the old myths."[5]

> We are asking America to turn from false glory, hollow victory, fabricated foreign threats, fear which threatens us as a nation, shallow pride which feeds off fear, and mostly from the promises which have proven so deceiving. . . .
>
> For many of us there is little to remember but the promises and . . . the loss of the symbols of those promises—of John and Robert Kennedy, of Martin Luther King, Jr., of Medgar Evers, of Fred Hampton, and Malcolm X, of Allison Krause, Sandy Scheuer, Jeffrey Miller, and William Schroeder from Kent State, and Philip Gibbs and James Green from Jackson State; the loss too of friends, the fifty-three thousand Americans who have lost their lives in this degrading and immoral war. . . .

> The New Soldier has come back determined to make changes without making the world more unjust in the effort to make it just. . . . There is greater dignity and power in the human spirit than we have yet been willing to grant ourselves.[6]

According to Kerry, this "greater dignity and power" requires an alternative to existing forms of military service and patriotism.

> I still want to serve my country. I am still willing to pick up arms and defend it—die for it, if necessary. Now, however, I will not go blindly because my government says that I must go. I will not go unless we can make real our promises of self-determination and justice at home. I will not go unless the threat is a real one and we all know it to be so. I will not go unless the people of this country decide for themselves that we must all of us go.[7]

The new soldier's creed calls for a tradition of service that rejects fear, finds the true American promise in the struggle for peace and justice, and demands democratic control over war and the military.

The memory of wars since Vietnam also figures centrally in the ceremony. Indeed, it was the 1983 car bombing of American marines in Lebanon that first provoked Madison's Veterans Day. Pastor Grogan returns to 1983 and his pastoral duties to read Randy Clark's last letter and eulogy. Grogan begs to understand young Clark's death in the Lebanon bombing. For Grogan "peacekeeping" seems more a bureaucratic rationale to be questioned than a compelling reason for going to war.

Chris Molnar, a Gulf War veteran, brings the historical review up to the country's most recent military past. He speaks about the unexplained health and social problems experienced by Gulf War veterans, and links his war to Vietnam. "When we got back," he said, "we were said to be heroes . . . the war that made up for Vietnam."[8] Yet the wages of war must seem the same to veterans and their families suffering from mysterious sicknesses.

The main speaker is Sukie Wachtendonk, Agent Orange activist, veteran's spouse, and mother of two. For more than a decade Wachtendonk, like scores of other activists, has been demanding that the government test, treat, and compensate the victims of Agent Orange. In the audience is her son Zak. Wounded by a war that happened before he was born, this Veterans' Day is for him and the thousands of young people poisoned by the Agent Orange sprayed on their fathers.

After greeting the audience, Wachtendonk's strong voice turns to the unending legacy of chemical warfare.

> It saddens and angers me that America has been unwilling and unable to honor the debt that it owes to these men and women. . . . I have watched

in horror the continuing budget cuts within the Veterans' Administration resulting in the loss of care . . . for ailing veterans while the appropriations for weapons of war have escalated.

My family and too many others here in America and in Vietnam have been devastated by the continued lack of responsibility for . . . Agent Orange veterans, our children, and the life-threatening illness and uncertainties which loom dark in our futures. . . .

Wars do not end when the soldier returns from battle. The burden is borne not only by the veteran, but by his parents, by his spouse, by his children, and us all.

The United States has in effect left its wounded on the battlefields to fend for themselves. . . . In the Agent Orange battle, the wounded include the wives and children of these veterans.[9]

Wachtendonk goes on to create a link between the special conditions of veterans and the broader public health threat posed by dioxin exposure.

The majority of the American people have chosen to close eyes and ears to our prolonged suffering and our warnings, content in the belief that such a horrendous thing could not be true. That America could not be capable of killing its own. Well, perhaps the terrible burden of knowledge that your children are also being sacrificed, that your air, your food, and your water are being contaminated by the same government, by the same corporations that sprayed veterans in the jungle of Vietnam twenty years ago. Perhaps then you will act in your own defense to save our children and to save our planet.[10]

Again the Winnebagos return, this time to help rescue the wounded we have "left on the battlefield." The drumming and singing of the "fallen warrior song" begins. The dance expresses the willingness and duty to put oneself on the line to retrieve fallen warriors. According to tradition, the fallen warrior song must be performed by a veteran. This time it is Joseph Whiteagle, a Gulf War veteran. This year's fallen warrior song has a particularly poignant meaning. John Beaudin, who had performed the dance for many years, is now dead, falling with six others from this community of antiwar veterans, people like Elroy Schultz, exposed to Agent Orange and now dead from cancer.

Whiteagle's buckskin regalia is festooned with bright blues and yellows, and with eagle feathers. Each feather represents an enemy that has been conquered, but it also symbolizes honor and respect for that enemy. For Winnebagos and many other Indians the eagle is the most honored creature. Flying high, close to god, the eagle carries greatness and bestows blessings. And so, eagle feathers may never touch the ground.[11] The dance begins when Whiteagle lays an eagle feather on a bandanna placed on the floor. The feather symbolizes the fallen warrior.

Again, waves of music well up to flood the rotunda. As the voices and drums mingle, an envelope of sound surrounds the audience. The drumbeats begin to feel like a great shared heartbeat drawing together the pulse of all present. Perhaps this is meant to summon the collective courage it takes to retrieve those who have fallen; perhaps it is to call out to them. Whiteagle circles the fallen warrior. Minutes pass as the spiral he dances slowly gathers and tightens. Finally he draws near the eagle feather and gracefully retrieves it, retrieves the fallen warrior. Proclaiming triumph he tosses his head back and gives a short, sharp cry of victory. This is the victory these veterans and their communities seek. To aid those with Agent Orange, those who are homeless, those who are still wounded—this is a victory worth fighting for.

As the song ends, a solo drumbeat continues beating. At the cadence call, an honor guard marches out from the wing of the rotunda with a smart, formal half-step. The audience rises. Composed of men and women, veterans and non-veterans, whites and Indians, old and young, the honor guard shoulders a litter weighted down with a stuffed body bag. They carry this symbol of the dead so that the young boys cannot mistake what war is always about. The honor guard stops at the center of the rotunda. They rest the litter on stanchions and solemnly drape it with a large American flag in proper military fashion. A moment of silence is called.

Then, in ponderously slow motion, the honor guard pulls a translucent black shroud over the flag. The whole flag is vaguely visible—the bright red, white, and blue remain uncovered along the edge. As they stand hushed, the ceremony's many authors turn to their thoughts of the shrouded flag.

> There are . . . three levels of experience to it. One of them is the body bag, that's stark and that's reality. . . . You have to accept that people really did come home in body bags. The flag in a sense is the honor that we want to put on it. That's the way we want things to be. And the black shroud . . . is the way things really are. . . . It is the pain of the bereavement for the person gone . . . the bereavement of what we're still doing. . . . To me it represents pain. And yet a pain for love, because you can still see it. . . . All those three things are there at one time.[12]

Like all symbols the shrouded flag evokes multiple meanings.

> The flag is there but there's a distress on the flag. . . . It represents a more accurate symbol of this country. . . . There's a shadow cast . . . over this country, and over its flag. The black shadow is there because of what we're failing to do for veterans and . . . what we have done as a military power. It's not just a bright, shining flag.[13]

> The flag is such a symbol. . . . What this country is doing is not what the flag symbolizes. . . . To me the shroud is what blind patriotism leads

to . . . the ultimate end to what that type of insane thought leads to. So the shroud is over the flag.[14]

After the shroud is in place the honor guard turns, and each member raises a fist clenched around a rose. A bugler breaks the silence with taps. In the huge dome the melancholy peace and sad power of that military signal overwhelms. The crowd is very still and silent. As the last strains of taps slip to nothing, the audience's spirits seem to ebb away as well.

Appearing at the center stage, Jim Wachtendonk cues our renewal by singing the old antiwar standard "Where Have All the Flowers Gone?" The audience answers in action. Moving slowly to form a procession, hundreds of people with roses in hand approach the center of the rotunda. Six or seven women workers from the capitol, still dressed in their yellow workshirts, join the line. All have come to play their part. As if they had approached an altar, each lays a flower upon the shroud, upon the flag, upon the body bag. Soon the sweet aroma of roses and a thick bed of rich, red color concludes the ceremony with a breath of hope and rebirth. Only quiet talk and hugs remain as the crowd drifts off into the cold Wisconsin night.

This is Madison's Veterans' Day, an observance that is truly in the spirit of that city's heroic namesake. It was, after all, James Madison and the American revolutionaries of 1776 who viewed large standing armies as a source of great mischief. The Constitution that Madison authored warns that a standing army under the control of an executive empowered to declare war is a combination hostile to liberty and government by the people.[15] It was Madison who said:

> That the people of the States should for a sufficient period of time elect an uninterrupted succession of men ready to betray both; that the traitors should throughout this period uniformly and systematically pursue some fixed plan for the extension of the military establishment; that the governments and that the people of the states should silently and patiently behold the gathering storm, and continue to supply the materials until it should be prepared to burst on their own heads, must appear to everyone like the incoherent dreams of a delirious jealousy, or the misjudged exaggerations of a counterfeit zeal, than like the sober apprehensions of a genuine patriotism.[16]

Madison's Veterans' Day expresses the potential for a new alternative tradition. It is part of a tradition that honors the warrior, not the war, and that forges the bonds of community from America's diverse cultures. This ceremony embodies a newly possible patriotism of community and peace.

The new Veterans' Day is part of a tradition rooted in a history true to America's original values. It may lift the shroud that covers the flag if we can recall America's history and ideals. Remember, the ceremony says, remember—remember the history and once-great promise of the American citizen–soldier.

The Soldier Ideal and American Culture: The Citizen-Soldier, the Fighter, and the Fifties

> What true myth concerns itself with is not the disintegration product. True myth concerns itself centrally with the onward adventure of the integral soul. And this, for America, is Deerslayer. A man who turns his back on white society. A man who keeps his moral integrity hard and intact. An isolate, almost selfless, stoic, enduring man, who lives by death, by killing, but who is pure white.
>
> This is the very intrinsic-most American. He is at the core of all the other flux and fluff. And when *this* man breaks from his static isolation, and makes a new move, then look out, something will be happening.
>
> —D. H. LAWRENCE, *STUDIES IN CLASSIC AMERICAN LITERATURE*

> In the bleak winter of 1776, when the men who had enlisted in the summer were going home because the way was hard and their enlistments were over, Tom Paine wrote, "These are the times that try men's souls. The summer soldier and the sunshine patriot will in this crisis shrink from the service of his country; but he that stands it now deserves the love and thanks of man and woman." Like the winter soldiers of 1776 who stayed after they had served their time, we veterans of Vietnam know that America is in grave danger. What threatens our country is not Redcoats or even Reds; It is our crimes that are destroying our national unity by separating those of our countrymen who deplore these acts from those of our countrymen who refuse to examine what is being done in America's name.
>
> —WILLIAM CRANDELL, *THE WINTER SOLDIER INVESTIGATION*

WHY THE ENDURING popular romance with war and war stories? For much of the world's history, war has been both a principal author of high-minded virtues and the supreme measure of human striving. War transcends everyday experience to touch the extremes of life; unbridled passions, momentous risk and decision, and the honor of fighting for some grand idea. At the heart of war's compelling drama is the soldier, one of humanity's great heroic ideals. The soldier ideal is a complex and sometimes volatile combination of symbols, feelings, values, ideas, and sentiments that is central to both a general mythology of military culture and a particularly American history of democracy, citizenship, and war.

The American soldier ideal is defined by the tension between two opposing historical traditions, each with its own meanings and myths. One aspect of the American soldier ideal is characterized by the fighter, the other, by the citizen–soldier. The fighter is evoked by Lawrence's observation of James Fenimore Cooper's Deerslayer. The fighter grew from America's frontier and imperial adventures. Arguably, the fighter figure is the dominant vision of the American soldier.

Yet even as some American soldiers fought and thought as the "stoic, enduring man, who lives by death," a substantial minority of Vietnam-era soldiers were transformed by the war experience. These men and women created an alternative vision of soldiering, basing this vision upon the figure of the "winter soldiers of 1776." Also deeply rooted in the American past, the citizen–soldier was not a "disintegration product" but the midwife and lifeblood of the American republic. Envisioned as free people fighting for the ideals of freedom, the citizen–soldier was a powerful political figure enlarging the scope of citizenship rights, wary of standing armies, and disdainful of deferential behavior. The soldier ideal, with all its contradictions, was transmitted to soldiers and young recruits of the Vietnam era by Hollywood, the military, and the communities in which they lived.

The heroic "soldier ideal" is crucial to an understanding of military culture because of its central role in the creation of soldiers.[1] By investigating the cultural inventory of American soldier figures, we may explain how soldier consciousness and military experience created the citizen–soldier, that common and virtuous soldier whose valor and sacrifices are memorialized in the historical accounts of Lexington and Concord, Valley Forge, Gettysburg, and Iwo Jima. For it is to the tradition of the American citizen–soldier that the antiwar resistance of Vietnam-era soldiers and veterans best belongs.

The universal tradition of the soldier ideal begins with the warrior–hero, a transcendent figure that populates the mythical and historical accounts of many cultures. This ideal is deeply embedded in centuries of mythology, war, and military culture. From Gilgamesh to Joan of Arc to George Washington, myth, religion, literature, and history all speak to the enduring presence of heroic consciousness. The power of the warrior ideal stems from its ability to satisfy the fundamental need for collective regeneration and a sense of immortality in the face of inevitable individual death. As Robert J. Lifton suggests in *Home from the War*, "Death is not eliminated or wished away but transcended by a newly envisaged enduring principle, by an activated sense of being part of eternal forms."[2] The heroic warrior may kill or die, but does so to serve truth, often in the face of an impending challenge. The heroic figure acts as a link between mind and action and between social life and individual death.[3] This ideal is a potent symbol that encourages selfless behavior and idealistic actions.

While the classical figure of the warrior has many different faces, each produced in its own historical context, this hero appears most often in stories that describe a time of national or cultural creation or rebirth.[4] Achilles, Charlemagne, and the Teutonic Knights, all central to European nationalist mythology, figure prominently in the imaginative construction of the warrior–hero. In the 1950s, the Mau Mau, Africa's first modern liberation movement, emboldened themselves by summoning up Kenya's heroic warrior tradition.[5] Chaminuka, the nineteenth-century Shona prophet, was evoked by Zimbabwean rebels seeking independence in the 1960s. Certainly for the United States the founding history and myth centers largely on stories of heroism and war. As Lincoln once claimed, Americans find their own "mystic chords of memory stretching from every battlefield and patriot grave to every living heart and hearthstone."[6]

This tradition is usually recalled as a male domain, but women have served as the warrior–hero in both myth and earthly engagements. Nzingha, the Angolan queen, achieved legendary status fighting the Portuguese in the seventeenth century. Yaa Asantewaa led the Asante against the British in the nineteenth century.[7] Madama Bhikaiji K. R. Cama, a Gandhi-style nonviolent leader of the early twentieth century, and Rani Lakshmi Bai of Thansi fought the British in India and became exemplars of national unity and independence.[8] No history of Ireland is complete without reference to its many warrior women. Although these figures embody characteristics particular to their cultures, they share a universal, creative, immortalizing, and life-giving power.

The American Citizen–Soldier

The citizen–soldier is the secular, historical, and democratic aspect of the soldier ideal and is best represented in American culture by the Revolutionary minuteman, rebellious seaman, winter soldier, and the white and the black abolitionist soldier and armed fugitive slave of the Civil War. The citizen–soldier leaves peaceable pursuits behind and departs on an honorable mission. Empowered by the nation's ultimate sovereign—the people—the citizen–soldier fights to create or defend freedom and democracy from calamity. The power of the citizen–soldier grows from both the regenerative and immortalizing functions of the mythic warrior hero and from the democratic implications of the historical figure of the American citizen–soldier.

Empowerment is central to the citizen–soldier figure. The struggle for universal principles such as "the consent of the governed" rebound upon the status of the citizen–soldier. The citizen–soldier wins not simply battles but freedom as well. Historically conceived of as a free man fighting for natural rights, the citizen–soldier was the classic hero for a revolutionary and democratic age.[9] From the minuteman to the Vietnam grunt, the citizen–soldier has been an important symbol in the American patriotic pantheon.

Despite the variety of ideals and interests that motivated the soldiers of the

American Revolution, their collective efforts created the citizen–soldier figure.[10] In colonial towns, common working people, young apprentices, sailors, and African Americans, both slave and free, played a central role in creating the revolutionary consensus in the years preceding 1776.[11] The soldiers of the Revolutionary army were drawn from the poorest, most common classes. In the wartime attacks on Loyalists, and of course as militia and regulars, the citizen–soldiers pushed events and consciousness toward revolution.[12] Indeed, the three most important popular organizations of the Revolution were the politicized mobs, the militia, and the army. Most important, the citizen–soldier experience became a cultural standard that bestowed citizenship rights.

During the Civil War, hundreds of thousands of free blacks and runaway slaves pressed for the right to bear arms and fought to destroy slavery. As military necessity pushed the Civil War toward revolutionary ends, African American regiments were organized and widely deployed. Thousands of fugitive slaves forced the point by gathering around Union armies and encampments.[13] For the African American citizen–soldier, enlistment meant freedom, a chance to destroy slavery, and held out the promise of economic advancement and citizenship for the entire community. Frederick Douglass, leader and organizer of the black insurgency, stated, "He who fights the battles of America may claim America as his country and have that claim respected."[14] At the heart of America's second revolution then was the citizen–soldier. As W.E.B. DuBois rightly argued, "Nothing else made emancipation possible in the United States. Nothing else made Negro citizenship conceivable, but the record of the Negro soldier as a fighter."[15] The African American citizen–soldier was central to the destruction of slavery and re-created, for a brief time, a vision of America consonant with its revolutionary roots.[16]

Although often overlooked in the record of America's revolutionary wars, women were also citizen–soldiers. Women's social roles changed in these times of revolutionary upsurge. Molly Pitcher was the original citizen–soldier, a symbol of warrior womanhood that came to represent the vast feminine contribution to the Revolutionary War. Tens of thousands of women served during the War of Independence in a variety of capacities, including combatant.[17]

Harriet Tubman and Sojourner Truth fought against slavery and for women's rights. On the Underground Railroad and as a scout for the Union army, Tubman did battle. The existence of four hundred documented female combatants only suggests a broader and forgotten female involvement in the military mobilization during America's second revolution.[18] Perhaps the most powerful contributions were the material and exemplary impact of the female fugitive slaves. As nurses, cooks, laundresses, and models of courage and commitment, African American women too became the American citizen–soldier.

In both the 1770s and the 1860s the citizen–soldier experience created a dynamic understanding of citizenship that demanded sacrifice of material, time, and perhaps life to the birth or rebirth of the nation and the principles it proclaimed. This popular military tradition won soldier allegiance and shaped patriotic belief. The act of sacrifice and mobilization empowered the common person or slave who became the soldier.[19]

The citizen–soldier produced political power for the soldier and nation in a contradictory way. While political positions and cultural differences were sharpened, the fight for freedom simultaneously inspired republican and patriotic sentiment. Involvement in revolutionary military action eroded preexisting patterns of deference to authority and created a historical moment in which people articulated cultural outlooks, values, and political interests distinct from those of political and cultural elites.[20] Yet the patriotic military struggle signified the collective and individual devotion to the universal ideals of freedom, equality, and justice.

The armed citizen of the republic not only defended popular governments from foreign threats but was a powerful guarantee against domestic tyranny. In *Federalist* no. 46, Madison made explicit references to the militia, "fighting for their common liberties" as the ultimate check on centralized power.[21] This was, of course, part of the rationale behind including the right to bear arms in the Bill of Rights. A republic based on shared commitment to universal ideals depended on a virtuous and dutiful citizenry, involved in the affairs of state, armed as its own militia, and vested with the right to rebel.[22]

The citizen–soldier was created in the same revolutionary times that introduced profound changes in the nature of war. In the American Revolution and Civil War the separation between soldier and civilian weakened.[23] These were intensely politicized wars in which the civil and military spheres of life merged. The American revolutions succeeded by mobilizing both national resources and national consciousness to an unprecedented extent. The newly created national governments were based upon an expanded popular sovereignty that could recognize and represent itself only through some degree of mass mobilization. These historical moments weigh heavily on the popular mind. Like the Revolution and Civil War they were a part of, the citizen–soldier figures fundamentally in our conception of America. A tradition of revolutionary republicanism was created when the citizen fought as soldier and the soldier thought as citizen.

The Fighter

The American citizen–soldier I have described is certainly not the single, or even the dominant, historical version of the soldier ideal. While many variations of the soldier ideal exist, the Indian fighter, chivalrous officer, and the Rough Rider are related historical constructions of soldiering that have exerted a powerful influence on American military culture. These three types are historical and mythical variations of what I call the fighter. They are associated with dominant positions, be they national, racial, social, sexual, or political.

The Indian fighter has been the single-most influential form of the soldier in

American culture. This fighter's acts of violence became America's first great national resource, clearing away all obstacles to continental expansion. From the first regular army organization in 1784 to Wounded Knee in 1890, the U.S. Army "was pre-eminently the Indian-fighting Army."[24] Poised between "civilization" and "savagery," the Indian fighter swept aside an "inferior" people certain to submit before the onward rush of civilization.[25]

The Indian fighter protected "civilization" by using savage violence because that, after all, is the way of the uncivilized and all that they can possibly understand. As D. H. Lawrence suggests, this figure "turns his back on white society," but is also "pure white." Ironically, the fighter becomes the heroic bearer of civilization by repudiating the very norms and values he claims to defend. For the Indian fighter, those beyond the pale, living in "Injun country," are beings of questionable humanity who must submit to civilized ways or be destroyed. The reservation system was the institutionalized expression of the same Indian-fighter mentality.[26] All Indians not on the reservation were deemed hostile, threatening, and subject to military reprisals. Those within the reservation system faced forced relocation, impoverishment, and cultural assimilation.[27]

The tactical problems posed by the guerilla warfare approach of the Plains Indians were often resolved through recourse to total war.[28] In a letter offering instructions for a foray against the Kickapoos, General Phillip H. Sheridan said, "When you begin let it be a campaign of annihilation, obliteration, and complete destruction."[29] Only in defense of villages would Indian warriors fight the fixed battles advantageous to the U.S. Army. Attacks on villages destroyed food and livestock, and resulted in numerous massacres of Indian people. This style of warfare was championed by General William T. Sherman, perhaps the most influential figure in defining the military tactics of the Indian Wars.[30] The soldiers who fought at Wounded Knee in 1890, in that last dubious battle of the frontier, represent the culminating experience of the Indian fighter.

This version of the soldier left a deep impression on American culture. The Indian fighter and the frontier experience profoundly shaped the psychology of the American military spirit.[31]

The chevalier, the honorable and gentlemanly officer, has also exerted a considerable pull on the military imagination. Marcus Cunliffe describes this figure well in *Soldiers and Civilians*.

> The supreme romantic image of a young man . . . probably of aristocratic lineage, alone . . . driven forward by some compelling noble purpose. . . . Dapper young officers in gloves pledge their troth to ringleted ladies . . . while soldier–servants . . . hold the steeds which are to bear them away to danger, to fame, perhaps to death. If they die they die immaculately . . . in the arms of politely aghast comrades.[32]

In American history the clearest expression of this soldier was the southern Bourbon officer of the Civil War. Drawn from the planter class, this chivalrous officer evoked the aristocratic past of Europe and fought to defend his way of life and commanding position. His paternalism and noblesse oblige extended to wives, children, slaves, and poor whites, and was rooted in the superiority of manhood, high birth, and Saxon blood. After the Civil War this officer was remembered sympathetically, as a figure symbolizing the grace and gentility of the Old South and the honor of the lost cause. General J.E.B. Stuart was eulogized as the "Chevalier of the Lost Cause." Similarly, Robert E. Lee was called the "Bayard of the Confederacy." Both of these references were to a French knight, Chevalier de Bayard, whose sixteenth-century heroics were celebrated in romantic literature.[33] This genteel fighter was part of a tradition bounded by chivalry, martial honor, and fighting spirit.

The Rough Rider appeared in American history during the Spanish–American war. Remembered for the charge up San Juan Hill, the Rough Rider thrived on the challenge and adventure of imperial expansion. The Rough Rider exemplified a vital masculinity, Anglo superiority, and a rugged individualism all destined to cultivate and civilize a world wasted by exotic and "backward" people. Like the Indian fighters, the Rough Riders are cavalry and so carry the spirit of an elite corp.

The essential similarity between the Rough Rider and the Indian fighter rests in part on the nature of their mission. According to military historian Russell Weigley, "The pacification of the Philippine archipelago brought campaigning essentially not unlike the army's historic campaigning against the North American Indians."[34] In addition, the army command of the Philippine–American war had all been experienced Indian fighters in the American West. Whether directly inherited from commanders or re-created, the frontier mentality informed the soldiers of the new American empire.[35] The Rough Rider shouldered the "White Man's Burden." That burden was lived as the onerous and grave duty to destroy the insurgent Filipinos because of their "inability to appreciate human kindness."[36]

Taken together, the Indian fighter, the Bourbon officer, and Rough Rider exemplify the dominant historical and mythical figures of the American soldier and foreshadow later incarnations of the fighter. Unlike the citizen–soldier who struggles for freedom, the fighter needs only to defend an established position of superiority. This superiority is rooted in an exceptional national character that bears the infallible wisdom of Western civilization. This superiority assumes patriarchy, white supremacy, and the survival of the fittest. The fighter and the citizen–soldier represent opposing currents in the history of popular American military culture. In the 1950s, however, the contradictions these figures present were united within a single imaginary rendering of the soldier.

The 1950s

World War II and its representations in popular culture produced an influential and ubiquitous soldier figure that drew on diverse cultural traditions. In its dominant variations, the soldier was presented by Hollywood and the military as a stoic and hypermasculine warrior motivated by a powerful fighter spirit. The heroic figures shaped by the armed services and the movie industry may be seen as the contemporary reinvention of the Indian fighter, chivalric officer, or Rough Rider.

The alternative version of the soldier, also reinvigorated by World War II, grew from personal commitment to community. The direct experience of class, religious, national, kinship, or racial community created a compelling image of soldiering related to the classic citizen–soldier.

Although the image of the soldier often appeared in popular culture as a monolithic ideal, historical developments of the 1950s subtly but significantly subverted the heroic figures of World War II America. World War II marked a special time in the technological and symbolic history of American warfare. Popularly understood as a just and necessary war, World War II promoted the moral and political character of the citizen–soldier figure.[37] Yet this same war completed long historical processes that would simultaneously undermine the soldier image it had created. The soldier ideal of the 1950s was produced by the contradictions between the popular, democratic, and moral legacy of World War II on the one hand, and the rise of both "total war" and the American empire on the other.

In total war the constraints upon violence, understood as a division between the civilian and military sphere of activity, collapse: civilians are as likely to experience war as soldiers. This is due not only to the destructive force of modern weaponry but because a nation's war-making ability has gradually come to rely upon its industrial capacity, trade arrangements, labor force, and national solidarity.

Since the early 1950s war mobilization has occurred on a regular, constant, and routine basis. Some historians call the new institutional arrangements of the Cold War the "national security state." Permanent war economies organized by a military–industrial complex, large standing armies, immense military budgets funded through regular taxation, international secret police forces, state propaganda to maintain a popular mood of fear, increasing executive war powers and governmental secrecy, and the militarization of both scientific research and popular culture are all indicative of a world where war has become institutionalized. Dwarfed by the unprecedented might of this radically new institutional arrangement both citizen and soldier are distanced from control or knowledge of politics and warfare.[38]

Similarly, the United States' dominant economic, political, and military position in the world undercut the democratic functions of the citizen–soldier. American policymakers came to define all world events, domestic or international, in terms of national security. Any popular political movement that aimed to upset the existing order of the "free world" could be interpreted as a dangerous threat.

As imperial war and total war dissolve key distinctions between soldier and civilian, so the individual soldier experiences a suspension of the accepted rules of combat and honorable service. Clearly demarcated battles become difficult to find, and honor—defined as the struggle between warriors—becomes difficult to defend. When war involves fighting whole populations, as it often does in counterinsurgency conflict, or potentially threatens human survival itself, as it does in nuclear war, then war cannot be conceived of as a special arena populated by heroic figures winning immortality through moral action. The citizen–soldier cannot exist under these military conditions and so was reborn as antiwar hero.

The Military Mind

During the 1950s scholars such as Morris Janowitz and Samuel Huntington recognized the problematic relationship between the developments in weapons technology, particularly nuclear weapons, the immense logistical and managerial demands of a global bureaucracy, and the traditional soldier ideal. These technological and bureaucratic developments removed more and more military personnel from the direct experience of battle. This promoted the outlook of the engineer and businessman, career-motivated models of behavior distant from the heroic warrior. Military intellectuals proposed several variations of the soldier to resolve the cultural crisis staged by World War II.

The deep tensions between soldier and professional and between citizen and bureaucrat led to a redefinition of the soldier ideal in military thought. Most significantly, the democratic, community-oriented, and immortalizing qualities—the dense core of values at the heart of the citizen–soldier ideal— were stripped away from the soldier and projected onto the state or military service itself. Instead of the classic citizen–soldier, a more militarized model prevailed. Citizen participation and spiritual regeneration were replaced with "an uncritical willingness to face danger." The tradition, honor, and way of life this military mind referred to were not universal values, democracy, or the people but "military honor, military traditions, and the military way of life."[39]

In *The Soldier and the State*, Huntington attempted to construct a theory of civil–military relations for the post–World War II period. Consider the construction of the "military mind."

> The military mind . . . consists of values, attitudes, and perspectives which inhere in the performance of professional military function and which are deducible from the nature of that function. The military function is performed by a public bureaucratized professional expert in the management of violence and responsible for the military security of the state.[40]

> The military profession exists to serve the state. . . . Since political direction comes only from the top, this means that the profession has to be

organized into a hierarchy of obedience. . . . Consequently, loyalty and obedience are the highest military virtues. . . . This highest virtue is instrumental not ultimate.[41]

The thrust of the military mind is the maintenance of rank and order. Its values relate solely to a "military function" that defends a "state" in which "political direction comes only from the top." There is no relationship between the soldier and civic community or universal values in the military mind. By shaping the conduct and expectations of the officer corps, this military ethic was an influential model held up for the American soldier to follow.

In *Professional Soldier* Janowitz attempted to explain the modern soldier. He claimed, "The fighter spirit is not easily defined, it is based on a psychological motive, which drives a man to seek success in combat regardless of his personal safety."[42] All the political and cultural functions of the citizen under arms are collapsed into a "psychological motive," whose sole goal is "success." In this version of the soldier ideal, managing violence and making war are the fighter's distinctive characteristics and career. In this elite rendition of the soldier, war becomes a way of life.

Such a definition severs the soldier from any democratic cultural roots or heroic motivation, leaving only a fighter. This fighter needs only deference, obedience, and sacrifice, and serves the state by killing for martial glory itself.

Boot Camp and the Fighter Spirit

The military mind was not the only rendition of the soldier ideal promoted by the military in the years before the Vietnam War. Another version of the fighter was transmitted and elaborated during boot camp.

Boot camp has been the military's central socializing experience. In boot camp, the fighter spirit was powerfully communicated to the new recruit by example, through training, and in ritual. While there were many variations among different services and camps, the marines, army airborne, and other elite units presented the starkest profile of the fighter in their training. Elite units enjoyed cultural status and held sway over the depictions of the soldier in military culture.

Boot camp was a shocking initiation into America's military institutions for the new recruits. Violence and denigration were used as the introduction to the world of the soldier.

When I got off the bus in San Diego the DI [drill instructor] was going around indiscriminately cold-cocking people. . . . The next morning after our first Marine Corps meal, probably 20 percent of us were throwing up . . . and when the drill instructor came out he chastised us for vomiting his good Marine Corps food and made who ever was standing in front of the vomit get down and eat it—in some cases it wasn't the people who vomited. . . . In fact, the whole boot camp was racked with sadistic violence.[43]

You pull up to this barracks. This staff sergeant gets on . . . [and]says, "All right you maggots, you got one minute to get off the bus and forty-five seconds are over!" He grabbed the first guy by his hair and threw him right out the door. . . .
  This DI, barking in your face, was coming down the line and got next to me, the guy on my right was picking his nose . . . with the guy's finger in his nose, he decked him, knocked him cold just like that. . . . I could hear his head hit the pavement. . . . I did not move. At that moment he got right in my face. . . . "You got something to say maggot?" . . . "No sir!"[44]

Violence and intimidation were mixed with strident and persistent appeals to sexual identity. Ex-marine Jess Jesperson recalls, "Especially in the earlier stages of boot camp, when people are real confused and real disorganized, they always said, 'Girls—you cunts—pussies.' " In boot camp sexist and homophobic appeals were used to train and discipline soldiers. In the exclusive all-male environment of boot camp, women were used as a negative example and positioned as the common 'other.' Bill Davis, an Air Force veteran, remembers that "the DI really poured it on. . . . 'It's OK, girls'—and 'you stupid cunts.' . . . If you screwed up—your name became some woman's body part.[45]

A number of sexual ploys were used to manipulate the foundations of identity. Machismo, misogyny, and homophobia were employed both as exemplary ideals and as weapons to destroy competing forms of masculinity.[46]

When . . . I got to basic training that's where all hell broke loose. . . . I was one of the people that was singled out because I was not a fighter. I didn't have any deep macho voice. . . . I couldn't growl. . . . I was not aggressive. . . . And I was called a pussy and a faggot through most of basic training.[47]

Both gay and feminine sexuality were used as threats and negative examples.

You'd get letters from home—and everybody's girlfriend was "Suzie Rottencrotch." "She's off fucking everybody in town while you're here and your mother's probably fucking everybody in town too."
  They emasculate you that way. They get you feeling totally helpless. . . . and that's when they start the rebuilding process . . . basically teaching you how to be a soldier.[48]

Female sexuality, personified as "Suzie Rottencrotch," was intended to evoke machismo and the spirit of an all-male world. Although the sexual strategy of boot camp portrayed conventional feminine stereotypes as the polar opposite of the fighter spirit, those stereotypes usually remained abstract ideals or distant realities, since almost all women were viewed as abnormal. Girlfriends, wives, and mothers were commonly presented as sexually perverse. Woman soldiers too were stereotyped as "whores or lesbians." Because a woman soldier was considered a contradiction in terms, her sexual identity could be understood only outside of conventional norms. Women soldiers cannot be viewed as sexually conventional without threatening the sexual rules used to discipline soldiers in boot camp.

The sexual appeals of boot camp training were supercharged by the suppression of sexual activity. The military enforced sexual depravation to create their vision of the soldier. Writing in the underground GI press, dissident soldiers used the ideas of radical psychologist Wilhelm Reich to suggest the link between sex, authority, and war.

> The goal of sexual suppression is that of producing an individual who is adjusted to the authoritarian order and who will submit to it in spite of all the misery and degradation. The suppression of natural sexual gratification leads to various kinds of substitute gratifications. Natural aggression becomes brutal sadism which then is an essential mass-psychological factor in imperialistic wars.[49]

The fighter was created by denying any positive connection, be it physical or symbolic, between male and female. In the production of the fighter spirit, masculinity functioned primarily as a psychological motive—essentially as a mystique. Masculinity became both a question and a quest.

> That's why I wanted to go into the marines. Let the marines make a man out of you—whatever that was. That was a big thing. What does it mean to be a man? . . . Join the marines, let them make a man out of you.[50]

The sexual politics of the military exploited the constantly shifting and ambivalent character of masculinity.[51] The sexual strategy of boot camp suggested that soldiers must have a macho, misogynist, and homophobic self-image to successfully learn the fighter spirit. The obsessive drive to create and maintain machismo drew upon an insatiable insecurity that may be momentarily slaked only by a display of domination against some threat. This hypermasculinity induced the fighter spirit.[52]

The military extended this sexual strategy by means of racial twist. For example the GI press cited,

> The attitude of the Asian woman being a doll, a useful toy, . . . and how they were not quite as human as white women. For instance . . . the

instructor would talk about how Asian women's vaginas weren't like white women's but rather they were slanted, like their eyes.[53]

Machismo was employed as a gateway to other forms of domination and dehumanization. Once a sense of male superiority was achieved, then other forms of dominating behavior were introduced. During the Vietnam era, Asians became the target of racist attacks.

When I went to the Marine Corps, I thought I was going to serve my country and be a brave marine and a good American. As I stepped off the bus . . . the DI came up to me and said, "Oh we have a gook here today in our platoon.' . . . All during boot camp I was used as an example of a gook.[54]

Dominance and manhood were equated with combat and opposition to the "other." This other was usually a "pussy" and then a "gook," sometimes a "commie," but always a potential victim.[55]

By the time I was in Nam at eighteen, I learned my identity, through a whole dehumanizing outlook on a culture of people that I knew nothing about. I was learning to identify with people through dehumanizing them, degrading them, humiliating them, killing them. That was my identity; that's how I learned my identity. They get you in the Marine Corps.[56]

The fighter is primarily motivated by a need to perpetuate a position of dominance, be it understood in sexual, racial, or imperial terms. Jesperson summarizes boot camp indoctrination:

It started when you went into boot camp. . . . There's a psychological terror . . . and physical torture. First, they dehumanize you, totally take away your identity, and then remake you . . . into what they want—just a fighter.

There are various psychological ploys that they use to do that. It's very easy if you refer to another person in a derogatory fashion . . . the racial slurs. . . . The Vietnamese were all dinks, and gooks and slopeheads . . . anything but a person. . . . You were dealing with a subhuman species at that point. . . .

The end result is that they want a highly disciplined, highly motivated killing machine. . . . There's ways to do it. One is if they are a threat to you, or if you perceive them as a threat to you.

They were pretty light on political ideology. . . . All we had to do was go kill them—we didn't have to understand them.[57]

In boot camp the military attempted to cue soldiers to respond to dominance and hierarchy. Violence, racism, machismo, homophobia, and misogyny were intended to replace all the other existing forms of soldier identity. This tradition of training, strongest in the elite services, was preparation to fight total war.

The Personal Heroes of Hollywood

In ways far different from the military institutions, mass media schooled millions of young Americans to a military culture populated by heroic actors and heroic actions. Mass media created a vital war mythology full of irresistible heroes and potent messages. Comic books, television, and movies informed the average American's imagination of war.[58]

> Growing up I always wanted to go into the Marines. Basically I was filled with Vic Morrow on "Combat" and Sergeant Rock of Easy Company. . . . As far as socializing us into the military and combat—the whole John Wayne image.[59]

> Always wanted to be a marine. Probably one too many John Wayne movies. In fact I'm sure it was one too many John Wayne movies.[60]

The John Wayne image was an incredibly powerful example to future soldiers. In the person of John Wayne the frontier figure of the Indian fighter was united with the heroic exploits of American liberators during World War II. The western and the World War II genre film were popular and compelling cultural experiences for young Americans in the 1950s.[61] Of the many movies referred to by Vietnam veterans as important to their military education, none is mentioned more than *The Sands of Iwo Jima*.

The Sands of Iwo Jima is a modern epic of heroic contest, death, and immortality that ironically politicized the private lives of its audience. Rather than referring to political ideals, *The Sands of Iwo Jima* resolves the problem of individual death through the personal story of a young soldier's passage to manhood.[62] A family drama between father and son subtly structures the action of this famous film.

John Wayne portrays Sergeant Stryker, a tough, battle-hardened warrior who becomes the symbolic father for Conway, a younger GI. Stryker's own family has deserted him, and the young soldier's father, a friend of Stryker and highly decorated officer, was slain in battle. The family drama begins with Conway's rejection of Stryker as father image and repudiation of warrior as ideal. Conway's "real" father is also rejected in favor of the future Conway claims for his own baby boy. In an argument with Stryker, Conway says, "I won't insist that he be tough. . . . Instead I'll get him a set of Shakespeare. . . . I want him to be intelligent, considerate, cultured, and a gentleman."

Conway is then tried and tested through the rigors of combat. After Stryker saves Conway's life and displays remarkable coolness and valor, the young GI comes to admire his indestructibility and greatness. Conway finally reveals that he will name his own son after his "real" martyred father. In the last scenes, the symbolic father and son are reconciled and depart together on their final mission, the conquest of Mount Siribachi. In the climatic moment, as the peak of the dormant volcano is taken under control, Stryker is killed by a sniper, and in a cinematic reproduction of the famous photograph, the flag is erected over Iwo Jima. As the film closes, the son adopts the expressions and language, indeed the personality, of the now-fallen father. Hard, stoic, and a fighter, the son has attained the full form of the Hollywood hero.

The film's second strategic approach to immortality is through marriage and reproduction. Boy meets girl, and Stryker's symbolic son falls in love. Meditating on his wartime romance, the son wistfully reflects as Stryker listens in, unobserved.

Why do men get married during a war? . . . Maybe something's got your number on it. You want to leave a little bit of yourself behind. Doesn't matter whether it's a boy or a girl, just so long as you know you won't be forgotten. There'll be someone who would never have lived if it hadn't been for you.[63]

In this musing, the son imagines a family that serves his desires to become both father and man. The loyalty here is to one's desire for a privatized immortality through fatherhood. Ironically, this heroic film considers immortality, not in terms of enduring principles but as a function of family—both symbolically and as biological reproduction. Creating a family is a form of becoming immortal, but was not conventionally seen as an immortalizing action—it was proper to everyday private life, not to the heroic realm. The fact that universal values or the struggle against fascism and militarism were never mentioned in *The Sands of Iwo Jima* did not diminish the attraction of its heroes but rather dissolved the distinctions between the personal and the political.[64]

This reading of *The Sands of Iwo Jima* suggests that John Wayne's powerful mythical role springs from the deeply ambiguous way the characters he portrayed resolved and presented cultural contradictions. This move toward the private realm bears the subtle traces of how empire and popular culture produced a powerfully personal utopian vision during the 1950s—a vision that nonetheless contained the seeds of its own transformation.

In one way *The Sands of Iwo Jima* suggests that the hero or citizen may depart from politics and the public domain because there is little work there left to do. As "number one" the United States became the best of all possible worlds blessed with a perfected moral authority. For an America basking in victory and global mastery there were no political ideals left to realize. If the empire was to maintain supremacy, then real historical change, the classical consequence of heroic action, must come to an end.

In such an end-of-history utopia, the public citizen of classic liberal political theory has no reason to act, and the citizen–soldier nothing to fight for. Only a subject or a fighter can remain to regenerate that which is victorious and dominant in self or nation. This regeneration cannot, however, be truly heroic, because the fighter cannot go beyond the existing principles of life; they are already present in their completed forms. In this way film helped to constitute a domestic culture of empire that featured a domesticated hero whose heroic turf became the family he led.

Similarly, *The Sands of Iwo Jima* and other World War II genre films treated the need for cultural immortality and regeneration by sanitizing and arresting the history of war. Conventional war was projected as the model for future wars, and the immortal hero was portrayed as the model for soldiers. World War II genre films disarmed the young for the real experience of counterinsurgency warfare, injury, or death. Steve Shuey discusses his own miseducation, and the way in which experience yielded terror and meanings beyond the command of the movie moguls.

> The way World War II was being projected in the movies is one of the things that screwed up a lot of Vietnam veterans. They never showed torn limbs or blood. The actors never project the terror that goes right to your guts. . . . But when you might die or be injured, you start looking for meaning in the war.[65]

Movie heroes survived through intense yet conventional combat, rarely died, and never suffered traumatic wounds. Through the portrayal of invulnerable heroes and clean deaths, film plots tended to lodge immortality in the persons themselves. And, as the title implied, comic books like "Sergeant Rock" also featured supertough heroes. Indestructible heroes hid the reality of war. By steering heroic action toward individual survival, reproduction, and the domestic sphere, the cinematic hero masked the motive of empire, the profound developments in the nature of war, and violent death—all essential aspects of the Vietnam War.

This desire to end history by directing the heroic toward the personal could well have had an unintended and strikingly opposite effect. The personal politics of *The Sands of Iwo Jima* suggested the impending expansion of politics into the arena of family, sexuality, gender, and the identification between universal ideals and private lives that would lend remarkable power and intensity to the social movements of the 1960s. It is no coincidence that *A Matter of Conscience*, a book of oral history and photos by and about antiwar veterans, has for its front cover an extreme close-up shot of veteran Paul Atwood's hand holding only a photograph of his father in uniform. As it was for many other antiwar veterans, Atwood's journey from soldier to peacemaker was also his engagement with a deeply personal representation of warrior idealism: his own father. Instead of corralling heroism within the boundaries of the private sphere, the cultural strategies Hollywood developed to maintain the existing order could not foreclose the possibility of their own transformation into dissenting political action.

World War II films played all the more powerfully on Americans because the national mission of "the good war" had resonated with deeply held American beliefs. Filmmakers were able to effortlessly valorize World War II events with a clear story line that portrayed a righteous victory of good against evil because audiences brought their beliefs with them. By using a shared system of symbols, heroic figures, and meanings, film helped establish an ideal around which soldier attitudes could circulate and refer. [66]

> Television, I really think, had some stuff to do with it. . . . I used to get goose bumps at the end of the movie, they'd play that stuff, the flag would go up, I'd stand up. You talk to marines who went in . . . they're all really a little "pie-in-the-sky"—unless you're ordered there by the court. [67]

By reinstating elements of classic warrior mythology, filmmakers helped to create the form of the hero. The evocative power of that ideal reinforced and merged with meanings from family traditions and the experience of World War II to create a view of the world that was beyond doubt or criticism. The child of Jewish refugees from Europe, ex-Green Beret Ron Arm looks back.

> I was raised understanding about what can happen to people who are oppressed . . . in terms of being Jewish. . . . My perspective was that the Americans had fought the Nazis. . . . America would only do the things that are right. It's the only reason we go to war. My family, my parents, were . . . benefactors of that.
>
> Growing up on things like John Wayne. We're the good guys; we're there to save villages . . . and be heroes. . . . Basically, the communists were the oppressors in Vietnam—were the parallel of the Nazis. . . . That's what we were told and I had no reason to doubt that. [68]

The popular legacies of the Second World War represented in both film and family merged to produce a personally compelling patriotic spirit. By identifying all war as justified and conventional, by submerging the historical development of American imperialism and total war, and by fusing the personal and the political, the World War II genre film succeeded in re-creating the hero figure. But the very dynamics of modern war that film concealed were real and nonetheless propelled young Americans into conflicts along the outposts of American influence—first in Korea, then in Vietnam.

Taken together, the military mind, the fighter spirit, and the Hollywood hero constituted the soldier ideal of dominant culture. However, the authoritative images presented by professional and military elites and conveyed in the mass media were not the only source of soldier idealism. An alternative set of military ideals existed in the culture of community.

Community Culture and the Community Soldier

An alternative soldier figure may be reconstructed from the beliefs and activities of diverse religious and civic traditions. It is in the community soldier that we encounter universal and democratic ideals, and the traces of the citizen–soldier figure. The community soldier was produced by personal commitments to kin, community, ideology, and nation.

Although American Indians represent a small fraction of the American population, their cultures produced a military figure that exemplified the community soldier in the years prior to the Vietnam War. With strong family and tribal traditions, American Indians served in numbers approximately three times that of their proportion in the general population. In "Forgotten Warriors," Tom Holm presented the results of a study of 170 American Indian veterans from seventy-seven different tribal groups. Holm claimed that "an overwhelming majority of veterans . . . entered the military to retain the respect of their own people and to carry on family or tribal traditions." Furthermore, Holm observed that many joined the military because "Native Americans seemed primarily interested in remaining a distinctive people."[69] Typical of the community soldier, young American Indians imagined soldiering in terms drawn from their own cultural traditions.

Similar notions of honor, family tradition, and community motivated many Chicano soldiers to service. Chicano veterans embraced a strong sense of loyalty to their nation and fellow soldiers. In "Perceptions of Race and Class Among Chicano Vietnam Veterans," Lea Ybarra suggests, "Their patriotism was based not only on national loyalty, but was linked to a cultural mandate that . . . they should fight well and with honor."[70] That mandate to fight came from within the Chicano community.

> I think that in the Chicano community there is a positive value placed on being a warrior. The substantive message . . . is this is how men behave, and we got that growing up. . . . We were aware of the racism. . . . But we were told this is the country that we are part of and . . . I think the implicit message is to prove that you are worthy to be a citizen. I've always, in my own heart, been proud of the warrior aspect of myself, maybe not so proud of Vietnam, but that's one of the contradictions between who I am and what the war was.[71]

For the Chicano veteran above, the soldier represented community, and his duty was part of the process of gaining full citizenship. This cultural mandate was a powerful force demanding risk, extraordinary effort, and action in service of ideals.

> I made an extra effort and it seemed to me all the Chicanos who came had this general tendency. . . . There was something that was driving us. We wanted it to be a good thing and . . . even if it wasn't, we were going to try to make it be if we could. And I think we probably tried too hard and too long. . . . It wasn't because we were . . . like John Wayne types. . . . I think we were trying to . . . be something like we were supposed to be there, even if it wasn't turning out to be that way.[72]

Despite the failure of combat in Vietnam to fulfill expectations, community culture motivated the soldier to "actually be something like we were supposed to be." The same strong community identities that motivated soldiers toward ideal behavior sometimes became a standard upon which the war was criticized. Although a working-class or ethnic background did not necessarily produce dissident soldiers, a strong thread of community commitment and culture ran through the lives of almost every antiwar soldier.

Most antiwar soldiers came from the working class. A survey of 172 Vietnam Veterans Against the War (VVAW) members in 1971 shows that a majority were from working-class backgrounds, with nearly every antiwar veteran having identified with conventional politics prior to the war. Although only 7 percent claimed to have been radical before their service, 67 percent described themselves as radicals by the time of the survey.[73] Twenty-four percent identified themselves as Roman Catholics. In the large New York City VVAW chapter the majority of members were also Catholics, many of whom had been altar boys.

The defiant soldier and antiwar veteran began their journey from places deep within the bedrock of American culture and society. For many, military service was a way of life. Ben Chitty grew up in the traditions of Tennessee. "Like many white southerners I come from a family that has a long tradition of military service. Without . . . a single exception, everyone in my family went into the military."[74]

Together, class, race, family, and community ideals formed a tightly woven web of meanings, commitments, and patriotic notions. Family, class, and religious identities were closely linked in the process of a community creating its own militant ideals.[75]

> I was raised Protestant. We quit the church, we walked out with thirteen other families. The minister had gone to the holy land. He came back inspired. . . . He had an attitude of like: You can't work for defense companies all week . . . come in here on Sunday . . . put a lot of money in the

collection and think that's going to buy you off. . . . He got fired, because the deacons of the church were all bigshots of different corporations. . . .

All the working-class families left the church. There was a big confrontation after the service. They were great role models. . . . I remember my father being kind of eloquent in defense of the minister. . . . So when I got into a confrontation and I knew I was right, I would stand my ground.[76]

Parents were often examples of community pride and civic action.

My mother has always been very political. . . . She was an activist. She was always community involved . . . but I never looked at it in terms of the way I look at activism today. . . . She was a committee woman, she had tried to start a co-op in our neighborhood, she was always involved in some type of social issues. She always had an opinion about things.[77]

The community soldier ideal was communicated from family traditions in which military duty functioned as a powerful standard.

Interest in the military went way, way back. Both my parents are veterans from World War II. Both of them served in the Pacific; my father was an army medic. . . . My mother, being a nurse, was also stationed in Hawaii and Guam. She was part of that layer of nurses that put up a fight to get commissioned. . . .

My desire was always to be in the marines. That was basically the way that we grew up. . . . There is nothing that has to be stated, verbally, explicitly, it just, in quotes, is the way society is. That's the way your paths lead.[78]

In other families the heroic heritage of a parent's war exploits shaped early belief with an almost sacred power.

My father was a perfect example of a modern-day warrior. Once I knew my father had been in the Marine Corps, I always knew that I would go in the Marine Corps someday.

When I was a kid my father kept these medals and ribbons and other Marine Corps paraphernalia in a little cigar box. . . . My brothers and I used to visit that little cigar box as though it were a shrine, in which these magic talismans were. I never tired of going there and opening the cover, tingling with anticipation, looking once again. I saw them as badges of courage and of honor, and there was never a time in my childhood that I doubted whether I would myself wear these emblems and earn these badges.[79]

Whether traveled as a "path" or revered as "a shrine," the power of family military traditions created the community soldier.

African Americans created their own version of the soldier drawn from the history of the African American community. Young African American men were often raised to see military duty as part of the struggle for full citizenship.[80]

> My father was in the military in World War II, and even though he was in a segregated army, it was very much a part of his life experience. Being a veteran wasn't something that was looked down on; it was one of the few things black men had that they could hold up as being honorable, as being accepted, as being proof that you had just as much right to anything . . . even though you didn't get it all the time. . . . He made us sit down and listen to the stories, but he didn't really elaborate on the negatives and the racism.[81]

Civil rights were an important tradition in which many of the community soldiers were raised.

> There's a lawyer in New Jersey called Ray Brown, and he had brought some young people up from Selma, Alabama. We had a little meeting . . . with these young people that were really experiencing the brunt—it's like going to South Africa . . . it's the same kind of situation. . . .
> I was aware of it and everything, but my political consciousness wasn't at a height where I was very vocal or consciously pulled into the civil rights movement as a young person.[82]

The alternative ways of thinking that characterized the community soldier were often latent prior to experience in Vietnam. Like civil rights ideology, trade unionism and other forms of class consciousness were formative ideas for the community soldier.

> Growing up my father would always tell us there is the rich class, the owning class, and the working class, and that was that. I never knew what that meant in society until I was in the war.[83]

For many antiwar soldiers, community values were so pervasive as to seem natural. Bill Davis explains his exposure to class consciousness and his perspective on military duty in nearly identical terms.

> Both my grandfathers had been union organizers. The grandfather I was living with had been a union organizer in the first sit-down strike in the rubber industry in Akron, Ohio. He had also been a mineworker and oil field worker and had organized in all those. He met Lewis and Big Bill Haywood [leaders of the United Mine Workers and Western Federation of Miners, respectively] . . . the union was natural, a totally natural thing. . . .

> I had no foreboding about it [the military] or anything. I figured eventually I was going to get there. . . . That's just the way it always was. Our family, both sides always went into the military. I was going to go in too.[84]

For many community soldiers, working-class values were a "totally natural thing" and military service was "just the way it always was." This community orientation rendered unionism or military service an aspect of family tradition. Dave Cline is a combat veteran and VVAW activist whose personal history unites many of the elements characteristic of the community soldier. Family, ethnicity, religion, class, and service merged to create the profile of the community soldier.

> We grew up in a German immigrant community. My father was a heavy-duty union man as well as his brother, who is now a Lutheran minister in Ohio. My father was involved in organizing the IAM-CIO and the UAW. He joined the merchant marine during the war. . . . My whole family had a strong religious training, and when I was young, I thought about the ministry.[85]

In addition to its community roots, the community soldier mediated messages from dominant culture. There seems to be a particular way that working-class and ethnic people live dominant culture on their own terms. Many of the community soldiers embraced an ideal of service, patriotism, and loyalty that ushered them into the military as dutiful citizens or sometimes as gung-ho volunteers.[86]

> I grew up in an average white, middle-class, Catholic, Italian family in Queens. I went to a Catholic high school and got a fairly normal conservative outlook. You had to fight for your country to defend us from communism. I even became interested in the FBI because it was honorable service.[87]

> I felt that it was my duty as a citizen of this country, the country that I considered the greatest country in the world, to join the service and fight for my country. . . . This was something instinctive in me. I had total faith and had always pledged total allegiance to my government. I never questioned the war; I never studied the history of Vietnam. It was sufficient for me to know that my government wanted me in Vietnam and that we were fighting to repulse a massive northern communist invasion which was threatening the freedom-loving people of South Vietnam. . . . Right from the beginning I wanted to be a good soldier.[88]

Anticommunism and service to the state were common ideals among community soldiers. These ideals, also typical of elite notions of soldiering, were reshaped by community concerns. The community soldiers' deference to the state was purchased through reference to idealism, honor, freedom, or equality.

> My mother . . . all she knows is what the propaganda situation is. She programmed us to be devoted to duty, God, state, and country. She said you got to do all these good things—like military service—to be a citizen here in America. "You're not white," she would say, "you're not as good as they are, but you got to work hard to strive to be as good as they are." And that's what you're brought up to believe. [89]

A few antiwar soldiers grew up with the military itself as their most compelling aspiration.

> For me the military is what I wanted to do. From the time I was ten or eleven I wanted to go to West Point. I had no other desire in life. Everybody in my family of that generation was in World War II. I had an uncle who was killed in the Philippines. . . . I don't think the family quite intended the message I was getting, but it was obviously coming across very strongly with pictures and medals—that it was a grand and glorious thing to go off in war and die. [90]

Early in their lives these Americans constructed a community-based version of the soldier ideal that grew from a strong sense of family, community, ethnicity, class, religion, and nation. Almost without exception antiwar veterans and rebellious GIs grew up with some traditional code of values or commitments that gave clear meaning to the world. Political or universal values, notions of citizenship, and honor were attached to some form of community. Just as World War II was lived by soldiers as a realization of community values, so did many soldiers go to Vietnam to fight against communism and for freedom and democracy.

The depth of belief experienced by the community soldiers is central to understanding the eventual transformation of their ideals into antiwar sentiment. [91] The compelling, personal, and seemingly natural quality of community beliefs were a shield from small deviations and departures from ideal standards. Idealistic soldiers were introduced into a situation of crisis powerful enough to push the latent contradictions in the soldier ideal to its very core. Even for those veterans radicalized prior to military experience, the war was a central reference point in their political development. The nature of community culture assured that change could not occur for light or transient reasons, but when it did occur, it would tend to be sweeping and sudden. The crisis of Vietnam rendered cultural contradictions painfully explicit, and a transformative leap occurred. [92] The raw materials necessary for the later political transformation of the antiwar soldier already existed in the culture of the 1950s.

The military mind, the fighter spirit, the Hollywood hero, and the community soldier constituted the complex and contradictory ensemble of ideas and feelings that touched and moved young Americans at mid century. The Vietnam War unleashed irresistible centrifugal forces, rending and transforming that seemingly unitary soldier ideal. In ways extraordinary and ordinary, thousands of American soldiers took hold of history and transformed the soldier ideal. That process of making history began in Vietnam as resistance and opposition to war, racism, and military authority.

GI Dissent and War Resistance in Vietnam

3

In grade school we learned about the redcoats, the nasty British soldiers that tried to stifle our freedom and the tyranny of George III. . . . Subconsciously, but not very subconsciously, I began increasingly to have the feeling that I was a redcoat. I think it was one of the most staggering realizations of my life.
—W. D. EHRHART, VIETNAM VETERAN AND POET

The first sergeant was telling me one day about gooks . . . gooks this, gooks that. That was the first time I [realized]. . . . "A gook's the same thing as a nigger," I remember telling him; then he said, "You're a smart nigger." He said that to me, just me and him
—GREG PAYTON, VIETNAM VETERAN

THE MILITARY ANTIWAR MOVEMENT grew from individual acts of conscience born of the moral and political ambiguities of the war in Vietnam. The Vietnam experience amplified awareness of the race, class, and imperial politics of war, the military, and American society. From the beginning of military escalation in Vietnam, soldiers began to question the wisdom of the conflict and acted to oppose it. They learned war resistance from the bitter experience of war itself.

Soldier and veteran opposition first became mass movements in 1968. On January 31 of that year Vietnam's Tet offensive surprised the American military and forced President Lyndon Johnson to temporarily curb the bombing campaign, refuse requests for more troops, and reconsider American policy. Although most historians consider Tet to be the turning point of the war and the event that precipitated declining troop morale, many of the protest tactics, organizational forms, and political characteristics of soldier and veteran dissent had emerged prior to 1968.[1]

It was the combined social, political, economic, military, and cultural crises of the late 1960s, however, that created new political possibilities. The contradictions latent within both liberalism and the Cold War consensus, already revealed by the civil rights movement, were intensified by the Vietnam War. The urban rebellions and the rise of Black Power, the musical and political explosion of the youth culture, the reappearance of feminism, the renewal of environmentalism, and the steady spread of antiwar sentiment among Americans expanded the political horizons for dissident GIs.

It is in this historical context that the Tet offensive is best understood. Tet revealed rather than created America's folly. The sources of Tet's power to dissemble the American war effort were ultimately rooted in the politics of the war and the culture of the American military. After all, Tet had not caused the American government to lie about the progress of the war, or to motivate officers to inflate the body counts, or to embrace a war of attrition in the first place. Tet had not created the confusing combat conditions of counterinsurgency war, or the bureaucratic mentality of the American war managers. Nor did Tet force American policymakers to ignore the history of the Vietnamese people or to define Vietnam as central to American security. These conditions were not the consequences of the Tet offensive; instead, they were created by the very nature of American empire-building in the era of the national security state.[2]

While less than decisive in a conventional military sense, Tet helped to clarify the politics of war and empire. Tet removed lingering doubts held by some soldiers about the popular support for the National Liberation Front and the weakness of the Saigon government. A massive attack on dozens of fronts could not be kept secret from American forces without the consent of thousands of ordinary Vietnamese people. Tet helped legitimize the ideas of the growing GI and veteran movements for peace and discredit ideas of soldiering, such as the fighter, that depended primarily on victory and dominance.

From 1968 to 1973 the soldier and veteran movements expanded rapidly in activity, effectiveness, and political sophistication. Collective action occurred first and most widely in the army and marines. Although the "Vietnamization" of the war by the Nixon administration did weaken the domestic antiwar movement by giving the impression of withdrawal, the slow retreat forced increasing numbers of soldiers to judge the meaning of the sacrifice they were making. Just as significant, Nixon's shift to a more technological role for the U.S. military, while removing more soldiers from direct combat, still resulted in increasing antiwar activity in the navy, air force, and among veterans. From 1971 on, the veterans' movement became a leading force in the antiwar movement at home and in Vietnam. Resistance in the military became a serious obstacle to the war makers and speeded the American withdrawal. Indeed, antiwar dissent in the ranks of soldiers and veterans grew rapidly until 1973, when the direct role of soldiers, sailors, and airmen ended. Even after the withdrawal of American troops from Southeast Asia, soldiers and veterans continued to act around an array of issues concerning amnesty for war resisters, racism, on-base living conditions, and veteran benefits.[3]

Conventional dissent in Vietnam was constrained by many factors. The draconian measures of the Uniform Code of Military Justice, the demands of survival, the transient nature of military life, limited communication, and official attempts at social control often corralled dissent.[4] Despite these limits, direct-action resistance by soldiers grew as the war continued. This resistance took its most desperate and immediate form as combat refusals, fraggings, and prison rebellions. Perhaps more important, GIs engaged in a pervasive pattern of activities intended to hinder daily operations and place the survival of troops before the success of the military mission. Thousands of soldiers slowed the pace of operations, went AWOL, or protested by inventing forms of peaceful resistance. Many sympathized with or joined antiwar or other social justice organizations, wrote letters or petitioned Congress, or sought conscientious objector (CO) status. The movement's unity and strength grew from a single reality: a large, committed, and significant minority of American servicemembers wanted an end to U.S. involvement in Southeast Asia.[5]

The War against War

The citizen–soldier's struggle for peace followed the country's march to war. The American military intervention in Vietnam began with advisers, technicians, and the elite troops of the special forces—Kennedy's Green Berets. These first soldiers serving in Vietnam began to question the legitimacy of the war. Jan Barry was an army radio technician in the 18th Aviation Company from 1962 to 1963. A young man steeped in military tradition and heading for West Point, Barry's appetite for the war slowly began to wane. His contacts with U.S. advisers were part of his eventual change of mind about Vietnam.

> Some of the special forces people would come back from their missions and say we should be supporting the other side, because these people have legitimate grievances and the other side is the only one . . . really trying to do something for these people. This was a rather startling thing to hear.[6]

One of those special forces, Master Sergeant Donald Duncan of the 5th Special Forces Group, 1st Special Forces, quit the Green Berets and Vietnam in September 1965. A deeply religious Roman Catholic, and once a militant anticommunist, Duncan became the first Vietnam soldier to stand publicly against the war. In many ways Jan Barry and Donald Duncan foreshadowed the type of soldier who would later compose the leadership of the GI and veteran antiwar movements. Both went on to play important roles in the military peace movement: Barry as cofounder of the Vietnam Veterans Against the War (VVAW) and Duncan as a prominent speaker and publicist for the GI movement.

Declaring that "the whole thing was a lie," Duncan wrote one of the first exposés of U.S. policy in Vietnam. The article appeared in the radical magazine *Ramparts*.[7] The many contradictions of fighting in Vietnam, which would also touch the minds of other Americans, moved Duncan to dissent. Duncan was discouraged by the military's futile reliance on massive firepower, by racism in the U.S. Army, and by the valor of and popular support for the Vietnamese insurgents. He acted upon a slow and painful education that occurred when his experience in Vietnam conflicted with his ideology and upbringing.

> The whole thing was a lie. We weren't preserving freedom in South Vietnam. There was no freedom to preserve. To voice opposition to the government meant jail or death. . . . Newspapers that didn't say the right thing

were closed down. People are not even free to leave. . . . It's all there to see once the Red film is removed from the eyes. We aren't the freedom fighters. We are the Russian tanks blasting the hopes of an Asian Hungary. It's not democracy we brought to Vietnam—it's anticommunism.[8]

Soldier resistance grew from the direct involvement of American soldiers in war and combat in Vietnam. Duncan's memoir, *The New Legions*, recalled the conflicts war experience created.

"Do you have any idea why we are here?" . . . Kovacs almost exploded. "Of course I know why we're here—to fight the Viet-Cong . . . the Commies . . . the people trying to overthrow the government." "Did you ever stop and think," Kane interrupted, "that the reason they fight the government is that they know it's as rotten as we do?" Kovacs looked ready to take a swing at Kane. . . . "You think you're smarter than the president?" . . . "Ah, that's why you are here. . . . The president sent you. Being God, he's infallible." . . . Kovacs glared at me and shouted, "You both talk like traitors . . . like beatniks!" Kane, probably thinking of his eighteen years in uniform, almost choked. "Why are we traitors?" [Kovacs] "Because you're talking about such things. The president is the commander-in-chief. If he says 'Go to Vietnam,' we go to Vietnam. . . . You obey orders. . . . A soldier is not supposed to get involved with politics." "Why not?" Kane asked. "We should be the first person concerned with politicians and what they decide." . . . "We must obey all orders—is that right . . . even if we know they are wrong?"[9]

For Duncan, deference to military and political commanders raised serious questions of power and morality. In one form or another this debate would echo through hundreds of barracks, bars, mess halls, and coffeehouses over the next decade. At stake was the nature of soldiering and citizenship, and the relation between democracy and war. These soldiers laid a claim to the rights and duties of citizens in a democracy.

Throughout the history of warfare defiant soldiers and seamen have resorted to mutiny to control the cruel or endangering behavior of brutal or overzealous officers. In Vietnam an array of mutinous activities culminated in what was called the "combat refusal." This was a form of mutiny that resembled a strike and occurred when GIs refused, disobeyed, or negotiated an order into combat.

As early as 1965 the expression of soldier discontent began to increase, with growing individual refusals to follow orders. In June 1965 West Point graduate and special forces officer Lieutenant Richard R. Steinke refused a direct order into a combat zone because of his disapproval of U.S. policy in Vietnam.[10] In June 1966 Private Adam R. Weber, Jr., of the 25th Infantry Division, was sentenced to a year in prison for his refusal to bear arms in Vietnam.[11] In a letter from October of that year, Captain William Wilders of the 1st Battalion, 28th

Infantry, 1st Infantry Division, described some of the rigors of combat and then the reaction of the troops.

> We don't have too many cases of battle fatigue, but we do have a goodly number of people who after a certain point just refuse to go out anymore and end up being court-martialed. And to tell the truth it's hard to blame them.[12]

What a "goodly number" meant and how widespread such resistance was in 1966 is difficult to tell. Wilders's sympathy for combat refusals does hint at a surprising acceptance of such acts by officers. These few cases are among the earliest documentation of combat refusal, which was later to become one of the most effective forms of GI resistance.

Starting in 1968, there was a rapid increase in incidents of combat refusal, resulting in at least ten major mutinies and perhaps hundreds of minor ones, many unreported.[13] Serving in the 1st Infantry Division from August 1967 to August 1968, Guillermo Alvidrez remembers, "We had a barrack-full of guys waiting for court-martials for refusing to fight. They felt it wasn't worth it."[14] There were sixty-eight recorded combat refusals in 1968 alone.[15]

The *Vietnam Courier*, a Hanoi-based newspaper, cited fifteen major events of war resistance by American GIs during the first five months of 1969.[16] In August 1969 Alpha Company, 3d Battalion, 196th Light Infantry refused an order to attack. In a response that can only underscore the political sensitivity of the refusal, the forty-nine men were not reprimanded.[17] In May 1970 sixteen soldiers from Fire Base Washington refused to go into Cambodia. Private Harry Veon wrote the GI press, "We have no business here. We have enough trouble in Vietnam. Sixteen of us refused to go. We just sat down. Then they promised we wouldn't have to go to Cambodia."[18] A week later, a group of men in the 3rd Battalion, 8th Infantry refused to board helicopters. In December 1970 Lieutenant Fred Pitts and twenty-three men of C Company, 2d Battalion, 501st Infantry refused a command to advance.[19]

Combat refusals were often led by squad leaders, men who maintained close relationships with the average soldier. Squad leader Dennis Kroll was a veteran of the 1st Cavalry Division (Airmobile) and led such an action in the spring of 1970. His recollection below re-creates the dialogue between the reluctant soldiers and their officer.

> One day there were these ARVN [Army of the Republic of Vietnam (South)] working out close to us. They kept going up this hill and the NVA [North Vietnamese Army] had a 51 caliber out there. They'd get halfway up—they'd come back down. Then the Phantoms would work out. They'd start back up—they'd didi-mau [run] off the hill. This went on all day.
>
> Our platoon leader says, "All right saddle up. . . . We'll show em!"

Everybody was just . . . "What's your problem?" "It's their hill, their objective." [Officer] "Well, they're refusing to go back up. Let's go show them what we can do." [Kroll] "Fuck you—it's their territory. If they don't want it, I don't want it."

That caused enough mumbling within the platoon that he lost face and said, "Fuck it." . . . He called me in the tent. He was going to be lenient and give me an article 15 for refusing an order. I just said, "I refuse the article 15, I want a court-martial."[20]

Scenes like this were repeated scores of times in Vietnam. In the 1st Cavalry Division alone, there were thirty-five cases of combat refusal during 1970. At times, entire units refused combat orders.[21]

In March 1971, fifty-three soldiers in Bravo Troop, 1st Squadron, 1st Cavalry, refused to go into combat, citing inadequate reasons for their mission.[22] In one of the most highly publicized of these events, fifteen men from Firebase Pace refused to go out on what they considered to be a suicide patrol. Sixty-six men from that base sent a letter of protest to Senator Edward Kennedy claiming that they were continuing to play an offensive role despite the officially declared defensive posture of Vietnamization.[23] In the C Company, 3rd Battalion, 187th Infantry, seven African Americans refused combat duty, claiming that racist commanders were exposing them to undue risk.[24] According to Representative Paul McCloskey of California, an entire platoon of the 1st Brigade, 5th Mechanized Division refused combat.[25] In the later years of the war combat refusals came to include increasingly large groups of soldiers. In April 1972, for example, one hundred men of C Company, 2nd Battalion, 1st Infantry, 196th Brigade, refused an order to advance.[26] In 1967–68 Colonel Tom Ware experienced two combat refusals of the men under his command. By 1972 Ware observed the increasing dimensions of combat refusal when the "Phu Bai 13," thirteen African American soldiers from the 2d Brigade, 101st Airborne Division, refused orders, occupied a barracks, and issued a list of demands.[27]

Combat refusals were complicated events in which good soldiers hesitated or chose not to court death for questionable goals or risky battle tactics. In *Soldados: Chicanos in Viet Nam*, infantryman Charley Trujillo recalls a 1970 combat refusal in the Americal Division. After a devastating direct assault on a Vietnamese position resulted in fifteen casualties, Trujillo and his company refused combat.

I was feeling very angry, especially toward the officers. . . . Some of the gringo soldiers would at times get angry at me because they thought I was gung ho. I didn't feel I was gung ho; I just felt that I had to do my best. Just because I felt that way did not mean I should be cannon fodder. . . . Some of the black soldiers were saying things like, "The war's at home." This made me think for a while.

We were told that we were going in again in the morning. I along with some of the other soldiers told them that we refused to go in again. There wasn't any sense in it. . . . A new company commander was brought in. He . . . gave us a real good pep talk, just like those charismatic football coaches do. However, that didn't convince me or many of the other soldiers. We argued among ourselves through the night, the majority being against going in.[28]

Although Trujillo's reluctant company eventually did return to combat, and this seems typical of many combat refusals, his story demonstrates how negotiations and debate had replaced commands and obedience.

The air force also suffered combat refusals. As a protest, combat pilots Captain Dwight Evans and Captain Michael Heck refused to fly missions. Heck, a veteran of 175 missions and holder of the Distinguished Flying Cross, realized that his targets were hospitals and civilian sectors; he cited Nuremberg principles and refused to fly.[29] He explained his position by stating, "I came to the decision that any war creates an evil far greater than anything it is trying to prevent. . . . The goals do not justify the mass destruction and killing."[30] Four other airmen who refused to fly B-52 missions joined Representative Elizabeth Holtzman of New York in a suit challenging the legality of the Cambodian bombings. These bombings, which exacted a heavy toll among civilians, led to a crisis of morale among B-52 bomber crews.

Mutiny in the Navy also took on significant proportions. The USS *Kitty Hawk* had suffered mounting racial tensions during its long 1972 combat tour. Heading back to the United States, the *Kitty Hawk* put in at Subic Bay, Philippines, but was unexpectedly ordered to return to Vietnam. According to a House Armed Services Committee report, the rescheduling seems to have been the result of sabotage on board the USS *Ranger* and the USS *Forrestal*, the *Kitty Hawk*'s sister ships and replacements.[31] Expecting relief from the tensions of war, the sailors found themselves back in the Gulf of Tonkin. A hundred African American sailors assembled for a protest meeting over racial discrimination. A foolhardy attempt to suppress the demonstration with a detachment of marines backfired, and fighting broke out. Roving bands of black and white sailors clashed for hours.

On November 3, 1972, one of the most serious mass mutinies in U.S. naval history occurred aboard the USS *Constellation*, paralyzing the ship. Following attempts to suppress a dissident organization of African American seamen, a sit-in over racism was staged by eighty African American sailors. Over 130 sailors, including some whites, were put ashore at San Diego, where they held another protest. The dissident sailors then refused to board the ship when ordered.[32]

These highly publicized and well-documented uprisings are only the most dramatic expressions of the GIs' refusal to fight in Vietnam or to obey military authority. Army documentation suggests that a thousand smaller incidents of combat refusal occurred. Court-martials for serious resistance, including insubordination, mutiny, and willful disobedience, show 252 cases in 1968 and 382 cases in 1970.[33] These figures reflect only cases brought to court-martial and certainly imply a more widespread impulse toward war resistance. These defiant actions pushed officers to test the troops before commands were issued.

The combat refusals exemplified the emergence of a more democratic form of military decision making in which soldiers exerted considerable power over command. Combat refusals and mutinous behavior took on a more desperate and violent form known as fragging.

The soldier revolt introduced a new word—"fragging"—into the English language. Taken from the fragmentation grenade, the term was used to describe violence directed at superiors. As early as 1965 folksinger Pete Seeger wrote a song entitled "King Henry" that alluded to fragging. On the back of the album cover Seeger explained that the song "uses the words of a young Kansas service-man in a letter to his wife a week before he was killed, the victim of a fragging. The following verses refer to an emerging breakdown in military discipline.

> 'It's my own troops I have to watch out for,' he said.
> 'I sleep with a pistol right under my head.'
> He wrote this last month, last week he was dead.
> And Simon came home in a casket.[34]

After 1968 the tension between enlisted men and officers would explode into an epidemic of assassination attempts. Since the army did not start collecting data on fragging until 1967, and an unknown number occurred in battle, it is difficult to estimate how widespread such attempts were. By war's end, however, between eight hundred and a thousand fragging attempts were made using explosive devices alone.[35] The Pentagon confirmed that eighty-six men were killed and seven hundred wounded solely through the use of explosive devices triggered by American troops.[36] A Defense Department source speculated that more officers were killed by their troops' rifle fire than grenades.[37] If one considers even a small percentage of unreported attempts and the difficulty in documenting battle-field assassinations, fragging was common in the U.S. Army from 1969 to the end of the war.

The assassination of officers happened during World War I, World War II, and Korea, but given the number of troops, it had occurred about half as frequently as in Vietnam. In World War I, with 4,700,000 men under arms, 370 cases were brought to court-martial, with approximately the same ratio in World War II and Korea. Army documentation admits to 563 incidents of fragging in 1969–70 alone.[38] From January 1970 to January 1972, 363 were cases in court-martial. Unlike earlier wars, in which soldiers assaulted officers during battle, Vietnam-era fragging was much more organized and deliberate: the largest number of documented attacks occurred on base.

Fragging was usually aimed at a rigid or overzealous officer who endangered troops. Cowardice, incompetence, or other forms of dangerous behavior could raise the call for a fragging. It tended to fall into two categories. The first was a form of bounty hunting, used in the Mekong Delta Region as early as 1967.[39] GIs would take up a collection to offer as reward for the soldier who killed a wanted officer. Angry GIs offered a prize of ten thousand dollars for the assassination of the officer who commanded the costly attacks on Hamburger Hill in the Au Shau valley.[40] Barry Romo led a platoon of the 2nd Battalion, 1st Infantry, 196th Light Infantry Brigade.

> My company commander had five hundred dollars on his head. And the reason was he was a coward. . . . We went up a ravine, it was about double canopy. . . . We walked right into a base camp . . . and fires were still burning. . . . The North Vietnamese started an ambush on us. My company commander di-died [ran] out of the area—took the other two platoons behind me and ran down the hill and left us there. We had to fight our way back down . . . until nightfall. . . . And after that my men collected five hundred dollars.[41]

The other and more common form of fragging consisted of a series of warnings, typically in three stages. Lamont Steptoe served in Vietnam from July 1969 to December 1970 with the 25th Infantry Division in both the 38th and 46th Scout Dog Platoons.

> Generally there was a pattern. If you were fucking with the men, they would generally warn you. When you came back to your bunk there would be a tear gas canister. . . . The next time there would be a booby trap, which when you tripped it would let you know it could have been real. The third time was the real thing. It's not like you weren't warned.[42]

A surprising number of fraggings occurred in the rear. This type of resistance was peculiar to Vietnam and underscores the tension between the lower ranks and the officers. Fragging was often a deliberate and collective struggle over power and became a grievance procedure parallel to official channels.

> We banded together, blacks and white, we banded together and said, "He's got to go, his sergeant's got to go. . . . We can't let them continue to run this platoon."
> We basically mutinied. At first we thought that murder was the answer. . . . It was going to be draw straws and frag the motherfucker, right. Somehow that didn't happen. The next move was we'll go to the IG [inspector general] as a unit [and] we'll lay out all of these things we disagree with . . . making us stand formation, shine our shoes, and shit like that. Since we were NCOs, I was a sergeant, number of other sergeants, we'd present our case. That's exactly what we did. They sent in new people. It was a question of dealing with him that way or the more violent way.[43]

Whether actually used or not, the threat of fragging was a means by which soldiers tried to discipline their commanders. In some areas, tensions were such that groups of officers were attacked. In 1969 a Claymore mine exploded in a tactical operations center, apparently designed to kill the entire staff. In March 1971 a fragmentation grenade was tossed inside a barracks at Bien Hoa, killing two officers and wounding a third.[44] At Camp Eagle, north of Hue, an officers' club came under attack by twenty to thirty enlisted men.[45]

The war between enlisted men and officers became so intense in some units—the American Division in particular—that counterfraggings occurred: officers sought retribution against soldiers.[46] Dissident veteran Ed Sowders, a medic at the Cu Chi base hospital from late 1967 and through the Tet offensive, remembers his fear of being fragged.

> We've all heard of fragging. We know what it is, so I want to be honest about this. Fragging is a two-way street. It's not always the GIs in popular rebellion against their NCOs and officers. It's also a very convenient way to get rid of any troublesome lower-ranking GI. I was afraid of that. Military intelligence is already on my ass. They already developed a file on me. They're already spying on me.[47]

Fragging had serious effects on army operations. In some cases access to firearms and explosives were actually curtailed. In the 440th Signal Battalion a colonel refused to distribute arms. Even more important, fragging hamstrung command capabilities. Captain Barry Steinberg, an army judge, argued, "Once an officer is intimidated by even the threat of fragging he is useless to the military because he can no longer carry out orders."[48] The fear of fragging certainly became a consideration in the formation and issuance of commands. Fragging created a sense of disorder and tension that fractured the military. John Lindquist served with the H & S Company, Communications Platoon, 7th Motor Battalion, 3d Marines, during the first half of 1969.

> One time they tried to frag the lifers' hootch [quarters], it didn't work because the grenade didn't go off. The lifers sat up there all night with a rifle waiting for somebody to try it again so they could blow them away. . . .
>
> They tried to get this CID [Criminal Investigation Division] guy, but the grenade got a gunney [gunnery sergeant] who had nothing to do with it and he lost a leg. . . . That rubbed me the wrong way.
>
> When I was down in Quang Tri they had three fraggings of first sergeants in 3d Division. . . . It got so bad that each battalion was concertinaed off from one another so they wouldn't fight. . . .
>
> We were . . . listening to Deep Purple and through the top of our hootch comes about five rounds of M16. That could of been lower . . . somebody could be dead or wounded because somebody's fighting next

door with other marines. The ground war was no longer really working. . . . You could see it coming apart.[49]

At its worst, fragging led to a war within the war. During October 1971 military police air-assaulted the Praline Mountain signal site to protect an officer who had been the target of repeated fragging attempts. The military police occupied the American base for a week until command was restored.[50]

The following anonymous story taken from *Spoils of War*, by Charles J. Levy, captures the war within the war. A marine recalls a series of attacks on his commanding officer.

> We started having war calls, which is like at midnight everybody in the outfit starts opening fire screaming, "Gooks in the wire." . . . And then you try to kill any of the lifers that you didn't like.
>
> So we tried to get the CO a couple of times with a machine gun. One time his rack took nine holes. His cot, nine bullet holes. . . .
>
> So one night this guy named H. booby-trapped his tent. And in the morning when he woke up it wasn't the CO that got it. It was the executive officer Captain J. . . . Captain K. was the one we wanted to get. But J., it was just as good to get J. 'cause he sucked too. They threatened to press charges against the whole outfit for mutiny. They were trying to figure out a way they could keep it hush-hush. Nobody wants to know the Marine Corps mutinied.[51]

Fraggings were sometimes attributed to drug dealers or "short-timers," men with few days remaining in Vietnam. The one-year tour of duty for soldiers and the six-month tour for officers also inhibited the development of good relations.

Although the motivations behind fraggings were varied, tangled, and complicated, at bottom lay issues of power and control. The realities of the war in Vietnam prohibited many soldiers from experiencing honorable combat and embracing the war's official justification. In lieu of fighting for democracy or following exemplary leadership, anti-authoritarian, antimilitary, and antiwar sentiment shaped soldiers' survival instincts. An officer who threatened a soldier's life with a mission unworthy of sacrifice was then seen as the enemy.[52] Desperate, effective, and often collective, fragging was the most extreme mutinous activity through which orders and authority were contested.

Part of the military's response to mutinous and disobedient behavior was to fill prisons with American soldiers. Rather than solve problems of discipline and morale, the prisons became schools of resistance and sites of rebellion. The largest were the army's Long Binh jail, ironically dubbed the "LBJ," and the marine and navy brig in Danang. The prisoners of the Danang brig rose up twice in August 1968, holding some parts of the prison for three days.[53] Later that month, the uprising at the Long Binh jail was the largest and most explosive episode of soldier resistance in Vietnam. The most immediate causes of the Long

Binh uprising were the cruel conditions for these prisoners of war. Greg Payton was a veteran of the 599th Supply Company, 1st Logistics Command, and served from November 1967 to December 1968. Sentenced to six months for going AWOL and other infractions, Payton was locked up in the "hell hole" of Long Binh jail.

> Long Binh jail was an experience in itself. It really was a hell hole. Ninety percent black, maybe more; young, eighteen to twenty-one. In there for a variety of stuff, most of it bullshit. Conditions were horrible. . . . There were a lot of sadistic kinds of guards in there. . . .
>
> I was in the box, solitary confinement. You can stretch your arms, it's long enough to put a cot in with one light, they let you out about twice a day for about fifteen minutes. It could drive you crazy. They feed you lettuce rolled in water, for two or three days—this is America.[54]

Long Binh meant solitary confinement in the "box," starvation diets, desperation, and the plain evidence that hard time was handed out with race in mind. The soldiers planned a riot.

> By the time they had a riot I had already been in the stockade for about four months. . . . The people who were organizing this were the toughest guys in that prison. . . . They had their little secret meetings . . . but I didn't believe they were going to riot. I half listened. . . . I'd be leaving the stockade soon. . . .
>
> My job was burning feces, which was a good job; you got a chance to leave the stockade and drive around the post all day. You use kerosene. What they asked me to do is like bring in an extra can of kerosene every other day.[55]

The prisoners fought guards, military police, and burned down large sections of the stockade. One group of soldiers barricaded themselves in and held out into the following day. Many escaped.

> On the night they had the riot . . . I remember twelve o'clock, waking up—everything was in flames, lot of chaos, there was gunfire. . . . Smoke everywhere and screams. It was a real nightmare. They actually did it— they burnt down the stockade. They went really wild, a lot of people got hurt. A lot of white people got hurt, a lot of people took out anger. That anger, like I said it was 90 percent black in the stockade, so they focused on the white man.[56]

While the LBJ uprising was sparked by the inhumane condition of military jails, it was also the expression of deeper social currents.

A lot of the GIs were urban America, man. They had what they called the black draft, what I call the poverty draft. . . . During that period . . . the rebellions were in the cities, here in Newark, Los Angeles. Certainly the same consciousness was there. People were well aware of what was going on. It was different in a lot of respects. The pain got to be so great that you just didn't care what happened.

And this was America. You tell this story and this sounds like Russia or Siberia; no this was the Americans in Vietnam. These are the stories that are not being told on the TV. . . . I don't see many movies about it.[57]

Events like the LBJ rebellion echoed the urban uprisings in the 1960s. Marine veteran Clarence Fitch remembers 1968 as an important turning point in Vietnam.

We weren't living in no vacuum in Vietnam. There was a certain growing black consciousness that was happening in the states, and also over there in Vietnam. . . . The militancy really grew after Martin Luther King got killed in '68. It made black people really angry. You remember the riots after Dr. King's death were some of the fiercest, and brothers took that up in Vietnam. People changed after that.[58]

The great rebellions, the assassination of Dr. King, the rise of militant black politics, and the soldier resistance to the Vietnam War merged to produce widespread black disaffection with the war.[59]

Combat refusals, fraggings, and prison rebellions were desperate acts often committed under the meanest conditions of service, combat, or incarceration and were the most visible events of the soldiers' revolt in Vietnam. These episodes were only the most dramatic expressions of a more covert, much more popular, and probably more effective movement of resistance. Thousands of instances of subtle insubordination and passive resistance occurred.

Military Disobedience and Peaceful Resistance

The most effective and creative antiwar actions reversed battle tactics and stood the military's mission on its head. Search-and-destroy missions were turned into search-and-avoid missions. In early 1969 Pete Zastrow was a captain in the 1st Air Cavalry Division, 2d Brigade, 1st of the 5th Battalion. Zastrow led his troops into search and avoid.

My feeling was that most of the Vietnamese we were fighting against . . . didn't want to shoot us anymore than we wanted to shoot them. They had their job, which was to carry supplies, and we had our job, which was to stop them. But if we stayed out of their way, they sure wouldn't come looking for us. So we stayed out of their way.

We did a very good job of avoiding the bad guys. As a matter of fact, we religiously avoided the bad guys. We worked hard on what we called search and avoid.[60]

Search and avoid was well suited to the mission of the antiwar soldiers.

The military teaches you mission first, men second. But because I felt the mission was stupid . . . the men were much more important to me than the mission. We were doing nothing I could see that was worth anybody getting shot for. It's as simple as that.[61]

It was this more covert resistance that characterized the most pervasive kind of antiwar activity in the military. In the spring of 1968 Greg Payton and others came upon the enemy. Occasionally, combat avoidance was mutual.

They didn't come after me. . . . We were walking in this high grass and we saw the grass moving so you knew somebody else was in the grass. We got to a clearing, it was Vietcong, they had weapons. . . . They looked at us, we looked at them; they went that way, we went this way. That was the end of that. There was identification, man. Oppression is a universal kind of thing.[62]

In addition to combat avoidance some soldiers tried to make friends with the local people. GIs often had access to food and supplies the Vietnamese peasants were grateful to have. Nicknamed "Hippie" by his fellows, John Lindquist worked in the lead truck of a supply convoy.

"They said we couldn't throw C-rations, but I'd do it anyway—nice and gently. I was usually pace vehicle. . . . Everybody's eating dust so they couldn't see me."[63] One such humanitarian mission in Cam Lo village ended in a kind of public celebration. Some American soldiers won the support of the Vietnamese people.

We'd listen to Cream and talk about how the war was messed up. . . . So as we went in the village. . . . Me and Buzz we gave the radio headset to the driver . . . we crawled out the back canvas window and stood there with a case of C-rations—very gently just throwing them. Well the word must of gotten out. By the time we're at the end of the ville they're throwing flowers and we're throwing C-rats. And we just had a great time looking out on the mountains of Laos. We'd throw C-rations, they'd throw flowers.[64]

Noncooperation with the military was part of a much larger style of nonviolent resistance that included shamming. Shamming, the use of deception, stealth, ruse, and petty sabotage, is a traditional form of working-class resistance, particularly effective under the condition of involuntary labor, slavery, or the military. Shamming was at times consciously promoted by the underground press. The GI paper *All Hands Abandon Ship* borrowed the title of the Simon and Garfunkle song "Slow Down, You Move Too Fast" to encourage sailors to resist military operations quietly.[65] Work slowdowns were a widespread and effective weapon. During 1969 Jack Klein served with Delta Company, 1st Battalion, 26th Marines, 1st Marine Division.

> If the officers pushed too hard there was generally a slowdown. People didn't directly disobey a lawful order, but they wouldn't comply as easily or as well as the officers wanted to. You could really piss them off and see the result right there in front of you. But people did the job well enough to survive. I was there in '69 as the common ground-pounder, the grunt, started becoming aware of the fact that the American public wasn't too pleased with what we're doing.[66]

Although shamming is traditional in the military, antiwar attitudes lent a political edge to everyday opposition to military life. Personnel clerks held considerable power in the giant military bureaucracy and sometimes resorted to a kind of paper sabotage or nonviolent fragging. Marc Leepson served with the 527th Personnel Service Company at Qui-Nhon during 1968.

> I loved my country when I went over there. Six weeks later I hated life, the war, Vietnam, America. . . .
> There were various things you could do. . . . One was the one-a-day method for dealing with lifers. Lifers in the army twenty years, they've got a file this thick. . . . Take one out—burn it—a day. They never notice until you do two hundred pages.
> Before I got there . . . when they were building a new mess hall . . . one night while the cement was setting, the sergeant's records of twenty years were—poof—mixed in there. He didn't get paid. He can't go home on leave.[67]

By the end of the war disobedient behavior and passive resistance had become commonplace. In January 1973 Tom Bradley of the Battalion Landing Team 2/9, 3d Marine Division was assigned to guard a prisoner on his flight home from Okinawa.

> As I'm boarding the plane they give me a record jacket for another marine who was facing court-martial. . . . I was supposed to make sure that he and his paperwork got to . . . Camp Pendleton, but I was being processed out. When we landed in California, I just gave him his paperwork and told him to do whatever he felt was right—shook his hand and I went my way and he went his.[68]

Bureaucratic sabotage, slowdowns, and shamming reined in the military machine. Although lack of civilian support and heavy official repression directed most resistance down these other avenues, a few public demonstrations did occur.

On Christmas Eve of 1968, approximately thirty stalwart dissenters in uniform, a number of civilians, and some Vietnamese students met at JFK Square in Saigon to demonstrate against the war. The rally site was placed off limits, and most GIs were confined to barracks. The local army commander showed up in person to threaten those in attendance.[69] In July of 1969 one hundred African American soldiers held an antiwar protest at Qui-Nhon. The soldiers marched through the port base and fought with police when the demonstrators approached a local airport.[70] Small-scale protests were common in many units. In February 1970 Lamont Steptoe organized the African Americans in his unit. "We wanted to dramatize the anniversary of the assassination of Malcolm X. I organized the blacks of my unit so that on that particular day we would all wear black arm bands."[71]

As domestic opposition to the war grew, dissident soldiers showed their support for antiwar demonstrations. On November 9, 1969, a full-page ad in the *New York Times* signed by 1,365 active-duty servicemen, 189 of them serving in Vietnam, called for Americans to support the November 15 antiwar moratorium. News of the moratorium and mobilization demonstrations were received warmly by antiwar soldiers.[72] The December 1969 issue of *Attitude Check* carried a photograph of over a dozen marines flashing peace signs and holding two banners. One banner was a peace sign; the other banner read Vietnam Moratorium, October 15, Danang Vietnam, U.S.M.C., End the Madness Now!

Soldier support for the moratorium even found its way into the pages of *Life* magazine. Correspondent Hal Wingo interviewed approximately one hundred men, many of whom were combat soldiers. Wingo asserted, "Many soldiers regard the organized antiwar campaign in the U.S. with open and outspoken sympathy." Wingo also believed that "the protests in the U.S. are not demoralizing troops in the field." Wingo's article quoted Private Raul Torres, 4th Division medic, as saying, "I never could see the sense in this war, but I enlisted partly because I wanted to get the true picture on what is happening. I'll go back now and carry my sign on the campus. Maybe I can influence somebody." Perhaps more poignantly, a soldier who had joined after the death of his brother at Khe San said, "I came partly for revenge, but now I have lost all faith. The demonstrators are right to speak up because this war is wrong and it must be stopped."[73] The article carried a photo of soldiers on patrol wearing black arm bands in solidarity with the moratorium.

GIs organized powerful demonstrations in Vietnam as part of the moratorium. Dave Blalock was a communications specialist stationed at Camp Long Thanh North.

> One night we were sitting around the barracks in Vietnam . . . and pass-ing around this full-page ad in the *New York Times* that a guy who had just come back from R&R [rest and relaxation] in Hawaii had clipped out. Everybody's . . . saying . . . "Why don't we do something on this date, November 15th." . . . We came to a decision that we're going to wear black arm bands and we're going to refuse to go out on patrol. . . .
>
> The next day we went around . . . and put out the word. . . . It seemed like everybody was going to do it. . . . The morning of the 15th we wake up at about five in the morning, and instead of playing the military shit, they put Jimi Hendrix's "Star-spangled Banner" on. . . .
>
> So we went to formation with our new commanding officer. The former CO was blown away . . . he was killed, fragged. . . . So we went out in morning formation and we're all wearing black arm bands. It was like 100 percent of the enlisted men . . . including some of the war doctors and the helicopter pilots. The CO comes out and he says . . . "I think we're going to give you guys a day off." He was real slick with it.[74]

The moratorium demonstrations accelerated public displays of dissent. That Thanksgiving, over one hundred members of the 71st Evacuation Hospital and the 44th Medical Detachment at Pleiku organized a protest fast called the "John Turkey movement." In *Home before Morning*, nurse Lynda Van Devanter recalls her change in attitudes.

> Earlier in my tour, when I had heard about the war protesters, I had felt angry at them for not supporting us. Now I wished I could march with them. . . . Most others in Pleiku felt the same way. We even held our own Thanksgiving Day fast—the John Turkey movement—as a show of sup-port for those who were trying to end the war through protests and morato-riums. We heard that the fast had spread to units all over Vietnam.[75]

The fast received considerable media coverage when Denise Murry, a nurse at Pleiku and daughter of a distinguished admiral, made antiwar statements to the press.

In the port city of Vinh Lam twenty-five GIs demonstrated publicly against the war. African American soldiers in the Americal Division protested high casualty rates among African Americans. A demonstration of forty African Americans occurred on January 15, 1971, at the U.S. Army headquarters and stockade at Long Binh. The marchers demanded an end to racial discrimina-tion in the army and the freedom of Angela Davis. The soldier–demonstrators held aloft a black, red, and green flag and a banner in honor of Dr. Martin Luther King.[76] Also in 1971 two hundred soldiers from airborne and medical units assembled at the headquarters of the 101st Airborne to protest the use of the powerfully armed Cobra gunships because they resulted in large civilian casualties.[77] A massive GI-sponsored rally and picnic on July 4, 1971, turned beaches near Chu Lai into what David Cortright called "the largest pot party in the history of the Army."[78]

Secretly circulated and short-lived, petitions were a common form of expression in Vietnam. The most successful petition was sponsored by the VVAW and collected approximately 2,000 names calling for an end to hostilities.[79] A petition with 136 names was collected by a Captain Alan Goldstein in support of the moratorium demonstrations.[80]

Hundreds of thousands of men wrote complaints to the president and Congress, or voiced similar sentiments to the news media. These letters helped to raise congressional doubts about the war. By 1971, soldier complaints to Congress totaled 250,000 a year and became one of the most popular forms of protest.[81] This wave of GI protest produced dissident organizations and began to reorganize the military itself.

GI Organization and Military Resistance

Formal GI movement organizations appeared primarily in the United States, Germany, and Japan. Yet soldiers in Vietnam did organize themselves to oppose the war. Together, the major antiwar groups, the VVAW, and the American Servicemen's Union (ASU), both founded in 1967, and the Movement for a Democratic Military (MDM), founded in 1969, had thousands of members in Vietnam by the early 1970s. For most, the affiliation seemed to provide antiwar information and an informal support network. After his tour in Vietnam, Bill Davis worked in Tactical Air Recon in Thailand.

> By the time I left Vietnam I was stone antiwar. . . . The following year in Thailand I did become an antiwar activist, circulating literature and stuff like that. . . . Some of the first stuff we got was from Movement for a Democratic Military. We had no real connection with the organization but had their literature and it sounded good, so that's what we called ourselves.[82]

GI newspapers provided a sense of connection to the organized GI movement. Writing from near the DMZ, one GI advised the editors of *Task Force* that their papers "are devoured by many GIs here, hungry for words that speak of peace in our time."[83]

African American soldiers were particularly involved in political organizing. Groups such as the Ju-Ju's, American Minority Servicemen's Association, Black Brothers United, US, the Zulu 1200s, and De Mau Mau were established to oppose racism.[84] Freddie Smith served with the 7th Marine Division from May

1970 to April 1971. For Smith, joining De Mau Mau was a routine part of being an African American in the armed forces.

> Just about every black veteran of the Marine Corps . . . was associated with the De Mau Mau at one time or another. . . . It was only to educate blacks that didn't know the UCMJ or laws of the marines. . . . We were well versed in it. Some Mau Mau's just assigned themselves as librarians . . . as far as the UCMJ . . . and also lawyers were assigned down at Danang City.
>
> Other activities might have been protests . . . If a black was given a court-martial and there was a justifiable doubt to his guilt. . . . Usually we try and ask questions, petition about the court-martial. . . . A lot of times they used to protest and maybe go on some type of semi-strike which was semi-illegal . . . sometimes it helped.[85]

Some chapters of the Black Panthers were formed in Vietnam. Due to repression and secrecy, it is difficult to determine how many Vietnam soldiers were members of the Black Panther party. In any event, it is more important that the Panthers enjoyed widespread sympathy from African American troops. In a survey conducted by Wallace Terry, 36 percent of the almost four hundred black combat soldiers questioned said they would join militant groups like the Black Panthers. Another 18 percent claimed they would "consider" joining Black Power organizations.[86]

More typical of African American organizing, however, were the Black Brothers United (BBU). Two related events in September of 1971 drew together both the character of black dissent and the nature of official reaction.

Cam Ranh Bay was a sprawling military base some one hundred miles north of Saigon. By the early 1970s its large soldier population had produced stable and established dissident organizations. The BBU was an openly organized equal-rights and self-help group much like dozens of other organizations in Vietnam. The BBU was well organized, with elected officers such as Sergeant Andrew Love, an able soldier with a clean service record. Mildred Majette, assistant director of the local USO, joined the BBU and became one of their most effective activists. "Sister Millie" gained respect for her abilities as a spokesperson and was elected to leadership in the BBU. Acting as an advocate for African American grievances, the BBU held regular meetings of several dozen members and investigated allegations of discrimination regarding promotion, punishment, and command. A pattern of conflict between African Americans and military police was particularly troubling to BBU members.

Typical of dissident organizations in Vietnam, the BBU's first defense was knowledge of military law and regulations and the use of proper chain-of-command channels. When these forms of protest were exhausted, the BBU moved to nonviolent forms of resistance such as petitions, letters, and demonstrations. Local officers held disparate views of such activities. Some officers saw

BBU as well intentioned but misguided while others saw it as subversive, militant, and dangerous. The BBU steadfastly opposed both the use of violence and the use of hard drugs, which they felt incapacitated soldiers' ability to be part of the movement for African American rights.

The BBU's struggle against racism took on a distinctly anti-authoritarian tone. According to Love and other BBU members, the racial tension between blacks and whites in the lower ranks was of little political significance.[87] The problems they sought to address were between lower-ranking African American soldiers and their military superiors: noncommissioned officer, officers, and military police. The BBU's main focus was the institutionalized expression of racism.

Local organizing came to a peak on September 25, 1971, when the BBU held a demonstration in off-limits Cam Ranh Bay Village to dramatize their demands. Forty GIs marched peacefully into the village and presented a list of fifteen grievances to superior officers who had hurried to the scene. No arrests or charges were made against the demonstrators. This action would have remained typical of GI dissent in Vietnam except for the attempt of African American GIs at nearby Whiskey Mountain to attend the demonstration.

Whiskey Mountain was an isolated construction camp that housed support troops responsible for maintenance along Highway 1. The work was dirty and boring, and opportunities for recreation few. In the months before the BBU's demonstration the mountaintop base had been ripped by a rash of fragging attempts, mysterious explosions, widespread hard-drug use, and sporadic work stoppages. Signs of the counterculture were common. Many of the soldiers wore long hair, bracelets, and beads, and did their hot work in less than regulation uniform. Some of the African American soldiers wore black berets, had afro's, or prefaced their military name tags with "Bro." There was periodic defiance of orders, and a number of African American soldiers began sporadic work stoppages.

When a new commander attempted to restore discipline, the NCOs began enforcing dress regulations, bed checks, and other military routines associated with stateside discipline. Seen as harassment by many soldiers, this new regime led to increased conflict between NCOs and enlisted men, both black and white. Several minor incidents prior to September 25 had also increased the feeling of racial tension.

It was against this backdrop of unrest and frustration that the local BBU chapter at Whiskey Mountain was attempting to reorganize. When fourteen African Americans, the core of BBU at Whiskey Mountain, tried to attend the demonstration in Cam Ranh Bay, a series of small protests by the BBU resulted in work stoppages, a violent confrontation, and charges of mutiny. [88]

Without elected leadership Private Douglas Stanford tried somewhat desperately to assert his direction and reorganize the group. Circulating Black Panther literature concerning the death of a young black girl in the United States, Stanford falsely claimed to both soldiers and officers that the demonstration scheduled to be held in Cam Ranh was a memorial service for the dead child.

In a series of stormy meetings, over a dozen African American soldiers requested transportation to the demonstration. The soldiers pleaded, warned, antagonized, and perhaps threatened some officers. In the company commander's office a first sergeant was so alarmed by the protest that he locked and loaded his M-16, refusing to unload even when ordered by his commander. After three failed meetings, African American leaders claimed they would march on foot the following morning. The group asked for and was granted permission to continue a meeting back in their hootches for a short time beyond curfew.

The next morning the fourteen African American soldiers, with the weapons they were officially required to have for such a trip slung over their shoulders, approached the main gate. On reaching the gate, the soldiers were given a direct order to return to camp. The sergeant major suggested that the men conduct a memorial service at Whiskey Mountain instead of going to Cam Ranh Bay. Slowly the men complied. They returned to a bunker and stayed there, refusing to report for duty. While witnesses disagree sharply over the stated intention of the protesters, the fourteen remained at the hootch, where "their intent and actions were peaceful and unassuming."[89]

The soldiers sat in the hootch, discussed the events surrounding the young girl's death, and talked over racial politics in America. Over the next few hours some went to the mess hall, some slept or read, a few hung around the area of the bunker. White soldiers approached the bunker several times without reaction from those inside. A white legal officer approached the bunker looking for his clients. Speaking to two African American soldiers, including Stanford, the officer saw no weapons, barricades, or other signs of tension or trouble.[90]

Almost immediately after the BBU returned to the bunker, however, a series of overreactions, rumors, false reports, and race baiting shaped official reaction. According to the army's own investigation, initial official reports contained "gross inaccuracies of both tone and fact," which were "based on unfounded rumor from unidentified personnel."[91] Without any attempt by company officers to investigate, the dissidents were reported as armed, barricaded in a bunker, and threatening officers. Rumors of violent intent against all whites spread rapidly through the camp.

Three armored personnel carriers were brought up to the gate of the camp on official command. A group of white soldiers began lining up approximately a hundred yards from the bunker.[92] The black soldiers were unaware that they were about to be attacked. Then at about noon an explosion rocked the entrance of the hootch. Within seconds the half-tracks, their fifty-caliber machine guns ready, and approximately fifty white soldiers, many of whom were armed, surrounded the bunker. Stunned by the blast, the protesters came stumbling out. All were unarmed except one, who turned his weapon over to an officer. Although never proved by the investigation, the coordinated nature of the attack on the black protesters, "indicated that this action was in response to an order."[93]

The dazed and injured protesters were taken to the dispensary, treated for wounds, and placed under arrest. When they attempted to leave the dispensary they were confronted and searched by a force of MPs, handcuffed, and taken to the maximum-security cell block in Long Binh jail. Except for two leaders all serious charges were dropped within two weeks and the soldiers were released with minor punishments. Stanford remained in jail for several months awaiting trial for disrespecting an officer and disobeying a direct order. The persons who bombed the bunker, gave false reports, ordered soldiers to load weapons, or were fully armed, were never identified or punished. The official inquiry concluded that "the instantaneous decision to place all of the men in pre-trial confinement served to further impair the lack of confidence that the black soldiers have in their commanders and further substantiated their belief that a dual standard of punishment exists."[94] The events at Whiskey Mountain showed an army fractured by race and also demonstrated the limitations of open organization in a hostile environment.

Cultural Revolution and Political Resistance

If the conditions of life in Vietnam made organizing difficult, the military also made it somewhat unnecessary. Since soldiers were already organized into work or fighting units, dissident sentiments coalesced on the level of platoon, squad, or "buddy group." The organization for antiwar resistance was often a transformed version of the original military unit.

The small buddy groups were centers of personal loyalty, mutual protection, and survival. Military sociologists consider these small, intimate groups to be a primary factor in maintaining discipline and fighting spirit.[95] Extensive research after World War II suggested that the solidarity and survival goals of these intimate networks engineered the commitment of its members to positive combat performance and discipline. The Vietnam War and the cultural explosions of the 1960s transformed some of these buddy groups into conduits for war resistance and for the expression of alternative culture and politics.[96] Dave Cline served in Delta Company, 4th Battalion, 9th Infantry, 25th Division near Cu Chi from June to December 1967.

> We were a combat unit. . . . Everyone stuck together. It was like racism didn't matter. Like . . . the one place where America could get past racism amongst its own ranks was going out and fighting someone else. There was a lot more racial divisions . . . in the rear. It was like America again.
>
> But when you came in from the field, people generally tended to break down culturally. It was culturally—musically. It was like what part of the country you were from, and it was also how you were going about getting wasted, because that's what we were doing. . . .
>
> And so you had the heads. You had the juicers. You had the brothers. . . . The juicers would be more into country music, and the heads would be more into the latest Jefferson Airplane, or Janis Joplin, or

Hendrix. . . . See '67 was when San Francisco—the hippie—all that type of stuff was coming up. . . . We were aware of some of that music. The Stones, of course.

Then they had the brothers, who were like into their own thing. And we used to like try . . . to have a pretty good relationship between the heads and the brothers, even culturally. You know, rock music incorporated soul music in that period. And there was also sort of a common bond because . . . at least a certain percentage of the black guys were getting high—smoking pot.[97]

The army in Vietnam was partially reorganized by American GIs into the "heads," the "juicers," and the "brothers." These new social arrangements, including a Latino-inspired group, "la raza," informally institutionalized some of the cultural developments of the late 1960s and early 1970s. Cline explains the ideas and motivations of the heads.

Well, we were in a situation of extreme brutality, and dirtiness, and funkiness. And I think that we used to look at the whole hippie thing—or at least I did—as being an alternative where people were living more in harmony. . . . Like, here are people living just the opposite of us. . . . And I used to really be attracted to that.

But it would just be like a fantasy because our reality is—you go out and smoke some herb and you're sitting there watching a fucking light show and the light show is a napalm strike over there fifty miles away. . . . You watch it and you say, "Wow, that was cool," and then you think someone's on the receiving end of that. . . .

For a long time . . . I had visions about these people in America that were really living together and working together, and I really wanted to come in contact with hippies.[98]

The transformed buddy groups were structured around an emerging youth culture of drug use, peace, and anti-authoritarianism. The purchase and use of drugs were activities that required group cooperation and trust to avoid being caught. Smoking marijuana was symbolically tied to antiwar resistance.

After six months I came to the conclusion that we were the aggressors. . . . I wasn't so concerned with winning or losing, but I started to see the injustice of it all. Truck drivers would just run people down on the road and laugh about it. We'd be riding in helicopters and people would be working in the rice fields and the door gunners would just kill them right on the spot and laugh. Something just started to go awry inside of me. This isn't right. This isn't mom and apple pie. This isn't what I came here for. So I was involved with smoking marijuana. At the time that was like the symbolism of the antiwar movement in the service.[99]

1 Monumental peace sign near Camp Eagle, where the 101st Airborne Division was headquartered. This David L. Terry photograph first appeared in the *New York Times Magazine* in 1971 and was circulated in the GI press. (Photo reproduction, Aubrey Haynes.)

The underground or alternative connotations associated with the heads helped to create an alternative set of social and political norms.[100] Long hair, peace signs, hippie beads, rock and roll, and pot smoking were the most common outward signs of an alternative youth culture in the military. The Country Joe and the Fish antiwar song "I Feel Like I'm Fixing to Die Rag" was one of the most popular songs in Vietnam after 1969. The peace sign in particular became a cherished symbol of the antiwar soldier. At least once the peace sign achieved the stature of monumental sculpture. Near Camp Eagle, where the 101st Airborne Division was stationed, a gigantic peace sign was sculpted into the landscape, perhaps by bulldozer.[101]

During the years that the youth culture was transforming the military, the assassination of Martin Luther King, Jr., and the urban uprisings amplified the need for an African American alternative.[102] Leslie Whitfield served in the 4th Division, 3d Battalion, 10th Infantry, from August 1967 to February 1968. The persistence of racial conflict in the United States pushed Whitfield to raise fundamental questions about military service and to strengthen his resolve to fight for his "own rights" and his "own people."

> Why can we be . . . fighting for this country . . . and then go back and we can't take advantage of opportunities that were offered us by the Constitution? That's the main thing. . . .
>
> When I was there this race riot was going on in Detroit and they sent . . . the 101st Airborne Division and they are a combat unit. . . . Actually it was just a war back here too. We couldn't understand why we had to be . . . fighting for a country that really didn't give a damn about us, when we should be back home fighting for our own rights and for our own people.[103]

African American culture within the military was represented by the brothers, or "bloods." The brothers were organized around distinctive African American qualities that distinguished them from other soldiers.

> Most of the heads were very critical of the war, looked down on lifers, condemned the military, wore peace symbols and beads with their uniforms, and smoked dope as much as they could. The juicers would be guys who believed in the red, white, and blue, and hated the word "communism"— who were prejudiced in many other areas. . . .
>
> I always hung out with the heads, but within that there were those of us who were black. The blacks were very tight in the military in Vietnam. . . . Black men in Vietnam would not pass each other without saluting one another. I'm not talking about military salute, I'm talking about a Black Power salute. . . . We all wore black arm bands that had been woven from our shoe laces.
>
> There was always some aspect to our attire that made a statement about us being black men. We had our own language. In terms of the way we gave up the "dap." . . . It was a series of very complicated handshakes. . . . If you came into a mess hall you would go around to all the tables and give up this dap to every black man in the place before you would sit down to eat.[104]

With the brothers an African American army began to emerge. The brothers promoted war resistance through a racial analysis of war and society.

> And we were constantly analyzing things. . . . You had this identity, the term "bloods." It just gave us this sense of nationhood, because we began

to see how even within the military, we would have to experience these racist things. . . . And that we would have to go through the rest of our lives in America as still being victimized by the various racist institutions that exist and people's attitudes. So it was a way of bringing us together and helping us overcome the stresses and strains of the military as black men.[105]

An identity based on the "sense of nationhood" was essential to the brothers. This sense of identity sometimes went beyond fellow African Americans to include the Vietnamese. Some black soldiers came to "the consciousness that the struggle of the Vietnamese was not so very different or far apart from the struggle of blacks."[106] Once that identification was made, antiracist attitudes took on an explicitly antiwar character.

The many symbolic expressions of black solidarity such as the black solidarity handshake or "dap," black leather bracelets, and soul music signified a cultural alternative to military life that laid deep claims on African American soldiers.

Latino soldiers also banded together. As "la raza," this diverse group of American soldiers expressed and shared their cultural similarities and differences. Miguel Lemus, a Chicano from California, served with the 25th Infantry and 11th Cavalry from March 1967 to March 1968.

Most of the platoon was from Arizona, New Mexico, Texas, and California. I met a lot of raza overseas. . . . In my company we had to protect each other 'cause no one was going to protect us. As for the races bit, we had to learn to get along because in time of action there was no color. . . . In the rear that's a different story. . . .

We'd get like Indians in our all Chicano platoon. . . . We would bullshit each other until someone would get mad, and sometimes we'd get into a fight. . . . And the next day we'd be friends. They were brothers-in-law . . . that's what kept the raza going.

The Puerto Ricans were a lot like the raza, in action they all did their job. . . . Everybody was a big family. It was togetherness.[107]

This "big family" began to articulate an emerging sense of Chicano identity. United by the Spanish language and a uniquely American mix of European and Indian heritage, the raza embraced a powerful code of honor and manhood. As with the heads and the brothers, the raza could also promote rebellious behavior through group "togetherness."

One time there were ninety of us smoking weed. . . . We were getting all crazy and celebrating our return from a mission—well it was party time. . . . There wasn't any killing of each other then except this one time we came back from a hard mission . . . and this officer tried to be a hero—bust ninety guys. We were along the trenches and . . . they shot him. . . . No one said anything. Someone called on the radio and told them the captain had been shot by the gooks. . . . Who saw it? Nobody saw it. . . .

I often ask myself, What did the war prove? Nothing! Was it worth it? No! I went and saw people get killed and slaughtered for nothing. You can prove you're a man without having to see men get slaughtered.[108]

Whether heads, brothers, or la raza, it certainly appears that by 1968 the dynamics of group solidarity and behavior were as likely to transmit political dissent as military discipline.[109] While the political views of the juicers was varied and ambivalent, most but not all antiwar soldiers who had contact with these subcultures identified with the heads, brothers, or la raza. The power of these groups to promote dissent cannot be overstated: they were the day-to-day organizations of the soldier resistance in Vietnam.

The desire for peace and racial justice motivated individual actions, led to the creation of political organizations, and transformed traditional buddy groups. These unparalleled actions by American soldiers were shaped both by a profound cultural revolution and by the military's own policies and practices.

The political fallout from the Tet offensive and the bureaucratic and careerist values permeating the military command resulted in a profound crisis of leadership. Soldiers grew to distrust officers they saw as interested only in making rank and who failed to act heroically or to articulate a compelling justification for the war. Serving only six-month tours, officers often failed to establish close bonds with common soldiers. The defiance of military authorities is just part of the story of American military failure in Vietnam. It has been persuasively argued that the military bureaucracy functioned in a way to promote dissent.

My image of leadership began to break down. They didn't care about the guys. Suggestions were punished. I saw a lack of courage and professionalism. Then I thought, What am I following these guys for?[110]

As one military observer commented, "It was a case of double deterioration, from the top down and the bottom up."[111] Poor leadership encouraged dissent.

While the war experience and the military itself catalyzed protest, it was the explosion of alternative cultures within working-class, African American, Latino, and youth communities that gave form and direction to the dissident movement. Yet the cultural revolution within the military was more than just a reflection of American society. Some aspects of this alternative culture seemed to reach an intensity of expression in Vietnam unparalleled back in the States. Soldier dissent was both consequence and cause of domestic political developments.

There was the whole Black Power thing. . . . It was a whole atmosphere. All that was a way of showing our camaraderie, like brothers really hanging together. . . . It was like a togetherness that I ain't never seen since.[112]

Soldier resistance to the war in Vietnam produced a powerful mass movement. Antiwar soldiers and their ideas circulated widely outside the theater of war. Created by the crisis of Vietnam, soldier dissent appeared everywhere the military was concentrated.

The GI Movement in the United States

Part of the larger struggle in this society for human rights, the GI movement is similar to the older Black and Brown struggles in that it was born out of oppression and fear. . . . Rather than reaction to fear and brute force in kind, many GIs are challenging the old order with active love and commitment to community and peace for all. . . . Its direction is the direction of the non-violent revolution in our society. . . . We believe that the struggles for peace and for social, political, and economic power for all peoples at home and abroad are intrinsically related.

—AS YOU WERE, APRIL 1970

IN THE UNITED STATES, Germany, Japan, and other locations where soldiers were stationed, the GI movement appeared. The movement outside of Vietnam took on forms more closely related to civilian protest and domestic disorders. After 1967 GI resistance grew from scattered groups and individuals acting largely in isolation into a domestic social movement. Widespread resistance from the rank-and-file soldier, the founding of the Vietnam Veterans against the War (VVAW), and the American Servicemen's Union (ASU), the beginnings of the coffeehouse network, and the start of the GI underground press marked the arrival of a movement unprecedented in American history.[1] As in Vietnam, sharp confrontations also marked the movement. A wave of prison rebellions and base uprisings racked the military.

Roots of Resistance

The earliest resistance, however, was characterized by individual acts of conscience, which usually incurred serious jail sentences. In November 1965 Henry Howe from Fort Bliss in El Paso joined a public demonstration against the war and was sentenced to two years hard labor for his act of free speech.[2] In 1966 the "Fort Hood Three" became the first widely publicized group of resisters in the military. David Samos, Dennis Mora, and James Johnson refused service in Vietnam and drew the attention and support of the civilian peace movement. Their joint statement, excerpted below, is evidence of the roots of the GI resistance.

We have decided to take a stand against this war, which we consider immoral, illegal, and unjust. . . . We represent in our backgrounds a cross section of the army and of America. James Johnson is a Negro, David Samos is of Lithuanian and Italian parents, Dennis Mora is a Puerto Rican. We speak as American soldiers.

We know that Negroes and Puerto Ricans are being drafted and end up in the worst of the fighting all out of proportion to their numbers in the population, and we have firsthand knowledge that these are the ones who have been deprived of decent education and jobs at home. The three of us . . . found we thought alike on one overriding issue—the war in Vietnam must be stopped.[3]

In their statement these three privates signaled the beginning of a rank-and-file upsurge against military authority and war. Ethnically diverse, these young men spoke "as American soldiers" against the injustices of a war they connected to injustices at home. Challenging the legality of the war, Mora appealed his case all the way to the Supreme Court, where it was denied review.[4]

In 1966 Private Ronald Lockman refused to go to Vietnam. Citing American atrocities and the illegality of the war as his defense, Lockman was sentenced to two-and-a-half-years of hard labor.[5] The son of a steelworker, this soldier typified the working-class and African American roots of the military peace movement. His action and those of marines William Harvey and George Daniels were among the first moves of African American GIs against war and racism. Harvey and Daniels called a meeting of soldiers during the 1967 Detroit rebellion to question the wisdom of the Vietnam War. In a later interview Harvey stated, "I feel that the black man's attitude is that the war is one of genocide toward the colored people of the earth in general, in that the military can kill two birds with one stone."[6] Both Black Muslims, Harvey and Daniels initiated war protest based on the racial politics of American policy. They were sentenced to six- and ten-year prison terms, respectively, but were freed after a two-year campaign for their release.[7]

Dissent among African American soldiers was linked to developments within other African American youth and community movements. After the 1965 combat death of civil rights activist John D. Shaw, the Mississippi Freedom Democratic party distributed a leaflet in protest, asserting that black Americans should not fight.

1. No Mississippi Negroes should be fighting in Vietnam for the White Man's freedom, until all the Negro People are free in Mississippi. 2. Negro boys should not honor the draft here in Mississippi. . . . 3. We will gain respect and dignity as a race only by forcing the U.S. Government and the Mississippi Government to come with guns, and dogs, and trucks to take our sons away to fight and be killed protecting Mississippi, Alabama, Georgia, and Louisiana. 4. No one has a right to ask us to risk our lives and kill other Colored People in Santo Domingo and Vietnam, so that the White American can get richer. . . . 5. Last week a white

soldier from New Jersey was discharged from the Army because he refused to fight in Vietnam; he went on a hunger strike. Negro boys can do the same thing. We can write and ask our sons if they know what they are fighting for . . . If he answers Freedom, tell him that's what we are fighting for here in Mississippi. And if he says Democracy, tell him the truth—we don't know anything about Communism, socialism, and all that, but we do know that Negroes have caught hell right here under this American Democracy.[8]

In various formulations, this argument articulated in McComb, Mississippi, in 1965 shaped the attitudes of a generation of dissident African American soldiers.[9] Growing out of the civil rights movement and reaching its most assertive form as Black Power—racial solidarity and antiracist politics constituted a central perspective from which military resistance grew.

Latino communities also mobilized a considerable level of opposition to the war. In September 1966 a public statement was circulated in Puerto Rico and eventually garnered the signatures of over a thousand young men. The statement took an anti–imperialist and republican position.

On . . . the ninety-eighth anniversary of the proclamation of the Republic of Puerto Rico, we . . . declare . . . our firm and determined purpose of each and every one of the undersigned to not serve in the United States Armed Forces under any circumstance.

In this way we express our repudiation of the tyrannical law of the Obligatory Military Service which is imposed by the North American imperialism on Puerto Rican youth as a part of the colonial subjugation of our country.[10]

Antiwar African American and Latino soldiers articulated dissenting positions shared by other members of their communities. Working-class communities also embraced antiwar sentiments expressed by the soldier resistance. In May 1966 socialist Andy Stapp joined the U.S. Army with the explicit intention to organize resistance. After a year of sporadic organizing attempts and court-martials, Stapp founded the ASU in December 1967. He searched for support from the antiwar movement and found a radical youth group, Youth Against War and Fascism, willing to organize publicity and public support for dissident soldiers undergoing court-martial trials and for other ASU activities.[11] The ASU promoted a working-class, antiwar, and trade union approach to organizing. Its basic demands were an end to saluting and "sir-ing" of officers, election of officers by vote of the troops, racial equality, rank-and-file control over court-martial boards, federal minimum wages, the right to free political association, the right to disobey illegal orders (such as orders to fight in an illegal war in Vietnam), and the right of collective bargaining.[12] According to Stapp, by 1969 the ASU union had grown to sixty-five hundred members in all services, and it signed on some twenty thousand members over the life of the organization. The ASU formed chapters on a hundred military bases and on sixty ships. Its paper, *The Bond*, one of the earliest GI newspapers, claimed a peak circulation of about seventy-five thousand.[13] Although the ASU failed to win a formal contract, it helped to establish a clear tradition of working-class resistance to military authority and unjust war.

Although the early working-class peace movement stood largely outside of the labor movement, important dissent began to undercut the prowar collaboration between powerful union and government elites.[14] As early as 1965 some unions had begun to dissent. A small New York City–based organization, Trade Unionist's for Peace, opened shop in the fall of 1965.[15] Local 1199 Hospital Workers, District 65 Distributive Workers, and a St. Louis Teamsters local were among the first to go on record against the war. In 1966 National Committee for a Sane Nuclear Policy (SANE) established a trade union division, and during May of that year, 173 union leaders from thirty unions attended the founding session.[16]

By 1967, union members began to move against the war in increasing numbers. Dissenting from the AFL–CIO leadership, union leaders from around the country condemned the war and bolstered working-class resistance. Calling themselves the National Leadership Assembly for Peace, 523 union leaders from thirty-eight states met in November 1967 to denounce the war as immoral and against the national interest. Their policy statement conveyed the depth of working-class opposition by claiming, "There exists at all levels in our unions the same disquiet, frustration, and opposition that characterizes the American people as a whole."[17] The unionists published *Labor Voice* to promote their antiwar position.

Although the dissenting GIs articulated antiwar ideas rapidly gaining currency in their own communities, American soldiers nonetheless faced a personal and often lonely struggle to express their dissent.[18] Alan Klein's turn away from the war and toward resistance to the military captures both the emergence and vitality of early antiwar resistance in the United States.

> On one of my trips home I was in O'Hare Airport. . . . This guy comes by and he's got . . . this doughy, pudgy hand, all pinkish. . . . And then I looked up at his face. He had been burned and he was all puffy. . . . I went home depressed about that. My father met me and he was telling me about a big killing he made on the stock market with a munitions company. Suddenly it became crystal clear. . . . He's the one who should have been in that young guy's place—he has a real reason to fight, he needs the war to make money. . . .
>
> From that point on it was never the same again. I came back and announced to my friends . . . I'm opposed to the war . . . I'm not going to Vietnam. . . . We decided what we could best do is destroy the efficiency of our outfit. . . .

> Everything we did was designed to be messed up, sabotaged, or basically deemed done by incompetents, and thereby they would exert more energy to keep us in line and less to wage war. So little by little, it might be a truck that was neglected, it might be the tip of a wing that was damaged, just anything to keep it off-balance.[19]

Opposed to a war for profit, the activities of Klein and his friends typified much of the military resistance. Small daily acts of resistance were designed to hinder the military's ability to function effectively. This covert resistance periodically welled up into group action and resulted in a broader consciousness of the military antiwar movement.

> Finally, in the fall of '66 a group of us decided we would go AWOL. . . . That was the end of it, I was in jail. Just before I was released I heard the reason I was being let out was because we got this directive that said all the people who committed the following offenses would . . . be dismissed. . . . So it dawned on me . . . there were thousands and thousands of guys who were doing time, costing the military a lot of money. . . . Unbeknownst to me, I was part of something larger. . . . I found tremendous solace in subsequently knowing there were so many people . . . groping along trying to find their way . . . but all of us . . . coming to the same point.[20]

As in prisons in Vietnam, jail became a place where a sense of resistance and community often developed. Conscientious objectors (CO) were sometimes incarcerated for their beliefs. Locked in the stockade, David Brown, a 1966 CO, recalls his experience in ways that hint at emerging trends in the military resistance.

> Looking at it in cultural terms, basic training was a blue collar atmosphere; the stockade was the street. . . . The games those guys played with the guards were amazing. It scared me to death. They were disrespectful, they broke the rules. . . . Also, it was now far enough into the Sixties to meet some kindred spirits. There were some semi-hippies who landed in the Army somehow and were doing their AWOL bit. I realized that in the stockade, more than anyplace else, I was with people who were most like myself. I had been put on CCCO's list of imprisoned conscientious objectors, and during Christmas 1966, I started getting Christmas cards.[21]

By late 1966 Brown encountered the youth culture, working-class resistance, and civilian peace movement support—all central aspects to the stateside soldier revolt. When the stockades became schools for antiwar activities, the military peace movement expressed its genius: it was able to transform the very means of oppression and control into the instruments of resistance and peace.

The War at Home

At least fifteen major prison uprisings occurred between 1968 and 1972. Perhaps the single best known event of the domestic GI movement was the October 1968 mutiny at Presidio prison in California. Led by antiwar soldiers Linden Blake, Keith Mather, Walter Pawlowski, and Randy Rowland, twenty-seven men attempted a sit-in-style demonstration at morning formation to protest harsh conditions and the recent killing of an inmate. The story has been well told by Fred Gardner in *The Unlawful Concert,* and more recently by Gerry Nicosia in an article entitled, "The Presidio 27."[22] Tried as mutineers, the protesters were given severe punishments, and a long legal battle ensued. Blake, Mather, and Pawlowski, all facing long jail terms for their leadership roles, escaped and fled to Canada. Mather remained at large until 1984, when he was arrested and jailed for four months.[23] The Presidio demonstration was a turning point for the GI movement in that it produced international publicity and proved that effective soldier protest was possible even under the worst conditions.

The June 1969 riot at the Fort Dix stockade involved 250 soldiers and resulted in the court-martial of 5 GIs targeted as leaders. One leader, Terry Klug, had long been AWOL in France and had founded Resistance Inside the Army, an early antiwar group. *Fort Dix Stockade: Our Prison Camp Next Door,* by Joan Crowell, portrays the brutal conditions of prison life, the inhumane treatment of prisoners awaiting trial, and the remarkable courage of GI resisters. Like the Presidio mutiny, the events at Fort Dix attracted widespread attention. On October 12, the "Free the Fort Dix 38 Committee" organized five thousand demonstrators, many of them Rutgers students, to march on the New Jersey fort.[24]

In July of 1968, 238 soldiers took over the Fort Bragg stockade and held out for three days.[25] The following January, 2,300 GIs went on a work strike at Fort Leavenworth to protest living conditions. In September 1969 the brig at Camp Pendleton became the scene of an all-night battle between hundreds of incarcerated marines and military police. Prison rebellions also occurred in West Germany and Japan.[26]

Jack Klein returned to the U.S. from Vietnam and found stateside discipline intolerable. Imprisoned at Quantico, Virginia, during the fall of 1970, this combat veteran sparked a riot with his resistance.

> It was basically a thing where they were going to break your will. . . . It was pretty cold in the hole. . . . They gave you your clothes during the day but took everything away at night. They wouldn't even give you a blanket. . . . One of the guards felt sorry for me so he let me have a jacket. One of the officers came by for inspection and saw the jacket and ordered me to give it up. . . . The weld was broken in one of the corners of the plate steel and I managed just to pull it up enough so that he couldn't slide the door open.

Well when I did that they really got pissed. . . . In the meantime the rest of the prison population got word of what was happening. . . . They sent about twelve guys this time—really kicked my ass. . . . There was just a lot of empathy and one thing led to another. . . . It pretty much went into a full-scale riot. . . . By the time it was over there was eight hundred marines out there with machine guns. I had had enough of Vietnam and really wasn't about to put up with their shit when I got back.[27]

Although ignited by the contest over prison conditions, other ideals animated the prison rebellion. Klein drew upon an array of political influences that encouraged him to act.

I had letters from my mother telling me that I could do anything. . . . She always told me . . . that whatever it would take to get me through a situation, I could muster the strength and the willpower. She didn't mean for me to be the bastion of radicalism in the prison, but that's what I turned out to be. . . .

At the time . . . they had me in the hole. . . . I could have books for two hours a day. . . . I'm reading Mao-Tse Tung's collected works, Angela Davis, and the Black Panthers. I'm getting more radical by the moment. . . . The jail was pretty much a radical environment. It was the time of Kent State—political dissent was mounting in the public at large. . . . More and more people were reaching for radical solutions.[28]

The example of his mother and the others struggling for social change created a tangible spirit of resistance for Klein. These influences merged with this soldier's combat experience to produce, in his words "a hundred-and-eighty-degree turnaround."

Here I was waving the flag in '67 and here I was leading prison riots in '70. So I guess there was a catalyst there somewhere. I'd say it was probably Vietnam. When I'd gone in I didn't think the government and the military could do any wrong, [but] after witnessing . . . man's inhumanity towards man, I just didn't believe in the system anymore.[29]

Prison rebellions linked the immediate reaction against prison conditions to larger political issues. These deeply rooted issues of power and injustice led to a series of uprisings, riots, and demonstrations on military bases.

In October 1967 the first large-scale rioting of American soldiers took place at Fort Hood. Scheduled to leave for Vietnam the following day, the 198th Light Infantry Brigade rioted, attacking the officers' club and destroying $150,000 in property.[30] This type of uprising was a typical expression of GI resistance. In a military environment where organized dissent was easily disrupted by harassment, transfer, or troop movements, spontaneous, seemingly leaderless outbursts were difficult to predict or prevent.

In May 1971 the most violent uprising of American soldiers in the United States occurred at Travis Air Force Base. A riot by over five hundred soldiers resulted in 135 arrests and national press coverage.

After a minor incident two African American soldiers were arrested and placed in the Travis stockade. Chanting "Free Our Brothers," approximately one hundred black airmen with some white GI solidarity marched on the stockade. Air force police armed with automatic weapons met them with tear gas, made mass arrests, and beat a number of demonstrators. As the fighting erupted scores of soldiers joined the fray. That night, the bachelor officer quarters were burned to the ground, and a colonel was dragged from his car and beaten. The next day a bomb scare was called in at the terminal where troops were being loaded for Vietnam. While military officials attempted to characterize the events as a "race riot," the GI press lent another interpretation to the rebellion.[31]

> Both the officers and the national press claim that it was a "race riot" . . . simply "mirroring" overall racial patterns in America. The airmen, especially those directly involved in the fighting and the arrests, have a different point of view. They see the incidents of the weekend not as a "race riot" but as a GI expression of frustration and anger with the officers at Travis, the oppressive system of the military, and the war.
>
> The fighting started around incidents . . . which may have been racial in character. But as the fighting grew and security police were called in, there appears to have developed black–white unity against the police. Fighting also developed against the officers. . . .
>
> It is significant that the only major property damage was done to an officer's quarters, and the heaviest fighting took place around the stockade. While it may seem surprising that such an eruption could occur in the Air Force, it is important to recognize that Travis has a very high percentage of black and white working-class airmen because it is primarily a support base.[32]

During June 1971 an army attempt to pacify GIs with a rock concert backfired into a riot. Canned Heat performed at Fort Ord for an assembly of soldiers heavily guarded by MPs, army intelligence, and Criminal Investigation Division agents. It seems that after a series of small incidents were met with excessive force by the police, a shower of rocks and bottles hailed down on the MPs. As the concert let out, buildings were broken into, trashed, and burned. A bus was stoned and overturned. Fighting between soldiers and police spread throughout the base. Over a hundred were treated at the base hospital for injuries.[33]

One of the largest base uprisings happened at Fort McClelland, Alabama, in November 1971. A series of racial incidents escalated when an off-duty MP drove his jeep through a crowd of African American soldiers, injuring several.

Following the incident, a number of African American servicemen and servicewomen rioted. The next morning a number of African American Women's Army Corps (WACs) refused to work. A demonstration the following Monday resulted in the arrest of seventy-one GIs and sixty-eight WACs when the protesters refused to disperse.[34] Major disturbances over racial issues also occurred in Okinawa during 1970 and 1971.[35]

Although stockade resistance and base uprisings cost the military millions of dollars in resources, absenteeism represented the greatest drain on military manpower. The most available form of expressing dissatisfaction was to withhold one's labor—as a striking worker deserts the job, so a worker in uniform strikes by deserting. By 1967 absent without leave (AWOL) and desertion rates began to climb precipitously. Army AWOL rates climbed from 57.2 per thousand in 1966 to 78 per thousand in 1967. Desertion, or absence over thirty days, grew from 14.9 per thousand in 1966 to 21.4 per thousand in 1967. For the same period, the Marine Corps registered an increase from 16.1 per thousand to 26.8 per thousand. By June 30, 1967, the end of the fiscal year, 40,277 servicemen were listed as deserters.[36]

While it is difficult to read explicit political content into these statistics they do speak to a general level of dissatisfaction. As early as 1965 Japanese activists formed the Japan Technical Committee to Aid War Deserters and successfully organized an underground railroad to Sweden.[37] By 1967 small communities of political deserters were forming in France, Sweden, Japan, and Canada. In October of 1967 four sailors from the *Intrepid* jumped ship to protest the war in Vietnam. Michael Anthony Linder, Craig William Anderson, Richard D. Bailey, and John Michael Barilla issued a statement from Japan that read, "Our decision to publicize our action in deserting from the military has been made in the hope that other Americans, particularly those in the military . . . can be spurred into action to work toward stopping this war."[38] In the following years soldier absenteeism would be increasingly politicized by the growing GI and veteran movements.

In July 1968 nine AWOL soldiers dramatized their antiwar beliefs by chaining themselves to sympathetic clergymen inside of a San Francisco Presbyterian church. One of the nine, Keith Mather, would later help lead the Presidio mutiny.[39] In August 1969, thirty-three AWOL GIs found similar sanctuary in Honolulu's Church of the Crossroads. The six-week protest drew considerable public support and media coverage. Military police eventually arrested the eight remaining servicemen who chose not to be smuggled abroad or go underground. A Honolulu ASU local was organized in wake of the increased antiwar activity.[40]

Between 1968 and 1973 AWOL offenses and desertions severely disrupted military capabilities. Military sources claimed that only 10 to 15 percent of deserters were motivated by opposition to the war, yet this would seem to be largely underestimated, even when we consider only one select group of deserters. Over one-fifth, or approximately 20,000 of the 93,250 deserters, were soldiers who had already completed their tours in Vietnam.[41] In light of the fact that Vietnam veterans were at the center of the GI movement, it is very difficult to see these desertions as arising from anything except their war experiences and disgust with the military. Vietnam veteran Ed Sowders volunteered twice, once for duty in Vietnam to "help the Vietnamese people" and once to desert for "the very same principles."

> When I volunteered for Vietnam . . . this is 1966 now, I tended to believe my political leaders—the president. They said we were over there helping the Vietnamese. . . .
>
> What I saw as a medic was massive civilian casualties that were the results of our firepower. Women, children, the elderly would come flowing into the hospital after certain missions as the results of our weapons and bombs. And there was the attitude of the GIs around me. How do you equate helping the Vietnamese people when your coworkers believe that everyone around them is the enemy. They're all gooks, slopes, dinks, chinks.
>
> I grew up during the McCarthy era. I was an anticommunist. All you had to do was label it communist and I automatically saw it as bad. . . . The greatest shock of all was the suspicion on my part that the communists were better for their people than we were. And given my state of mind, my education, that was a blow to the system. It was like having many or most of the things you had believed in so strongly for so many years pulled right out from under you.[42]

Ironically, Sowder's decision to desert was clinched by his fidelity to values he had held earlier, that the U.S. presence in Vietnam was to help the Vietnamese win self-determination and security. Sowders claimed, "I can honestly say that I deserted the Army on the very same basic principles that I volunteered for the war." For this GI, continuity with traditional values demanded dissent.

A group of six soldiers publicly left the military in May 1968 claiming that war atrocities had made their participation intolerable.[43] When Green Beret Gerry Condon refused an order to go to Vietnam, he was sentenced to ten years in prison at hard labor and a dishonorable discharge. Condon deserted and remained a fugitive well into the 1970s, defying authorities by speaking publicly about Vietnam and amnesty issues.[44] Like many deserters, Condon remained part of the military antiwar movement.

> We've often been asked a question by the media. "Even if there was an unconditional amnesty wouldn't you be afraid to go back to the U.S. with all those people who served honorably over there?" We're always happy to be able to tell them that our main support in the U.S. comes from the veterans, many of whom were in Vietnam, and that's extremely important.[45]

The political content of desertion is suggested by the way in which desertion rates mirrored and contributed to the decline of military effectiveness and political control.[46] From 1966 to 1971 army desertions rose from 15 to 70 per thousand, an increase of 400 percent.[47] As the war shifted to greater reliance on air and naval power, the desertions continued. With reduced combat stress and personal risk, the disruptions in these more technical services certainly reflected the political unpopularity of the American war effort in the last years of the conflict. Although the absolute numbers were considerably lower than among ground forces, air force AWOL offenses increased 34 percent in 1970, 59 percent in 1971, and 83 percent in 1972, at the peak of the air war.[48] The events in the navy portray a similar trend. Starting in 1970, navy AWOL and desertion rates began to climb, and by 1973 navy desertions peaked at a record 13.6 per thousand.[49]

In 1971, three junior officers aboard the USS *Coral Sea* resigned and publicly denounced the war. Before leaving Alameda Naval Station, thirty-five sailors jumped ship, and when it put in again at Honolulu, another fifty-three went AWOL.[50] In July 1971 Sergeant Norma Welshams, a WAF technician, became the first woman to refuse duty abroad based on anti–imperialist principles. The *Fatigue Press* reported Welshams as stating, "I do not believe that the United States Military is in foreign countries to allow the inhabitants self-determination, but rather to occupy their land to maintain financial and military power."[51]

In October of that year nine sailors missed the departure of the *Constellation* when they sought sanctuary in a Catholic church. The nine men from Missouri, California, Pennsylvania, Georgia, Wisconsin, Arkansas, Iowa, and Texas were declared deserters, arrested in the church just before daybreak, and flown back to the carrier.[52]

In his 1971 book *New Exiles,* Roger Williams offered a detailed description of deserters in Canada during 1969 and 1970. The highest-profile group of deserters Williams found were GI organizers. Although a small minority, these deserters fled the United States to avoid punishment for GI movement activities. Most were draftees, many were well educated, and often they entered the service with some antiwar feelings or ambivalence about the military and war. These deserter activists had life experiences and attitudes similar to draft resisters except that they became activists after induction or enlistment into the service.

Williams found the largest group of deserters to be "nonactivists" who "knew that the war in Vietnam was wrong."[53] This majority were "all-American boys," who were radicalized by the politics of the Vietnam era and chose desertion when confronted with war duty. According to Williams another 30 percent were very young and confused because "the world they knew was collapsing around them. The Army which they had been taught was the noble defender of goodness and freedom turned out to be ugly, brutal, and evil."[54] Politically confused by war and the military, these young men sought refuge from a world beyond their control. Williams found that a slim minority, perhaps only 5 percent, fled to Canada for personal, criminal, or other desperate reasons.

In general, deserters tended to be young volunteers with minimal education and from poor or rural backgrounds in the South, Midwest, and mountain states of the West. Twenty-five percent of the total were African Americans, and one hundred were women. One Pentagon study found that of the deserters exiled abroad, fewer than 5 percent left for family or personal reasons.[55] Unlike World War II deserters, few fled under fire, with only 3 percent deserting from Vietnam itself, and 1 percent from combat.[56]

In 1971 army absences were the highest in modern history, 170 AWOLS and 70 desertions per thousand. This was three times the Korean War rate, and while the overall World War II desertion rate was higher, 1971 exceeded the 1944 record of 63 per thousand.[57] Furthermore, the length of absences was far greater during the Vietnam era. It is estimated that absenteeism deprived the military of about one million man-years of service, almost half the total time actually disposed of in Vietnam.[58] Absenteeism forcibly curtailed military capabilities and contributed to the aura of chaos that hung over the armed forces by the early 1970s.

Exile organizations frequently worked in tandem with draft evaders and other war resisters. In London, the exile community united draft evaders and deserters and was organized as a chapter of the VVAW. In France deserters formed Resisters inside the Army (RITA) and published *ACT,* an early GI newspaper.

The American Deserters Committee and some twenty other organizations helped the thousands of military exiles and draft resisters who sought refuge in Canada. The Canadian resisters were the largest community of exiled Americans and published *Amex-Canada* from 1968 until 1976.

Deserter communities held conferences, addressed issues of amnesty, and continued antiwar outreach to U.S. servicemen. When the USS *Hollister* docked at Vancouver in March 1969 the crew was met by groups of civilians and deserters who had organized leafleting, entertainment, and a demonstration on the last day of leave.[59]

Just as important as the formal organizations abroad was the loosely coordinated "underground railroad," which supported AWOL soldiers.[60] The underground functioned like a community in which resistance and protection of the resister were the common values.

My experience with the underground, if that's what you want to call it, is just a string of people who are nonmembers of any organization what-so-ever, but they're so damn sympathetic and one person knows another. It's a string of people, it's not an organization. It's a couple . . . thousand people who give a damn and who would help someone in trouble.[61]

The underground relied upon two communities; the network of peace activists, and the fugitives' own local community.

I used to sneak home in the wee hours of the morning to visit my family in Detroit. What I didn't know at the time was half my neighbors . . . knew that. . . . Somebody always saw me but nobody ever reported me. In fact my mother told me one time . . . the FBI had been around questioning neighbors about my whereabouts. She got calls from neighbors. . . . "If you see Ed tell him to get out of town—they're serious this time."

If people wanted to they could have done a McCarthy number—ratted on dozens of kids who didn't register for the draft. Everybody knew somebody who resisted the war in one way or another.[62]

Community members, neighbors, activists, churchgoers, students, and teachers, all were strands in the string of underground organization. The underground sheltered soldiers, arranged jobs, and shuttled GIs back and forth across the Canadian border. Border crossing involved the greatest risks for AWOL GIs and the underground's activists.

It was terrifying, every time you did it you could be busted. We had tricks crossing the border. You got an old hippie van, you put "Jesus Saves" all over it, and you take a bite out of the stinkiest onion you can find. Just as you're pulling up there you roll down the window and go, "Hi," and the guy goes "Whew!." . . .

Coming back into the country was harder. . . . They knew what we were doing. Occasionally you would run across a customs guy who said "I just got back from there myself, man. Right On! You get them guys out of there."[63]

Desertion was only one form of disobeying orders. The figures on the general level of disobedience within the military are considerable. Estimates of less-than-honorable discharges vary, with a minimum number of 563,000.[64] However, amnesty advocates writing in *Amex-Canada* claimed that 790,000 war-era veterans were punished with bad discharges. While it is difficult to determine what percentage of disobedient acts were politically inspired, disorderly soldiers certainly disrupted military effectiveness. The impact of military disobedience becomes greater when viewed against the background of GI protest.[65]

A Protest Movement

While extralegal forms of resistance were important, legal dissent involved even more servicepeople. Like their civilian counterparts, soldiers marched in demonstrations, organized protests, started discussion groups, founded peace organizations, and built an extensive network of underground newspapers and coffeehouses. GIs responded to the political issues of the time.

The 1968 assassination of Martin Luther King, Jr., prompted spontaneous demonstrations and dissent. Ben Chitty was a petty officer aboard the USS *Richmond K. Turner.*

> [King's] assassination was quite a shock to me. What was even more upsetting was that I was assigned to shore patrol duty the night . . . he was assassinated. And . . . the shore patrol's job was to go into the black community and put down riots. There weren't really riots in San Diego. . . . It was mostly black people . . . gathering on the streets outside in marches . . . to protest the assassination of Dr. King. . . . They gave me a .45, expected me to go out into the street against fellow citizens who were protesting what I also felt was a great injustice. . . . My heart was with the people . . . so I refused to go.[66]

Chitty's personal insubordination led to a shipwide protest and a shift in consciousness.

> That day me and three friends . . . cut out strips of black cloth and wrapped them around our arms as a sign of mourning, and by midafternoon I had easily half the ship wearing black arm bands . . . maybe a hundred people. . . . Every black person on the ship—nearly half the whites.[67]

In September 1968 San Francisco was the site of the first antiwar march led and organized by active-duty soldiers.[68] The GI-Veteran March for Peace was an outstanding example of GI activism. Susan Schnall, a navy veteran, recalls how the limitations of military organizing were creatively and dramatically overcome in preparation for the GI march.

> We needed publicity. . . . It was also the time the United States was flying B-52 bombers over Vietnam with leaflets . . . urging the Vietnamese to defect. And I thought if the United States could do that in Vietnam, I could do it in the United States. . . .
>
> I had a friend who was a pilot. . . . We loaded up the airplane with leaflets urging people to come to the GI-Veterans March for Peace. And we dropped the leaflets on Treasure Island and Yerba Buena Island and of course on my hospital. And on the deck of . . . the *Enterprise*, that was stationed at Alameda Naval Air station, and also in the Presdio. . . . It was on the news and in the newspapers.[69]

Schnall's leaflet bombing mission was learned from the logic of the military itself. Like other dissident soldiers, Schnall insisted on wearing her uniform to the demonstrations. Again she relied on the example set by military leaders.

> The military . . . issued a regulation which stated military . . . personnel couldn't wear their uniforms while talking about religious, social, or political ideals in a public forum. . . . I knew I was going to the peace march. I went there and I wore my uniform. My feeling was, I was not a civilian, I was a member of the armed forces. And if Westmoreland could wear his

2 The fall 1968 GI-Veteran March for Peace was the first major demonstration of active-duty GIs. Michael Locks, Susan Schnall, and Hugh Hester (first, second, and third from left, front row) led the march. Hester was a retired army general and supporter of the Veterans for Peace in Vietnam. Locks and Schnall were later court-martialed for demonstrating in uniform. Schnall continued to be a prominent activist in the military antiwar movement. Student Mobilization Committee poster; photo reproduction, Aubrey Haynes.

uniform talking to Congress about increasing aid to fight with Vietnam, I could certainly wear my uniform talking out against the war publicly.[70]

Although Schnall was court-martialed for her actions, she continued to organize the GI movement—traveling and speaking across the country. The five hundred soldiers and veterans who participated in the GI-Veteran March for Peace created what would become a tradition in the antiwar movement.

Later that year Bay Area marches drew up to 300 uniformed GIs and reservists. In July of 1968, 200 troops from Fort Hood attended a "love-in." In April 1969 soldiers led civilian demonstrations in six major cities.[71] That August dozens of marines from Camp Pendleton joined with thousands of civilians to march on Nixon's San Clemente home.[72] The moratorium demonstrations drew a groundswell of support from GIs in Vietnam and at home. The gigantic November demonstration in Washington was led by 150 active duty GIs and 400 veterans.[73]

The issue of riot control also sparked considerable protest by soldiers. Fort Hood was an important base for training soldiers for domestic duties. Dave Cline recalls the resistance at the time of the Chicago convention.

> Fort Hood was one of the forts slated for Chicago. Troops from Fort Hood were actually committed to the streets of Chicago . . . when there were rebellions after Martin Luther King was assassinated. There was a lot of opposition to it among soldiers. . . . A lot of black guys were against it because they saw it as directly aimed against black people. Some guys identified with the youth movement. . . .
>
> We had a meeting on the base. . . . There must have been seventy-five [or] a hundred guys there. . . . We discussed the issue, and we came up with the idea that we would agitate against riot control. . . .
>
> We produced a sticker, which was a black hand and a peace sign. . . . And then we began to go around among the troops, distributing [the stickers] to people who said they were against riot control. And the plan was that if they committed us to the streets of Chicago against the demonstrators, we were going to put these stickers on our helmets to show that we were against it and in solidarity with the demonstrators.[74]

Later that week at Fort Hood, over a hundred African American soldiers gathered at an all-night meeting to expose army racism and to oppose the use of troops against civilians. Later deemed the "Fort Hood Forty-three," a group of African American GIs were arrested the following morning for refusing to disperse upon orders.[75] GIs would continue to protest their use as riot troops during the Republican convention and during the demonstrations surrounding Nixon's inauguration in 1973.[76]

Beginning in 1970, GI and veteran demonstrations assumed their classic antiwar form during Armed Forces Day. Armed Forces Day was transformed from a ritual of respect for militarism into a rite of defiance. One thousand GIs at Fort Hood held the first large public demonstration Killeen, Texas, had ever seen.[77] The march in Killeen was just one in a day of coordinated antiwar actions around the country. GIs and their civilian supporters demonstrated at nineteen military bases. The threat of demonstrations shut down the regular Armed Forces Day ceremonies at another twenty bases. Soldiers in Vietnam wore black armbands in support of the demonstrations. The *Fatigue Press* reported that the larger demonstrations fielded a thousand soldiers at Fort Bragg, twelve hundred at Fort Riley, and eight hundred at Camp Pendleton.

Renamed "Armed Farces Day," the 1971 demonstrations were the peak of these nationally coordinated actions. Servicepeople from every branch and nineteen major bases joined for simultaneous protest against the war.[78] Armed Forces Day emerged as a new tradition in the antiwar movement and was celebrated by dissident soldiers and veterans well into the 1970s. The 1972 Armed Forces Day activities drew thousand of GIs from twenty-five bases.

The demonstration at Wright–Paterson Air Force Base in Ohio was characteristic of Armed Forces Day activities. Three hundred and fifty airmen, Vietnam veterans, and civilians shut down the official program. The base commander was so rattled he assigned 500 soldiers to riot duty, canceled all leaves, and reinforced security at the main gate. GI ingenuity was particularly sharp at Cherry Point Marine Corps Air Station in North Carolina, where a marine parachuter dumped three thousand antiwar leaflets on the official Armed Forces Day rally. *About Face* reported that the day's events had stretched across this land, "from California to the New York islands."[79]

While the focus of Armed Forces Day varied from base to base, the 1970 demonstrations at Fort Dix was organized around a political manifesto that represented the diverse currents within the GI movement. Signed by Joe LeBlanc, Sue Slovak, and Leroy Connely, *Shakedown* issued a series of sweeping demands. They called on Americans to stop Armed Forces Day and the glorification of weapons, end the repression of the GI movement, free all political prisoners, abolish the stockade system, and end the enforcement of unnatural and oppressive sexual roles (including sexual stereotypes, attacks on homosexuals, and sexual segregation). *Shakedown*'s program went on to call for the "self-determination of Blacks, Puerto Ricans, Mexican-Americans, American Indians, and Orientals, stop the use of class oppression which makes poor people fight the rich man's war" and, of course, the "immediate withdrawal of all U.S. troops from South East Asia." *Shakedown* instructed its readers that all of the demands "are necessary, if we are to be free."[80]

As of 1970, dissent spread to every area where major troop concentrations existed. Germany was the scene of considerable African American protest. A demonstration held by a soldier organization called the Unsatisfied Black Soldiers was organized around racism. Their top priority was to get "all GIs out of

South East Asia now." Over one thousand soldiers, mostly African Americans, attended that Fourth of July 1970 rally, making it the largest GI protest in Europe.[81]

The campaign around the "Darmstadt Fifty-three" was one of the better-publicized examples of antiracist organizing in Europe. African American activists had long cited a pattern in which only African Americans were arrested or punished after racial conflicts occurred. A protest over just such an incident resulted in the arrest of fifty-three demonstrators, including a handful of white dissenters. Twenty-nine were slated for court-martials, which were eventually canceled after the National Association for the Advancement of Colored People and the American Civil Liberties Union became involved in the case.[82]

Other organizations such as the Black United Soldiers and the Black Action Group fought racial discrimination on German bases and in the surrounding communities.[83] African American marines and sailors in the Mediterranean organized the People's Freedom party. Like many other African American GI organizations, the People's Freedom party articulated black pride and a race-centered critique of the war.

By the end of 1971 navy and air force dissidents emerged in greater numbers. With the decline of the ground war, sailors and airmen reacted swiftly to the increasingly technological war.[84] The 1971 Christmas bombings and the 1972 Easter raids sparked intense protests. Bases at Mountain Home, McGuire, Lackland, Wright–Paterson, Minot, Lowry, and Westover were stung by picket lines, rallies, and marches organized by airmen.

The resistance aboard the USS *Coral Sea* styled itself as the Stop Our Ships movement (SOS). Inspired by a public referendum to keep the USS *Constellation* at home in San Diego, the SOS movement soon spread to the *Coral Sea*, where the campaign started around an antiwar petition. Over fifteen hundred seamen, one-third of the crew of the USS *Coral Sea*, signed on to end the war. When reporters came aboard ship, SOS staged a demonstration.

> About a hundred antiwar sailors and Marines overwhelmed the fantail passageway. . . . The crowd was beautiful, headbands, POW stenciled on T-shirts, peace symbols, clenched fists. WOW! I didn't even know half of the brothers there. What a grapevine! Chicanos, Blacks (though not in large numbers), and straights . . . . The lifers freaked and the pigs were powerless.[85]

As part of the press conference, SOS released a statement to the media stating their determination to end the war.

> It has become apparent that the majority of the Americans oppose the war in Vietnam. But the government has refused to be guided by public opinion. Members of the USS *Coral Sea* have begun taking a part in ending the war by starting the Stop Our Ships movement, which began with a peti-

tion to Congress with the goal of stopping our ships from deploying to Vietnam. This petition has now been signed by over 1,000 members of the crew. We are going to stop our ships, and we, the military men, are going to stop this war.[86]

Official repression followed the demonstration, but jailings, beatings, and other punishments failed to weaken their determination. On October 12, two hundred crewmen demonstrated on the flight deck as the *Coral Sea* passed under the Golden Gate Bridge. Thirty-five crewmen, including three officers, stayed behind in San Diego.[87] Another fifty-three jumped ship on November 24 when the carrier put in at Honolulu. In a related activity, eight hundred sailors and supporters demonstrated at Subic Bay in the Philippines in October 1972, the day before the *Newport News* was to return to Vietnam.[88]

As in Vietnam, much of the real resistance within the military came in small-scale daily expressions of dissent. "FTA," a military acronym meaning "fun, travel, adventure," was commonly used by recruiters. Typical of the military resistance, the meaning was reversed to "free" or "fuck the Army." FTA became one of the most common slogans expressing soldier discontent. In his memoir *Quang Tri Cadence*, Jon Oplinger recalls that "in 1968 FTA was scratched on the walls of every latrine on every army base in the world. In bright paint it materialized briefly on water towers and the walls of NCO and officer clubs. It decorated bus stations."[89] Writing in the GI press, a Vietnam veteran suggested a subtle, tactical approach in an article entitled "How to FTA."

> Remember, you don't have to pass out *Abovegrounds* . . . to hurt the Army. You can rip off supplies, break trucks . . . punch holes in walls, go AWOL. . . . Everyone of you could come up with hundreds of ideas. If we all tried our best to slow down the Army at least once each day—in whatever way we choose—it would go a long way toward causing the Army's death. . . . The deaths of over 40,000 of our fellow soldiers in Vietnam points out the real threat.[90]

The editors of *Aboveground* went on to lend a political rationale to day-to-day resistance.

> If we really lived in a . . . truly democratic country the GI would control the Army. . . . It's time the GI stopped being used by the Brass and rich corporations of this country to fight their dirty wars. . . . It's time the GI gained full citizenship. It's time the GI gained control of his own life and his own destiny.[91]

Informal discussion groups were also a common way antiwar sentiment was spread.

At Fort Houston . . . a couple of recruits came up. . . . You should have seen it—two guys walked up to me and before I was done speaking there'd be twenty or twenty-five sitting around. There'd be a mini rally going on.[92]

Less politically articulate than rap sessions, acts of sabotage impeded the war effort, particularly in the navy. After 1970 acts of sabotage increased dramatically. The USS *Anderson, Chilton, Forrestal, Ranger,* and *Constellation* were all subject to incidents of sabotage significant enough to cripple operations.[93]

Although sabotage, shamming, and gripe sessions have occurred in all wars, the Vietnam-era antiwar resistance was distinct from other periods of soldier resistance in its collective, principled nature and vast scope.

Building the GI Movement

Following the ASU, the Movement for a Democratic Military (MDM) was founded in 1969, and organized primarily in the navy and marines. Two GI organizations in the San Diego area, Duck Power and Green Machine, came together to form the MDM. Some of the African American GIs who led the merger had previously been associated with the Black Panthers, and the MDM both promoted and borrowed from the Panthers. Its initial program included demands to extend all constitutional rights to military men and women, stop all military censorship, abolish all mental and physical cruelty in the brig and basic training, hold trial by jury of one's peers by rank, abolish the class structure of the military, end all racism, free all political prisoners, stop the glorification of war, abolish the draft, and end the war in Vietnam.[94] As the war went on the MDM developed strong radical overtones. Eventually MDM styled its appeal to be anti–imperialist abroad and revolutionary at home. The group's statement of purpose read in part:

The goal of MDM as an organization is to educate GIs to the real causes of their oppression and to help them move to put an end to the problem. Through a black–brown–white coalition, we will educate one another, struggle together and defend one another . . . . The Vietnamese freedom fighters have shown us the way: A united force of brothers and sisters determined to free themselves can defeat the U.S. military monster.[95]

Although both black and white GIs joined the MDM the organization later split along racial lines. One observer estimated that the MDM had signed up between five thousand and ten thousand members.[96]

Although the GI and veteran movements were overwhelmingly composed of the lower ranks, officers also played important roles. In 1967 Captain Howard Levy, a military doctor at Fort Jackson, refused an order to train Green Berets. Levy's case was widely publicized, and he became an important figure encouraging military dissent. Despite large demonstrations for his release and an appeal to the Supreme Court, Levy was sentenced to nearly three years at Leavenworth for his act of conscience.[97] The same year Captain Dale E. Noyd, an air force officer with eleven years of service and instructer at the Air Force Academy, sought conscientious objector status because of his opposition to the war and spent two years in jail.[98]

Sometimes officers were placed in positions that allowed access to information that directly contradicted the official version of the war. In a remote barroom, navy officer Captain Michael Sutton learned an important and disturbing fact.

> I found out the Gulf of Tonkin incident was wrong. . . . We were in this officers' club on a rainy day. . . . Myself and other officers . . . off either the *Joy* or the *Maddox*. . . . We've been drinking and we've come to like each other. These guys finally . . . say, . . . "It didn't happen. There were no motor torpedo boats." They were tracking each other, there were no motor torpedo boats. In the first incident there had been, but we fired first. . . . But in the second they were tracking each other around in fairly high seas. . . .
>
> The Fulbright hearings in 1971—that's when it came to light for the American community. I knew about it in a bar in 1965.[99]

Due to their positions of authority, officers often played a role in the military antiwar movement greater than their numbers would indicate. The Concerned Officers Movement (COM) organized junior officers against the war. The COM eventually established some twenty locals totaling three thousand members. The COM went public in September of 1970, staging a press conference with twenty-eight officers. The principles of the COM tied together war resistance with domestic concerns.

> Paramount in the program of the COM is a fervent opposition to the continuing military effort in Vietnam. COM decries the military policies that turned an internal political struggle into a nation-destroying bloodbath. . . .
>
> COM further abhors the military mentality that promotes absurd measures like the body count; that leads to the indiscriminate slaughter of innocent civilians; that destroys land and villages and calls it victory.
>
> COM is opposed to the preponderant share of national resources devoted to the military. While Americans go hungry, while cities decay, while our natural resources become more despoiled, the Pentagon is able to get billions of dollars for an ABM system that may not even work. National defense is important, but so are poverty, education, and the environment.[100]

The COM sponsored antiwar advertisements in local newspapers. In 1971 twenty-nine COM members from Fort Bragg and Polk Air Force Base and thirty-eight from Fort Knox publicly signed antiwar statements.[101] On April 23 of that year junior officers from the COM organized a memorial service at the Washington National Cathedral to honor all of the war dead. Over 250 officers in uniform attended the service despite warnings that the military considered it a political demonstration.[102] At least one smaller group of officers called the Junior Officers against the War organized in California.[103]

A letter signed by forty officers and sent to President Nixon in 1971 is particularly revealing of the political shift of junior officers in the early 1970s. Although political elites publicly ignored the GI revolt, few junior officers could afford the luxury of such ignorance.

> We, too, find the continuation of the war difficult to justify and lead others . . . into a war in which few of us really believe. . . .
>
> If the war is allowed to continue much longer, young Americans in the military will simply refuse en masse to cooperate. . . .
>
> You often contrast the disaffection of the American student protesters with the devotion and patriotism of our soldiers in Vietnam. We want you to know that in many cases those "protesters and troublemakers" are our younger brothers, and friends, and girlfriends, and wives. We share many common causes with them. Please get this country out of Vietnam before we too become disaffected.[104]

Many dissenting soldiers opposed the war by declaring conscientious objector (CO) status. CO applications increased in numbers as the war proceeded and gave rise to large counseling organizations. In 1965, 940 claims were processed by the Office of Legal Counsel in the Justice Department. In 1966 that figure rose to 1,862. In the first four months of 1967, 763 soldiers applied for status, suggesting a yearly figure near 2,290.

James M. Taylor was a Christian and early CO. Taylor began to understand Christian morality as an antiwar ideology.

> I made a mistake—I joined the army. I did not know the spirit of this thing. I thought of it as a job and a chance for a free education. . . . Since that time I truly realized that the only thing of any importance was "seeking the Kingdom." I have used this as a factor by which I determine whether a thing should be pursued or not. . . . If "Christ is the Answer"— I am of the opinion that the Armed Forces isn't.[105]

Both Christianity and secular pacifism became important philosophical references for the thousands of active-duty COs that would eventually flood the military with their protests.

The Pacific Counseling Service (PCS), founded in May 1969, provided legal and counseling help and assisted thousands of soldiers seeking to oppose the war. Jackson Lears was a navy officer with doubts about war.

I was talking things over with Karen and we were getting closer . . . to the time when the ship was . . . going to be sent back overseas again. . . . I was . . . actually considering Canada, just deserting. . . .

I had met an enlisted man . . . named A. W. Powell, former prep school teacher and backwoods Baptist minister from Tennessee—wonderful man—he happened to be gay. And he had a friend . . . who was a graduate student at UC San Diego. . . . They were a window into another radically different world. . . . It was a world full of information about how to get out of the military if you wanted to. . . .

The most appealing . . . was to apply for CO status. I discovered . . . I fully qualified for it. . . . The guy who was running the counseling service was himself a guy who had gotten out as a CO. He was a former Army officer. . . .

It was the Pacific Coast Counseling Service. . . . They would meet every Sunday. The one I remember was a couple dozen people. . . . It was the spring of 1970.[106]

This and other types of soldier support work led the PSC to grow to eleven offices, including several overseas.[107] Military counseling and the people who pursued CO status helped to hone the political, philosophical, and ethical basis of war resistance.

What they were doing was helping people to articulate an inchoate sense of disaffection, and there was plenty of that . . . . Early I had had vague doubts to be sure. . . . I was without question opposed to the Vietnam War, but that seemed to me part of this larger package of which nuclear war was the ultimate and most insane expression of the military–industrial complex. . . .

When I got on board this nuclear armed ship then I began to think about nuclear war. And then I began to make the connection between nuclear war and . . . imperial adventures like Vietnam. And to me it made intellectual and ethical sense to put the two together and separate myself from both of them.[108]

Legal knowledge and skill were required to manipulate the military bureaucracy and obtain CO status. The impact of groups like PCS was a factor in the 400 percent increase in COs in the army, and a 200 percent increase in the marines. During the 1971 peak of CO applications, the army had 2,827, the navy 861, the marines 157, and the air force 536 men under CO status.[109] The rise in military conscientious objection paralleled the sharp increase in civilian CO exemptions in the early 1970s.[110]

The United States Serviceman Fund (USSF), founded in 1969, collected and distributed money to scores of GI organizations, newspapers, and coffeehouses, and provided legal funds for court-martials. The USSF was the financial lifeblood of the organized soldier movement. Its fund-raising activities and the "Support Our Soldiers" campaign enabled an international network of soldiers and veterans to pursue antiwar work among GIs. The list of sponsors and contributors to the USSF reveals that antiwar soldiers were supported by the mainstream antiwar movement. Bella Abzug, Shirley Chisholm, Noam Chomsky, William Sloane Coffin, Ossie Davis, David Dellinger, James Forman, Betty Friedan, Nat Henthoff, Arthur Kinoy, Adrienne Rich, Benjamin Spock, Andrew Stein, I. F. Stone, Cora Weiss, and many others contributed to the USSF. Similarly, USSF publications were sponsored by the Fur, Leather, and Machine Workers Union, Local 1199 Drug and Hospital Union, District 37 AFSME, District 65 Distributive Workers, and the United Farmworkers.

The 1971 USSF publication *The New Army* claimed a total of seventy-six organizing projects, coffeehouses, and newspapers that enjoyed their services from a network of six support offices. The USSF material support was also important in that the institutions it aided were often a political crossroads between the military and the civilian movements.

The Fort Bragg Women's Project was a key example of fusion between feminist and military organizing. Funded by the USSF, the women's project set out to build a movement of GI wives. The project was remarkable because it confronted the necessity of linking together myriad social differences and contradictions into a single political campaign. Writing in the *GI News and Discussion Bulletin* the project leaders fused military, class, and gender issues.

> We have done an analysis of women in GI towns with our main emphasis being on which group of women have the most potential consciousness and power at this point in our history. We decided that working women have more power because of their relation to the means of production; but we felt more strongly that our main emphasis in Fayetteville should be GI wives. It is our opinion that the GI movement is the only mass working-class movement at this time; their awareness comes from their close relationship with imperialism. Wives are similarly touched except that they don't literally go to Nam themselves. . . .
>
> Because of the Army's blatant sexism regarding "dependents" and its overt objectification of women, we do feel that most women in an Army town are a potential force against the Army.[111]

By merging a critique of sexism and classism within the context of empire, the Fort Bragg women's project displayed the political broadness that characterized the GI resistance at its best.

On the lighter side, the USSF sponsored the popular FTA show. The FTA show was an alternative USO that brought together show business celebrities such as Dick Gregory, Jane Fonda, Peter Boyle, Holly Near, Ben Vereen, Ossie Davis, Nina Simone, and Donald Sutherland to deliver entertaining political messages. The 1971 debut of the FTA show drew five hundred GIs near Fort

Bragg. That November the show packed New York City's Philharmonic Hall for a civilian fundraiser.[112]

The GIs United Against the War in Vietnam grew out of local events but became an influential nationally recognized group. GIs United was largely black and Latino, yet also included white soldiers. Growing out of a campaign to defend the "Fort Jackson Eight," a group of soldiers arrested for antiwar activities, the GIs United launched a successful petition drive demanding constitutional rights for GIs.[113] GIs United turned nearby Fort Bragg into one of the most active centers of the GI movement. The Fort Bragg area supported several coffeehouses and produced *Bragg Briefs*, one of the most sophisticated and enduring GI papers. The case was well documented by Socialist Workers Party (SWP) leader and antiwar organizer Fred Halstead in his *GI's Speak Out Against the War*.[114]

Indeed, GIs United against the War was one of the outstanding examples of GI organizing by left-wing groups. Led by Halstead, the SWP and its youth organization, the Young Socialist Alliance (YSA), committed considerable effort to promoting antiwar sentiment in the military. The socialist organizers, including drafted YSA members, focused on expanding the constitutional rights of soldiers to speak against the war. The Student Mobilization Committee, also influenced by the SWP, created contacts between the civilian and military antiwar movements by organizing GI–civilian marches and conferences. Andrew Pulley, one of the Fort Jackson Eight, became a prominent SWP member and the party's vice presidential candidate in 1976.[115]

Although the GI movement produced national groups, much of the political activity was led by locally based and very diverse organizations often consisting of a few activists reaching out to the larger population. In early 1970 four army privates from Fort Gordon were charged with promoting "disloyalty and disaffection among the troops" for planning a war crimes investigation. These young men, who hailed from Maryland, New York, Tennessee, and Minnesota, banded together "to arouse . . . an antiwar and an antimilitaristic response" in the American people.[116]

On November 29, 1968, the day they graduated from basic training, sixty-eight soldiers from Company B, 6th Battalion, 2nd Basic Combat Training Brigade from Fort Jackson, South Carolina, mailed an antiwar petition to president-elect Nixon. After completing a training cycle without AWOLs, court-martials, or administrative discipline, these model recruits banded together to declare "our fundamental opposition to the war in Vietnam."[117]

Local groups of gay and lesbian soldiers and their supporters challenged the sexual politics of the military and the homophobia of the military peace movement. Gay and lesbian GIs faced harassment, abuse, and discharge for their sexual choices. A small number of soldiers raised these issues in the GI movement. At least one dissident newspaper *GIGLE* (GI Gay Liberation Experience) spoke directly to gay and lesbian issues. Gay GI leaders like Vince Muscari circulated leaflets and papers, wrote for the underground press, attended gay liberation meetings, and joined the VVAW.

GIs United Against the War. Ft. Jackson.

Fighting men.

GI Civil Liberties Defense Committee
P.O. Box 335, Old Chelsea Station
New York, N.Y. 10011

3 Arrested for discussing the war, the "Fort Jackson Eight" helped to promote the military antiwar movement particularly at Fort Jackson and Fort Bragg. From left, Andrew Pulley, Eugene Rudder, Delmar Thomas, Edilberto Chaparro, Tommie Woodfin, Dominck Duddie, Joe Curtis, and Curtis Mays. GI Civil Liberties Defense Committee poster; photo reproduction, Aubrey Haynes.

Two lesbian Waves stationed at Great Lakes Naval Training center filed suits to block their dismissal based on their sexual preference.[118] The *Navy Times are a Changin'* came to the support of the Waves. The dissident soldiers claimed, "Although some of the accused sisters may or may not be gay, they all agree that the question of homosexuality is irrelevant. The main issue is the persecution of women."[119]

In 1972 an article attacking homophobia ran on the front page of *All Hands Abandon Ship*. After quoting a Vietnam veteran who said, "I got a medal for killing two men and a dishonorable discharge for loving one," the article went on to explore the use of macho imagery in producing soldiers.

> "Fag-baiting" is one of the typical techniques used. . . . Since gayness does not conform to the John Wayne syndrome of manliness, it is seen as threatening to military discipline. If you're not a *man,* if you're not into power relationships, then how can you be expected to fight, subdue, and kill others. Homosexuals are the opposite extreme of what the military expects men and women to be.[120]

Similarly, an article calling for "sexual self-determination" appeared in the *Bragg Briefs* January 1971 issue. That article located the question of sexual identity and gay liberation as part of the larger struggle for human freedom. Like women, gays were outside of the conventional model for soldiers and threatened the existing recruiting techniques that often exploited youthful insecurity about masculinity and manhood.

FED-UP, based in Tacoma, Washington, reached out to the servicemembers at Fort Lewis and operated the Shelter Half coffeehouse. The FED-UP program went beyond criticizing the war to offering a positive vision of society and the military.

> We believe this country is run by very few men. These men run it for their own profit. We believe the function of the present Army is to serve the interests of these few men and to put down people who challenge the system. . . . We believe further that a society can be built that serves the needs of all the people. We believe an Army could exist in such a society run by soldiers and working people not by generals and businessmen. . . . It is our goal to build such a society and such an Army.[121]

Another local attempt, the Anniston Women's Project, displays the complexities and difficulties of organizing women in the military. The contradictions of race, class, gender, and sexuality sculpted a challenging political terrain as reported in *GI News and Discussion Bulletin.*

> Lots of WACs see the Army as a means of upward mobility. Often they were trapped in bad family, school, or social situations that they hope to

break out of by joining the Army. Gay women are in certain ways the most vulnerable and have even greater reason for staying in service. . . . There is an unspoken understanding—people kind of know who is gay, it's fine—but if you step out of line, it's the ever-present excuse for booting you out. . . .

We were surprised at the number of black women in general we've been meeting. . . . From what we've seen, it appears that black and white gay women are especially tight. Perhaps since they tend more to be career women and there's not the whole white woman–black man thing to keep them apart. This whole dynamic has been very difficult for us.[122]

Local groups and individuals scored considerable successes against military sexism. Unequal pay, dress codes, and discriminatory benefits were the expression of the institutionalized sexism of the military. Lieutenant Sharon Frontiero initiated a lawsuit that resulted in a Supreme Court decision that women were allowed the same fringe benefits and allotment as men.

These activists helped to broaden antiwar constituencies and discourse by fusing their antiwar appeals with issues of sexuality and sexism, as African Americans had with racism, and working-class dissidents had with questions of wealth and power. The intellectual leap that connected war to other forms of oppression was an essential part of the antiwar movement. Indeed, the antiwar movement treated war not simply as some extraordinary event but rather as a well-established cultural system with its own structure of human meanings and identities. War and empire became understood as activities that both created and were dependent upon oppressive sexual and gender identities, racial chauvinism, and economic exploitation. From this perspective the war in Vietnam was not only a question of poor policy choices, diplomatic errors, and even national aggression, but also the most extreme expression of America's democratic shortcomings.

The focus of many GI groups was the publication of a base newspaper. From Alabama to Alaska to Southeast Asia the underground newspapers provided an important forum for the GI movement. Written by active-duty GIs, veterans, and civilian supporters, the movement press was far more than an elaborate gripe sheet. Although these papers allowed GIs to sound off about the many grievances of military life, they articulated a political analysis and promoted organization and feelings of solidarity between resisters as well. The very production and distribution of the papers was a political challenge to the brass.

Underground newspapers succeeded in reaching tens of thousands of servicemembers. The largest papers, such as *Vietnam GI*, *Camp News*, and *The Bond* claimed circulation in the tens of thousands. Some 15 papers had national or international distribution networks.[123] More typically, papers like *Aboveground* were distributed to between thirty-five hundred and ten thousand readers.[124] Many papers were short-lived, simple, mimeographed sheets. In 1972 the State Department counted some 245 papers published since 1967. Recent research now suggests the number to be close to 300. In 1972 the House Investigation of

Attempts to Subvert the Armed Services identified 46 papers being published that year, 6 of which were located in Germany and Japan.[125]

The papers' first function was to spread news of the GI movement. The many acts of resistance and the military response to it were featured. War news and stories relating to domestic and foreign political movements filled most issues.

In language and style the papers reflected the cultural explosion of the late 1960s and early 1970s. Papers like *Aero-spaced,* from Grissom Air Force Base, championed the peace, pot, and personal expression of the hippie counterculture. A marine paper from Camp Pendleton called *All Ready on the Left* was steeped in the political style of Black Power. Fort Ord's *Right-on Post* proclaimed its purpose to be:

> GIs dedicated to freeing themselves and all exploited peoples from the oppression of the U.S. military. We recognize our true enemy . . . it is *the capitalist* who sees only profit. . . . They control the military which sends us off to die. They control the police who occupy the black and brown ghettos.[126]

Other papers employed a trade union style. The *Fort Campell's People's Press* stated, "We want to make our living conditions on base as bearable as possible, and we want to make America a better place by ending the war, sex discrimination, racism, and poverty."[127] This type of paper promoted the ideas of trade unionism and collective bargaining within the context of the military, a tendency typical of GI newspapers. The *GI News and Discussion Bulletin* presented more theoretical and sophisticated debate encouraging military organizers to join the political controversies of the time.

The *Women's Newsletter,* dated April 1970 and addressed to "USSF Sisters," was one of the few publications dedicated to women's history and feminist concerns.[128] Soldiers in the WACs put out *Whack,* a newspaper created by the Anniston Women's Project. *Whack* attacked sexual discrimination in its many forms.[129]

The underground press worked to create a historical context for the movement. Papers were peppered throughout with articles and images from American history. Under a photograph depicting the Latino group the Young Lords, *Fatigue Press* discussed "Our Inherent Right."

> The Constitution of the United States was written to provide a basis for the continuous change in accordance with the will of the people to maintain a free and just society. However . . . we have reached an elixir of social repression and militarism which can no longer be tolerated.[130]

The Ally referred to America's Revolutionary army in calling for a militia of citizen–soldiers who elect their own officers, enjoy full constitutional rights, and are free from unnecessary discipline.

You may wonder why, if the election of officers was so important to early Americans, the practice is now completely absent from our military establishment. . . . Propaganda from high ranking lifers in favor of centralized officer appointments won out over facts about historical liberties. The meaning of the Constitution itself gradually became obscured. . . .

The result is that now you are fed a distorted version of your past. . . . The lifers are scared . . . that you would have enough sense and courage to vote against such traitors to American liberty, and to elect in their places patriots who would lead you into battle against the corrupt establishment, instead of following you into battle against the Vietcong. But maybe some day the United States will be a free country, and American fighting men will regain their traditional right to elect their own officers.[131]

For the *Ally* democracy in the military meant the election of "patriots" who would do "battle against the corrupt establishment." In their statement of purpose the editors of *Attitude Check* summed up the philosophical posture of the underground papers. "*Attitude Check* is written by active duty Marines and ex-Marines who are sincerely dedicated to placing the military man's struggle for liberty and human dignity in the proper historical perspective."[132]

As the above examples suggest, "the proper historical perspective" was sometimes linked to the American Revolution. In its coverage of a soldier demonstration broken up by police, *Fatigue Press* carried a graphic of a British soldier bludgeoning a rebellious colonist. Captioned with Benjamin Rush's 1787 observation of American politics, the GI journalists claimed, "The American War is over, but this is far from the case with the American Revolution. On the contrary, nothing but the first act of the great drama is closed."[133]

To some degree all the papers contained the different styles and influences that characterized the movement. The *Fatigue Press*, for example, carried explicitly historical, working-class, African American, youth, and feminist perspectives in addition to the news of the soldier revolt. The more sophisticated papers arranged this chorus of insurgent voices.

Many of the underground papers were produced or distributed from a system of coffeehouses that were established in military towns. The coffeehouses brought GIs into contact with antiwar literature, military counseling, and each other in a relaxed setting. Free coffee, live music, and political conversation drew thousands of soldiers into the coffeehouses. Soldiers seeking alternatives to the war and established military life could gather, safe from the eyes of the brass. The first coffeehouses were established by civilian activists and remained one of the primary ways that the peace movement supported dissident GIs. Antiwar activist and later president of the USSF Fred Gardner and GI organizer Donna Mickleson began the coffeehouse movement in late 1967. Together they founded the "UFO" in Columbia, South Carolina, near Fort Jackson, and within a few months helped to organize a "pray-in."[134] A number of coffeehouses were initiated in 1968 as part of the "Summer of Support," a campaign organized by Students for a Democratic Society to assist antiwar soldiers.

From their beginnings in 1967, the number of coffeehouses rose to nineteen in 1970, and as many as twenty-six in 1971.[135] The coffeehouses were often affiliated with larger GI organizations. In 1970 seven coffeehouses identified themselves as being part of the MDM. The effect of the coffeehouses, like that of other GI movement tactics, was considerable, even if difficult to quantify. Thousands of servicemen and high school students passed through coffeehouses. The level of on-base political activities usually increased following the founding of a local coffeehouse.

GI coffeehouses were subject to legal harassment and violent attacks, some being mysteriously firebombed or riddled with gunfire. Local officials, military authorities, landlords, and right-wing terrorists harassed these organizing centers. Members of the Oleo Strut coffeehouse at Fort Hood confronted the Ku Klux Klan.

> We were under a lot of harassment from the Klan. . . . We were going to go down to this rally in Houston once, and we had four carloads of us. . . . We got . . . out on this empty road and all of a sudden this car comes zooming by us and this guy is hanging out the window with an M-16 rifle shooting at the front wheels of the lead car. . . .
>
> I guess they thought we were going to get intimidated and quit. We went back and got our guns and then the Texas Rangers came because we called them. . . . So then they told us we could take . . . one weapon in each car. And we proceeded down to the rally. . . . It was a big event, you know, the Klan shooting at GIs coming to a rally.
>
> They used to circle our house sometimes, too. . . . They would leave these stickers: "The White Knights of the Ku Klux Klan are watching you."[136]

The struggle to establish and maintain coffeehouses was an important focus of GI activity. In Muldraugh, Kentucky, a protest movement formed around the right of soldiers to establish a coffeehouse near Fort Knox. Officials were apparently alarmed that "more than a hundred Fort Knox GIs and even a handful of commissioned officers were participating in nightly rap sessions under posters of Mao Tse-tung and Black Panther luminaries and a huge, upside-down American flag symbolizing 'the nation's distress.' " In an attempt to block eviction nine persons were arrested by local authorities. Among them were Larry Shapiro, a Rutgers University ROTC graduate, and Kathleen Jackson, "one of the dozens of young GIs' wives who have involved themselves in the coffeehouse."[137]

Coffeehouses were sometimes staffed by civilian dissidents and provided an important link between the civilian and military antiwar movements. At the Oleo Strut in Texas, the Home Front in Colorado, and other coffeehouses, women played an important role in introducing soldiers to a feminist outlook.[138] As counselors, organizers, and supporters, women promoted GI organizing and were the central point of contact between the GI and women's movements. The USSF in particular seemed to promote women as GI organizers.[139]

Although sexism remained a real problem within the movement's ranks, some military dissenters identified their own interests with those of women. In *Sixties Going on Seventies*, Nora Sayre recalled meeting antiwar GIs at a Fort Bragg coffeehouse.

> I was staggered to hear four of them contemptuously referring to some others in their unit as sexist pigs. Almost all of the antiwar GIs I met were stronger supporters of the women's movement than many civilian radicals—perhaps because GIs are beginning to rebel against their own experience with machismo. One huge . . . GI, just back from Vietnam, said, "Macho is still the army's biggest drawing card for enlistment—it's even more powerful than patriotism. . . . The army's still capitalizing on their insecurity. So I think civilians' and women's liberation groups can help GIs a lot: by continuing to expose the absurdity of the male role." "Right on!" came from the GIs in earshot—to my astonishment.[140]

Like many coffeehouses the Oleo Strut had a library stocked with alternative literature. The pamphlets for sale at the Oleo Strut were a good indication of the broad political orientation of the coffeehouse movement. They included *The Problems of U.S. Capitalism, Vietnam: A Thousand Years of Struggle, To the Point of Production* (an interview with the founder of the League of Revolutionary Black Workers), *The Earth Belongs to the People, An Introduction to the Black Panther Party, I Am Furious (Female)*; and *The Political Economy of Women's Liberation.*[141] Environmentalist, revolutionary black nationalist, feminist, working-class, and historical, the Oleo Strut embraced a diverse political outlook. In mobilizing these diverse communities the military antiwar movement struck hard at the cultural sinews of empire by challenging the racial, gender, class, and sexual strategies used by American war-makers.

Although the war had been the central focus and motivation for action, the soldier movement continued after the peace accords were signed. After U.S. withdrawal from Vietnam, soldiers continued to oppose military aid to the Thieu-Ky dictatorship. Racism in the military and issues of working and living conditions were particularly important after 1973. While the pace of GI organizing slackened by the late 1970s, some organizing initiatives continue to the present.[142]

Official repression and limited reforms slowed organizing. The citizen-soldiers often paid a high price for their freedom of action. Jail, beatings, harassment, and bad discharges were the lot of soldier activists. By 1972 the military began large-scale systematic repression of activists. Typical of these moves was the navy's attempt to purge dissenters. The first wave of discharges alone targeted three thousands servicepeople for "mutual benefit" discharges.[143] Antiwar and antiracist GIs were discharged from every branch of the service. Dissenters were the subject of military intelligence, FBI, CIA, and congressional scrutiny. Intelligence agents penetrated GI newspapers and coffeehouses. The dap and other signs of black solidarity were banned from some bases.[144] The "new volunteer army" of the mid 1970s brought minor reforms such as increases in pay and a relaxation of some dress regulations. Ultimately, however, it was the end of the war that changed the pace of GI dissent. It had been the experience of Vietnam, carried by the Vietnam veteran, that had moved and motivated the military democracy movement.

Over the course of the war tens of thousands of people had made their political and moral values identical with their personal concerns. The antiwar soldiers had truly become citizens and had done so under the most challenging possible conditions. The dissident soldiers had created a rich alternative culture. Changed by the Vietnam War, America's citizen–soldier had transformed deference and obedience into a movement of defiant resistance against illegitimate authority and war.

The following story by a Chicano veteran is remarkable for the way in which it encapsulates many of the major aspects of the GI resistance.

In fact, when I was in Camp Pendleton, nineteen marines were dishonorably discharged because they had signed a petition condemning the U.S. war in Vietnam, and these were mostly blacks and Chicanos. . . . They were Vietnam vets and they were getting ready to get out but they got dishonorable discharges and they lost their pay, their benefits, everything. They were just very angry because of what had happened to them as individuals and then because they knew, now that they were home, nothing had changed, the poverty and the discrimination. So . . . they had a total disdain for authority. I mean, they didn't salute anymore, they didn't get up in the morning if they didn't want to, and they cussed at their officers. This is '67, '68, by then and it was a total breakdown, so that the Vietnam vets that were coming back were kept on a totally opposite part of the base from the new recruits.[145]

The presence of the Vietnam veterans was so disruptive that the commanding officer of the 197th Infantry at Fort Benning constructed a special correctional facility. Referred to as a concentration camp by Fort Benning dissidents, this special detention center was an attempt to control the unruly 197th, a unit overwhelmingly composed of Vietnam veterans who bristled under stateside discipline and harassment.[146]

Vietnam veterans had been at the heart of the GI movement. When the veterans returned to the streets and towns of the United States they built a new kind of peace organization and changed the character of the antiwar movement itself.

The Veterans' Antiwar Movement

5

> The moral of the story son,
> Death for profit is not fun.
> If they want to start a war
> Be sure of what they're fighting for.
> Sound off—one, two,
> Sound off—three, four,
> Bring it on down.
> One, two, three, four,
> One, two, three, four.
> I do believe the CO lied
> When he made us use that herbicide.
> They said it only killed the trees
> But now I've got this strange disease.
> Sound off—one, two,
> Sound off—three, four,
> Bring it on down.
> One, two, three, four,
> One, two, three, four.
> —VVAW MARCHING CADENCE

RETURNING VETERANS confronted many challenges: physical and psychological injury, unemployment, discrimination, and readjustment to civilian life. Although homecoming was sweet for some, most faced a nation weary of war and the troubling questions raised by that war. Too often the American people chose to ignore, forget, or denigrate those who had been sent to Vietnam, as though doing so would make the war itself go away. Yet thousands of antiwar veterans steadfastly struggled to keep the issue of Vietnam in the public eye. Between the founding of the Vietnam Veterans against the War (VVAW) in 1967 and the end of the war the veterans' movement became an important force in the national antiwar movement.

As individuals, dissident veterans also participated in other movements for peace and justice. The long legacy of racism, the persistent cultural and personal distance between whites and blacks, and divergent political agendas led many veterans into other social movements. The heightened racial awareness experienced by dissident African American, Latino, and American Indian veterans, and the more desperate situation facing ethnic minorities, motivated veterans to join struggles that focused primarily on the challenges facing their communities.[1] Organizations like the National Association of Black Veterans reached out to

African American veterans. The Special Ministries/Vietnam Generation of the National Council of Churches, the Ministry with Veterans of the Lutheran Council in the U.S.A., and the National Association of Concerned Veterans all sought to improve the conditions facing veterans in the aftermath of war.[2] This chapter however, focuses on the thousands of ex-servicemembers who felt compelled to identify themselves as veterans and to act by joining the protests for peace.

The most significant veteran antiwar organization of the period was the VVAW. The first organization of veterans from the Vietnam conflict, the VVAW had a special appeal to combat veterans who composed the majority of its members. What follows is not an organizational history of the VVAW, but rather the story of a veterans' movement that produced the VVAW as its most organized, coherent, and enduring representative.[3] Beginning with a few peace advocates, the VVAW grew into a membership organization of at least twenty-five thousand. Their protests for peace assailed the injustice and futility of war and brought a new historical consciousness to antiwar organizing.

Speaking Out

Authoritative and convincing as few civilians could be, returning veterans were the vanguard of the military resistance.[4] By 1967 thousands of returning soldiers began to talk publicly and privately about their Vietnam experiences. In September 1967 David Susskind hosted four veterans in a televised discussion of the war. To the surprise of many viewers two of the veterans championed strong antiwar positions.[5]

The stories the antiwar veterans articulated were a once-familiar, now-forgotten litany of official corruption and incompetence, the atrocities of war, racism, injustice, and futile violence. The letter excerpted below was published in the October 1967 *Veterans Stars and Stripes for Peace* and was typical of the emerging perspective of antiwar veterans and the transformations they endured and embraced.

> I went to Vietnam, a hard charging marine 2nd Lieutenant, sure that I had answered the plea of a victimized people in their struggle against communist aggression. That belief lasted about two weeks. Instead of fighting communists . . . ninety percent of the time our military actions were directed against the people of South Vietnam. . . .
>
> I wanted to tell you that there are many, many of us in the military who oppose this war and appreciate your efforts to bring out the truth and get this thing stopped.[6]

The compulsion to speak out against the war typified the antiwar veterans' movement. In 1967 a group of Vietnam veterans acted in a way without precedent in American history. While veterans have been considered problems following all wars, only after Vietnam did veterans form a popular nationwide organization to protest the very conflict in which they had fought. Jan Barry, co-founder of the VVAW, remembers going to a peace demonstration at the UN in the spring of 1967.

> There was this great big contingent . . . at the entrance of Central Park, wearing Veterans for Peace hats. These guys were all older, World War II, Korean War, some of them were Spanish civil war veterans. Just as we got close . . . somebody said, "Vietnam veterans go to the front." . . . Somebody had provided a banner that said Vietnam Veterans Against the War. . . .
>
> So I tracked down this Veterans for Peace group, went to one of their meetings, and discovered there was no Vietnam veterans group, they just brought along the sign, hoping some Vietnam veterans would show up.[7]

The six veterans who marched together at the front of the demonstration informally founded the VVAW on that spring day.[8] The VVAW's early statements declared the Vietnam conflict to be a civil war to which there was no American solution. They asserted that the Saigon government had only the support of its officer corps, and the American people had not been told the truth concerning the nature of U.S. involvement.[9]

Planned for Veterans' Day 1967 but mysteriously delayed by the *New York Times,* a full-page ad declared the principles of the VVAW and was signed by sixty-five veterans.[10] That same year veteran Jeff Sharlet founded *Vietnam GI,* which became one of the most successful soldier newspapers of the period. The early VVAW served as a speakers bureau—engaging debates and giving talks. A 1967 statement of principles hints at the founding political vision of the veterans' movement.

> We are veterans of the Vietnam War. We believe in the United States of America, its Constitution and laws. We believe in freedom to speak, to think, to change our mind, and to dissent. We believe in democracy. We join the dissent of millions of Americans against the war. We support our buddies still in Vietnam. We want them home now. We want an end to the war now. We believe that this is the highest patriotism.[11]

Fidelity to the United States' original principles demanded the "highest patriotism" of dissent from the war. Although the VVAW was unique in that it was organized while the war was still being fought, it carried on a tradition of democracy and peace embraced by World War II and Korean War veterans.

The first group of American veterans to demand peace in Vietnam was the ad hoc committee of Veterans for Peace in Vietnam (VFP). On November, 24, 1965, members of this committee ran a full-page ad in the *New York Times* declaring their support for an upcoming peace demonstration. Hundreds of World War II and Korean War veterans, including a number of women, signed the protest. On February 1, 1965, in New York City, the VFP held its first large action, protesting renewed bombing of Vietnam. Seventy-five veterans from World War II and Korea led this demonstration, the earliest veteran action against the war in Vietnam. On February 5, 1965, approximately one hundred veterans foreshadowed later VVAW activities by returning medals and discharge papers to President Johnson. Similarly, a group of fifty veterans participated in a Veterans March to End the War in Vietnam in January 1966. Marching from the town of Gettysburg to the Eternal Peace Light Monument on that hallowed battlefield, World War I, World War II, and Korean War veterans held a "speak-in." These early veteran protests were often organized around adherence to the Nuremberg principles. [12]

The actions of this small but significant group of veterans suggests their continuing allegiance to the democratic ideals they fought for in World War II. In fact, a few of America's top World War II soldiers became early public critics of the war in Vietnam. In "Division, Dilemma and Dissent," historian Robert Buzzanco thoroughly documented high-level military dissent. [13] As early as 1954 Army Chief of Staff Matthew Rigeway opposed American intervention in support of the French. By 1966 former Marine Corps commandant general David Shoup, retired army brigadier general Hugh B. Hester, and ex-army plans chief General James Gavin all publicly opposed the war. They combined appeals to the national interest with dire warnings about the moral and political costs of continuing the war. In a January 1966 letter to the VFP Hester supported the dissident veterans.

> I am very much interested in your plans to organize a veterans' group to help end the illegal and immoral war the U.S Government is imposing upon the Vietnamese people. . . . This war is degrading our past, dishonoring our present, and if continued will destroy any possibility of us as a people and nation ever leading in building a worthy future for man. [14]

In December 1967 Shoup appeared on a radio talk show hosted by Congressman William F. Ryan of New York. Shoup attributed the failure of the United States to win in Vietnam to "a failure to conceive the real devotion of these people to their cause. . . . That what they're fighting for is something that belongs to them. That they're right and they're going to fight to the death."[15]

With Colonel James A. Donovan, Shoup later wrote a stinging critique of the modern military. In "The New American Militarism," Shoup extended the analysis and warnings about the military–industrial complex first made famous in President Dwight Eisenhower's farewell address.[16] These high-ranking officers stirred the national debate and encouraged the antiwar movement. Indeed, even Gavin, the most moderate of the high-ranking dissenters, concluded that the antiwar movement was "the only real hope of our country."[17]

On January 28, 1966, a convention of antiwar veterans ended their ad hoc status and formally organized the Veterans for Peace in Vietnam. In March 1966 full-page advertisements appeared in the Chicago *Daily News* and the Chicago *Defender* calling for an end to the war. A leaflet for a public protest meeting stated the group's perspective.

> No one is better qualified than veterans to make the public aware that it is *patriotic* to oppose the war in Vietnam . . . . And speak out we must against a war contrary to both America's interests and its best traditions, a war *destroying our honor* before the whole world.[18]

The theme of dissent as patriotism connects Vietnam-era dissenters to their World War II forerunners. VFP activities powerfully predicted elements of the cultural changes that Vietnam veterans would later experience. Both dissident World War II veterans and antiwar Vietnam veterans opposed the war out of respect for America's "best traditions." Years before American defeat was apparent and GI dissent pervasive, American veterans were transforming military culture, appealing to America's revolutionary past, and acting within the citizen–soldier tradition. Tellingly, they opposed the war because it was "destroying our honor." The VFP provided the initial support, encouragement, and example for the Vietnam veterans' peace movement.

After 1968 a number of developments pushed veterans toward a more activist stance. The Tet offensive, the growing youth culture, the Black Power movement, and feminism had a deep effect upon soldier consciousness. As earlier chapters suggest, a pervasive anti-authoritarianism swept the lower ranks. After Tet, the political direction of the war faltered, and any sense of mission began to deteriorate rapidly. More and more veterans became convinced of both the injustice and futility of American intervention in Vietnam. After 1968, veterans had experienced a higher level of discontent in the military, and many had been touched by the GI and veteran movements. The growing influence of the VVAW became apparent when a 1970 full-page advertisement in *Playboy* brought in twelve thousand responses. Veteran, David Curry remembers the impact of the veterans movement on soldiers in Vietnam, during the 1970s.

> In 1971 . . . I was on orders for Vietnam. . . . It meant a lot to me . . . in my thinking and values at that time, that you . . . were protesting against the war that I was on my way to.
>
> By the time I left Vietnam, VVAW was a name that was important in Vietnam. I was a captain in counterintelligence, and it was decided at the top that the reason our morale problem was so bad in Vietnam had to be because of outside agitators. And it had to be because of the Vietnam Veterans Against the War—who were disguised as soldiers all over Vietnam at that time. So when I returned to the United States one of the first things I did was join Vietnam Veterans against the War.[19]

Increasing numbers of veterans were radicalized by the time they left Vietnam. They were joined by a second wave whose shift to an antiwar stance occured slowly, after their return to civilian life. Without the pressures of survival, and given time to reflect on their experience, thousands of veterans came to reevaluate the war.[20]

The civil rights movement also continued to produce dissenting views among veterans. Of Mexican and Iroquois descent and raised on the Oneida reservation, Vietnam veteran Jesse Torres was among those who began to see the connections between civil rights and the war in Vietnam. Torres served on the Mekong River with the navy's 151st Assault in 1966–67.

> Martin Luther King . . . started pointing out how most of them being killed were ethnic and poor whites. . . . It started to fall in place when I saw the antiwar movement as more than just a bunch of college kids.
>
> Then I started thinking about it and started reliving some of the experiences I had there. I could really relate. . . . There really wasn't a whole lot of difference between . . . the oppression there and the Native Americans or blacks and slavery.[21]

The peace trend in the civil rights movement prodded minority veterans to explore the antiwar implications of their cultural identities.

> There was a group going around the country called the White Roots of Peace, which was an educational group. . . . The Iroquois have a tradition called . . . the Great Law of Peace, which was supposedly the start of what is now called democracy.
>
> The whole ideal of democracy that evolved from the Iroquois was to end all the bloodshed—that there should be no more war. That you should try talking, having great councils . . . having representation from people to decide whether they want to go to war or not. . . . This group really had a lot of influence on me because I was seeing . . . my roots.[22]

This overall shift toward activism was also accelerated by the force of events. As individuals and as a part of the VVAW, veterans participated in the wave of protests following the Cambodian invasion and the Jackson State and Kent State massacres. At the University of Wisconsin, Milwaukee antiwar veterans joined the protests.

> In '70 they invaded Cambodia. We were on campus. We hadn't heard of VVAW yet but they were in green and they were obviously Vietnam vets and they were obviously trashing the ROTC building with great glee. . . .
> It was great fun. And the students ate it up: "The Vietnam vets are going crazy!" The next morning we found out about the students getting killed at Kent State.[23]

The killing of four students at Kent State was another important turning point for many GI and veteran activists. When the National Guard fired upon the student demonstrators they also polarized differences between soldiers. Kent State became a call to action. Bill Davis had returned from Southeast Asia and was on active duty in Ohio when the Kent State shootings occurred.

> The actual day that the Kent State thing happened we had a big brawl at the NCO [noncommissioned officers] club. Guys who'd been to Vietnam and were young first-term guys were more antiwar and opposed to it. . . . Other guys were quarreling—how things were going to be put right in the country—when they start shooting commies here too. . . .
>
> That's what pushed me over the edge to some degree. . . . I went AWOL. I went to antiwar stuff all over the state and Washington, D.C. Eventually they court-martialed me. . . . I joined VVAW right after Kent State . . . and redoubled my activism.[24]

In the years after 1970, when the organized civilian peace movement had begun to fracture and stall, the veterans emerged as important leaders of the increasingly popular disaffection from the war in Vietnam. Their actions added a dimension of historical awareness largely absent from the peace movement.

Reclaiming America

In September 1970 the VVAW conducted its first national demonstration, called Operation Rapid American Withdrawal. One hundred and twenty veterans marched through New Jersey and Pennsylvania on a three-day mission to bring the war home. Hiking from Jockey Hollow to Valley Forge, the veterans retraced the old roads used by America's Revolutionary army. Valley Forge exerted a strong symbolic pull on the antiwar veterans. It was there, two hundred years before, that the first citizen–soldiers endured the worst days of the Revolution and had been immortalized by Thomas Paine as the "winter soldiers."

Dressed in fatigues and carrying toy weapons, the marchers trailed through small towns receiving support from some and condemnation from others. Whistling "Yankee Doodle Dandy," the new winter soldiers delivered the war to America's doorstep. As they passed through quiet villages they reenacted violent scenes from search-and-destroy missions. During a break a young soldier explained his reasons for joining the march.

> Where do a person's loyalties lie when he finds that the goals of the service are in conflict with what he believes to be his loyalties to humanity? Even though I'm a West Point graduate and even though I'm a first lieuten-

ant . . . on active duty—I'm many things before I'm an army officer. Among them what Richard Nixon has stated . . . he said all of you are citizens first and soldiers second. . . . As a human being, as a citizen, as a military officer, I reject the Vietnam War in its entirety.[25]

On the last day the marchers approached Valley Forge. The Veterans of Foreign Wars (VFW) appeared in a small counterdemonstration. A dozen members of post 1507 stood by the roadside. One man called out, "Why don't you go to Hanoi? They need boys like you."[26] As the marchers passed they silently saluted or flashed peace signs. Turning from the procession another VFW member blamed the soldiers for losing the war.[27]

The counterdemonstrators defended the dehumanizing anticommunism that the peace marchers had struggled to recognize and overcome. Referring to the Vietnamese, one counterdemonstrator raged, "They're not people, they're animals. . . . Any communist—I don't care what his nationality, color, or what . . . if he's a communist—he's a beast—he is a godless beast!"[28]

As the marchers reached the fields of Valley Forge a crowd of fifteen hundred supporters waited. Excited and festive, yet serious, everyone seemed to know that the VVAW's first national action had scored a great victory. As the new winter soldiers paraded on the fields of Valley Forge, the crowd began to applaud and chant "Peace now! Peace now! Peace now!" The antiwar veterans, assembled in military rank, joined the crowd, calling out, "Peace now! Peace now! Peace now!" As the chants were repeated quickly and more intensely this new army smartly presented their mock weapons for public review. The drill climaxed with the final orders called out in military cadence, "Company present arms— break arms!" The new winter soldiers willingly obeyed: breaking and smashing their plastic guns in a wishful parody of American withdrawal. Cheering and applauding, the whole assembly celebrated the scene. The march was captured on film and entitled *Different Sons*.

As the VVAW grew, new attitudes and objectives emerged. Anti-imperialist sentiment within the group took more explicit forms. First, the VVAW called for the U.S. forces and the CIA to withdraw from every country. Then, stronger links of solidarity were forged with the Vietnamese. At the invitation of North Vietnam, Joe Urgo, a VVAW organizer and national officer, became the first veteran to visit Hanoi. In the following years a number of other veteran contingents would visit North Vietnam. Combat veteran Barry Romo got to see the war from a different perspective.

In December of '72 I went to North Vietnam. I was in North Vietnam . . . when Nixon bombed Hanoi. . . . We were having lunch and . . . all of a sudden it's boom! boom! boom!. . . . Then we went down in the shelters and for the next ten days, the thunder of the equivalent of two Hiroshima bombs a day. They bombed every single day including Christmas.[29]

4 The VVAW at Valley Forge for the 1970 Operation Rapid American Withdrawal. The three-day march for peace concluded with the new winter soldiers symbolically destroying the weapons of war. This Sheldon Ramsdell photograph first appeared in Jan Barry, ed., *Peace Is Our Profession.*

The My Lai massacre and the military reaction to it moved antiwar veterans to respond. Frustrated by the scapegoating of individual soldiers such as Lieutenant William Calley, several war crimes hearings were held. In 1969 Jeremy Rifkin and Tod Ensign began organizing the Citizens Commissions of Inquiry. The first American hearings, cosponsored by the VFP, were held at Annapolis, Maryland, in February 1970 and later that spring in Springfield, Massachusetts. The National Veterans Inquiry into U.S. War Crimes in Vietnam was held in Washington during December 1970 and drew support from the Concerned Officers Movement.[30]

The largest of these events was held in February 1971, when the VVAW organized a three-day war crimes testimony dubbed the Winter Soldier Investigation. Structured by unit, by year, and by sector, the VVAW hoped to prove that the use of terror and mass destruction tactics against Vietnam's civilian population was a pervasive phenomenon directly resulting from U.S. war policy. Al Hubbard, the executive secretary of the VVAW, staked the veterans' claims.

My Lai was only a minor step beyond the standard, official United States in Indochina. It is hypocritical self-righteousness to condemn the soldiers at My Lai without condemning those who set the criminal policy of free-fire zones, strategic hamlets, saturation bombing . . . from which My Lai was the inevitable result.[31]

The overall tone of the testimony reiterated the sense of betrayal that ran throughout the veteran movements. The opening statement by William Crandell exemplified the rhetoric of betrayed ideals.

> We went to preserve the peace, and our testimony will show that we have set all of Indochina aflame. We went to defend the Vietnamese people and our testimony will show that we are committing genocide against them. We went to fight for freedom and our testimony will show that we have turned Vietnam into a series of concentration camps. We went to guarantee the right of self-determination to the people of South Vietnam and our testimony will show that we are forcing a corrupt and dictatorial government upon them. We went to work toward the brotherhood of man and our testimony will show that our strategy and tactics are permeated with racism. We went to protect America and our testimony will show why our country is being torn apart by what we are doing in Vietnam.[32]

Over one hundred veterans gave shocking testimony to the pervasive nature of war crimes. Beatings, rape, murder, and the destruction of crops and livestock—the veterans portrayed a war, not against an enemy, but against a people. The war crimes tribunal produced an important book entitled *The Winter Soldier Investigation: An Inquiry into American War Crimes*. A documentary film, *Winter Soldier*, which recorded the veterans' testimony, was released in 1972. Later that year similar hearings were held in Boston and Washington, D.C., under the leadership of Congressman Ronald Dellums.[33]

After coming home many veterans headed to college and university campuses and organized a network of VVAW chapters. Many veterans not previously involved became antiwar activists. A Chicano veteran remembers:

> While I was in basic training and when I went to Vietnam . . . I really thought we were doing something for our country. I really believed we were stopping communism. . . . I wasn't aware until after I got out how I was used and how we all were used and what a lost cause it was. . . . It took . . . four months after I was out to really understand what was happening. It was in that period of time I joined the Vietnam Veterans Against the War and I was in every protest . . . on Vietnam while I was in college.[34]

Like thousands of others, Guy Osmer headed for college. "I went to Montclair State in 1970, and as soon as I got there things started to shift. I went to an SDS meeting and joined the VVAW." In activities typical of campus chapters, the

Montclair, New Jersey, VVAW joined with other student organizations for joint actions, including the disruption of the local Selective Service Bureau.[35]

Veterans also opposed the presence of military recruiters on campus. At City College in San Francisco a group of angry veterans chased marine recruiters off campus and convinced the student council to ban their activities.[36] One of the best-publicized campus actions occurred at the University of Michigan homecoming football game in October 1971. Tens of thousands of fans stood hushed as a hundred veterans silently released black balloons and offered up a clenched fist salute to the war dead.[37] The campus campaign was very successful and a primary source of the organizational strength that would make the VVAW's appearance in national politics possible in 1971.

Intensely frustrated by the continuing war, a national convention of organizers unveiled the plan for Dewey Canyon III. Its name inspired from the military code name of the 1971 Laotion invasion, Dewey Canyon III was to be a weeklong "incursion into the land of Congress." Former Marine Corps commandant David L. Shoup and retired Army brigadier general Hugh Hester, both longterm opponents of the war, joined the VVAW in announcing the protest.[38] Scheduled for the third week in April, Dewey Canyon III was a lobbying effort targeting congressional representatives. Hundreds of veterans met with their elected leaders and presented their case against the war. Speaking on behalf of the VVAW, veteran John Kerry testified before Congress, drawing together in his message the need for remembering the war, the fate of war veterans, and the importance of social change. The excerpt presented here captures the spirit of that new breed of citizen–soldier.

> This administration has done us the ultimate dishonor. They have attempted to disown us and the sacrifices we made for this country. . . . We wish a merciful God could wipe away our memories of that service as easily as this administration has wiped their memory of us. . . . All that they can do by this denial is to make more clear than ever our own determination to undertake one last mission, to search out and destroy the last vestige of this barbaric war. . . . To conquer the hate and fear that have driven this country the last ten years and more. And so thirty years from now . . . we will be able to say Vietnam and not mean a desert, not a filthy obscene memory, but mean instead the place where America finally turned and where soldiers like us helped in the turning.[39]

Remembering not forgetting, acting not acquiescing, the new winter soldiers came to the nation's capital to "turn" America. Over a thousand veterans camped out on the Mall at the center of Washington, defying a Supreme Court ban on their tent city. Washington, D.C., police, many of whom were veterans, refused to evict the protesters. When local army units were put on alert, the GIs of these units sent word to the veterans and sabotaged trucks.

With the steps of government buildings as their stages, the veterans orchestrated antiwar theater. Over 100 were arrested for disturbing the peace when a large group of veterans, singing patriotic songs, assembled on the steps of the Supreme Court to demand that the justices stop avoiding the issue and rule on the war's constitutionality. When a group of veterans and Gold Star Mothers, women whose sons died in Vietnam, were barred from laying a wreath at Arlington Cemetery, the veterans returned 250 strong to win entrance to the nation's military graveyard.

On Thursday night a candlelight march was held around the White House. At the end of the procession a group of veterans carried a giant American flag flying upside down as a symbol of distress. Hundreds watched as the final contingent mounted the stage and a group of veterans pulled together to raise the flag.

> There was this spontaneous feeling of pride. I sort of drew a parallel with Iwo Jima. I guess you had to, because it was with the same type of pride that they put up the flag in Iwo Jima. And when that was done—instead of burning the flag, they took it and they folded it up because as Phil Lavoie, one of the vets with the flag said, "We love America. We're not here to destroy it."[40]

This new Iwo Jima struck a responsive chord deep in the childhood memories of the new winter soldiers. A photograph of the flag raising was used on the cover of *The New Soldier,* a book of words and pictures John Kerry and the VVAW published to commemorate Dewey Canyon III.

The week of activity peaked in what was one of the most dramatic and influential events of the antiwar movement. On April 23, approximately two thousand veterans marched toward the nation's Capitol building. Dressed in faded uniforms and combat fatigues, the veterans had come to return their war-won honors. Finding a fence erected to block their passage, the marchers gathered around the Capitol steps and cleared a space for the ceremony.

One by one the citizen-soldiers approached a microphone. Pronouncing declarations of anger and peace, of rage and repentance, the veterans hurled their honorable discharges, medals, and ribbons onto the Capitol steps. "My name is Peter Branagan. I got a purple heart and I hope I get another one fighting these mother-fuckers." An African American veteran approached the stage, "I pray that time will forgive me and my brothers for what we did." Tossing a handful of medals toward the Capitol another citizen-soldier solemnly said, "This is for the brothers and sisters at Kent." Then, "Second Battalion First Marines—power to the people." Representing a number of veterans, Paul F. Wither shouted, "Spec 4, army, retired. I'm taking in nine Purple Hearts, Distinguished Service Cross, Bronze Star, Silver Star . . . and a lot of other shit. . . . This is for my brothers," he declared as he heaved a heavy handful of medals. An African American spoke calmly and deliberately, "Robert Jones, New York. I symbolically return all Vietnam medals and other service medals given me by the power structure that has genocidal policies against nonwhite peoples of the world. All power to the people." Pointing at the U.S. Capitol walled off from its people, a veteran claimed, "We're not gonna fight anymore, but if we have to fight again it will be to take these steps."[41] For three hours Vietnam veterans passed in review. As the ceremony wore on, the emotional pitch strained to a breaking point.

> After I threw in my medals I moved beyond the mike and was . . . helping herd the newsmen away from the fence so that the vets could get through. Then I saw some newsmen beginning to pick up medals. I grabbed the mike and said: "Listen, you newsmen, we're not giving you the medals. We're turning them in to the country . . . don't touch them!"
>
> And then another newsman picked up a Purple Heart and put it in his pocket. And I snapped. It was just . . . the most sacrilegious thing I'd ever seen. . . .
>
> And I just turned to go when Ron Ferizzi from Philadelphia got up and said, "My wife is divorcing me for returning these medals. She wants me to keep them so my little sons can be proud of me." And went on to say how three of his best friends had died so he could get that medal. And that finally snapped everything, and a whole bunch of us, you know, just

5 Veterans prepare to raise the flag after the Candlelight March at VVAW's Dewey Canyon III in Washington, D.C. This Jim Pathe photograph first appeared in Jan Barry, ed., *Peace Is Our Profession*.

6 Dewey Canyon III. VVAW members line up to return their medals to Congress at the U.S. Capitol. Barry Romo, one of the current national coordinators of the VVAW, stands third from right. Photograph courtesy of the VVAW.

7 Dewey Canyon III. This Jim Pathe photograph first appeared in Jan Berry, ed., *Peace Is Our Profession.*

started crying. . . . We couldn't take it anymore. And we walked away and were crying really hard for two hours. . . . Right at that instant . . . we wouldn't have been surprised if somebody said, "Hey Nixon just announced that all the troops will be out of Nam and back home by suppertime." We would have believed it at that instant. . . . We thought we'd finally done it and we'd reached everyone.[42]

By returning war decoration en masse, the veterans had created a meaningful alternative to the military's award ceremony and the sense of honor it held. For the participants of Dewey Canyon III, honor and the authority to confer it came from the people, the ultimate source and agent of democratic principles. As soldiers who knew that the people no longer ruled and that principles of democracy had been violated, the veterans publicly reclaimed their citizenship and honor through resistance to illegitimate authority.

Dewey Canyon III, to me, is a representation of patriotism . . . . I love what this country is supposed to stand for. What is says it stands for, and the mystique it carries.

But, that's not what it really is. When you say the word "patriotism" . . . I think of somebody blind who really doesn't want to see truth.[43]

The internationally televised images of Dewey Canyon III stunned many who had previously dismissed the antiwar movement. Perhaps as important as the media impact of the demonstration was the fact that participants at Dewey Canyon III represented a broad segment of veteran sentiment.

I brought not only my own, but I brought about fifteen guys' medals that could not go to Dewey Canyon III. They would have if their job, or family, or something, hadn't got in the way. So I brought my medals there—it was a . . . bucketful. . . . Those were some of the most touching things. These guys . . . saying, "Hey I can't go but . . . I want you to take mine and throw them for me." I also took notes and guys said, "Please say this for me."[44]

On the last day of Dewey Canyon III the veterans planted a tree on the Washington quadrangle at the site of the encampment. As a symbol of rebirth, the tree announced the spirit of the new winter soldiers. The soldiers had become peacemakers. Not a single act of violence had occurred.

A massive antiwar demonstration occurred the following day. According to a prominent antiwar activist, these VVAW activities helped to draw the hundreds of thousands of protesters that would make April 24 one of the largest demonstrations in American history.[45]

In the wake of Dewey Canyon III, VVAW membership skyrocketed. Organizations in Germany and Japan blossomed, and over five hundred letters seeking membership were received from soldiers in Vietnam. The VVAW logo was emblazoned on fatigues, buttons, and automobiles. Hundreds of actions were taken by local groups in the name of the VVAW. At one time nearly thirty thousands names appeared on formal VVAW membership rolls, but possibly twice that number acted in the VVAW's name. After Dewey Canyon III, the VVAW claimed nine thousand members on duty in Vietnam.[46]

A wide array of activities spun off from the VVAW's newfound prestige in the peace movement. Veteran rap groups, an experiment in group counseling, were started in New York with the cooperation of a number of psychiatrists, most notably Robert J. Lifton. These sessions helped troubled veterans and laid the clinical basis for the eventual recognition of post-traumatic stress disorder (PTSD). The rap groups offered the solace of therapy and mutual understanding. Inspired by his experiences, Lifton went on to write the 1973 antiwar classic *Home from the War*.

In May 1971 Massachusetts veterans organized the most striking Memorial Day observance in American history. Designated "Operation P.O.W." because "we are all prisoners of this war," the VVAW planned a weekend march from Concord to Lexington and from Bunker Hill to Boston Commons. Retracing the path of Paul Revere, the dissident veterans hoped to rekindle the spirit of liberty at its historic birthplace. On the first night hundreds of veterans camped peacefully on Concord's Old North Bridge to honor the memory and sacrifices of the first American citizen-soldiers.

As the parade of five hundred veterans marched off, no one thought they would soon participate in what was to be Lexington's most authentic reenactment of that famous battle. When town officials barred the veterans from camping on Lexington Green, a local radio station and an activist telephone tree sent out a peaceful call to arms. Hundreds of people quickly gathered on Lexington Green to support the VVAW's right to free speech and dissent. The crowd swelled to a thousand veterans and their supporters, and "called forth two hundred years of revolutionary ghosts who assembled at the Vietnam veterans' side."[47]

Despite all this, town officials refused to budge. Late that night, after many local residents had returned to their homes, the police advanced on Lexington Green and conducted the largest mass arrest in Massachusetts history. By daybreak 458 persons had been arrested without resistance. Many gave only their name, serial number, and a birthdate of April 19, 1775.

The arrests sent political shockwaves throughout Massachusetts Bay and provoked comparisons with Shays's Rebellion and the Boston Tea Party. For weeks the *Lexington Minutemen* published letters discussing the event. Local citizens organized a public apology in the *Boston Globe* and petitioned to pardon the arrested demonstrators. A leading Lexington official, responsible for the arrests, was voted out of office. In 1991 a committee of local historians—some arrested on that night—organized a research project to reclaim the public memory of Memorial Day 1971.

By August of that year the VVAW began to publish a nationally distributed veteran newspaper. The veterans drew its title from the Aeschylean dictum "In war truth is the first casualty." *First Casualty* displayed the political broadness that typified the veterans movement. The first cover story treated not the Vietnam War but the racism and racial riots plaguing Cairo, Illinois, a community that had asked the veterans for help.[48] Later retitled *Winter Soldier*, the veteran's newspaper reached tens of thousands of readers. An overview of cover and centerfold stories from *Winter Soldier* suggests the multi-issue orientation of the VVAW. The *Winter Soldier* read like an inventory of the social movements of the early 1970s: the coal miners' strike, the uprising at Wounded Knee, the Attica Revolt, support for the Farmworkers Union, calls for prison reform, a constant demand for the impeachment of Nixon, and freedom for political prisoners. International Woman's Day and International Workers' Day were celebrated on the covers of *Winter Soldier*, unemployment, the Chilean Coup, and U.S. policy in the Middle East were attacked and criticized. These were not merely news stories; they often reflected the political associations of the veterans movement. For example, when a group of Indian activists occupied a building in Wounded Knee, South Dakota, dissident veterans responded.

Jesses Torres traveled to Wounded Knee.

> I had met a couple of veterans at Pine Ridge. One was a Navaho . . . and one was a Kiowa—both these guys were heavily decorated combat veterans. . . . We went right underneath the Guard's nose and the FBI. . . . I had some money, some clothes, and some medical supplies. . . . I gave that willingly to the group. . . . There were at least a half a dozen or maybe more veterans that were there.[49]

Torres was not unique. Many American Indian veterans became active in Indian politics or joined the American Indian Movement.[50]

The VVAW's involvement with the Wounded Knee uprising typifies its members sense of solidarity with other social movements. They attempted to bring humanitarian and medical support to the besieged Lakota. Bart Savage and Bill Branson of the VVAW were arrested while transporting medical supplies to the Sioux reservation. Nurse Ann Hirschman was smuggled into the siege, where she served as medic during the armed assault on Wounded Knee.[51] The *Winter Soldier* devoted both front, centerfold, and back pages to Native American issues. In the centerfold the veteran journalists reproduced a statement from the Six Nations Iroquois Confederacy that read in part:

> We are a free people. . . . This is the greatest gift we gave you, the concept of freedom. You did not have this . . . now that you have taken it

and built a constitution and country around it you deny freedom to us. There must be some one among you who is concerned for us and if not for us, at least for the honor of your country. In 1976 you are going to have a birthday party proclaiming 200 hundred years of democracy, a hypocritical action. . . . The solution is simple: be honest, be fair, honor the commitments made by the founding fathers of your country.[52]

While staking a claim for the American Indian contribution to American republicanism, the Iroquois statement also pronounced a sense of betrayed ideals that the veterans knew all too well. The *Winter Soldier* went on to link the veterans' solidarity with Wounded Knee to the Vietnam experience.

VVAW thinks it is important for all of America to seek the reason behind Wounded Knee, as America must seek out the reasons behind the Vietnam War. . . . We can see the roots of the Vietnam War in the way the United States had treated . . . the American Indian.[53]

Beyond a liberal sympathy for the downtrodden, the VVAW acted out of an egalitarian solidarity that recognized American Indian history as part of their own lives.

The Christmas bombing of 1971 set off another round of protest. Valley Forge again became the site of a veterans encampment. Antiwar veterans and civilian supporters from around the country returned again to the winter refuge of the Revolutionary army. Using Valley Forge as headquarters, the new winter soldiers planned "Operation Peace on Earth," a campaign to recapture the symbols of the American spirit.

In Philadelphia, the Betsy Ross House was occupied, and Independence Hall became the site of antiwar protest.[54] One hundred and fifty veterans rallied at the White House and marched in Washington. Shouldering a casket, the veterans sang "As Johnny Comes Marching Home," "The Star-spangled Banner," and the "Battle Hymn of the Republic." As the demonstration approached the Lincoln Memorial the veterans marched up the steps, placed the casket at Lincoln's feet, and blocked the entrance to the monument. Eighty-seven veterans were arrested and spent the night in jail.

On December 26, fifteen VVAW members blockaded themselves in the Statue of Liberty. One of those veterans recalled his mission.

The idea came forth to take over the Statue of Liberty. . . . So we ran it like a military mission. . . .

Fifteen of us, plus a reporter from WBAI, went over on a Sunday afternoon. Gradually all of us got in. So we were in the arm and the last ferry took off and it was pitch dark. . . . We were told that some vets in a drug rehabilitation ward in San Diego had taken over their hospital floor in solidarity with what we were doing. . . .

> Meantime the people in Valley Forge with hundreds of vets—they were buoyed. We hung the American flag upside down from the crown. Everything was very positive. . . . I was the only noncombat vet there. . . . I remember being entirely empowered. We were changing the way the message was coming out.[55]

On the protesters' demand, an article and photograph was carried in the military's newspaper *Stars and Stripes*. From "within this international symbol of liberty," the veterans claimed to have "captured the hopes and imaginations of a war-weary nation."[56]

That same week the VVAW also joined other vets in protesting poor conditions in the Travis Air Force Base hospital, disrupted an air force recruiting station in Massachusetts, petitioned the UN to stop the war, and organized an antiwar protest at the traditional New Year's Eve celebration at Times Square.[57]

By the end of 1971 the antiwar veterans and the peace movement generally had contributed to a basic shift in public opinion against American involvement in Vietnam. The people had turned against the war.[58] The remaining problem was how to pressure the government, party, and military elites to accept the popular will.

In 1972 the VVAW mounted "the Last Patrol," which organized hundreds of veterans to demonstrate at the Democratic and Republican conventions, both of which were held in Miami. Despite intense police harassment that would eventually end in a conspiracy trial against eight VVAW leaders, the veteran contingents from around the country found their way to Miami. In *Born on the Fourth of July*, Ron Kovic describes his cross-country trip to Miami.

> I . . . see the convoy behind me . . . cars and buses, trucks and jeeps, painted with flowers and peace signs, a strange caravan of young men wearing war ribbons on torn utility jackets and carrying plastic guns. . . . It is a historic event like the Bonus March. . . . And now it is we who are marching, the boys of the fifties. We are going to the Republican National Convention to reclaim America and a bit of ourselves. It is war and we are soldiers again, as tight as we have ever been, a whole lost generation . . . coming from all over the country to tell Nixon a thing or two. We know we are fighting the real enemies this time—the ones who have made profit off our very lives.[59]

They were "soldiers again," but this time for peace, and this time representing the will of the people. From all over America veterans tramped their way to Miami.

At both conventions the veterans were the leading force of the public demonstrations against government policy in Southeast Asia. The veterans were allowed to enter the Democratic Convention and speak to delegates. Perhaps the most significant political actions of that week occurred away from the conven-

8 The VVAW march at the 1972 Republican convention in Miami. Three wounded veterans in wheelchairs (left to right, Bobby Mueller, Bill Wienman, Ron Kovic) would also protest from the convention floor. Ann Hirschman (standing at right) was a nurse, VVAW medic, and participant at Wounded Knee. Photograph courtesy of the VVAW.

tion floor. Ann Hirschman recalls the tensions between the veterans and the surrounding community.

> They put the encampment in a part of South Miami Beach that is a predominately working-class retirement area. . . . The neighborhood was scared to death. They had been told that all these crazy vets were likely to eat their children, kill their dogs, blow up their homes . . . set fires . . . get drunk, and act crazy. The community bought that hook, line, everything. . . . They closed the stores. They literally boarded up their windows. This was serious fear.[60]

The appearance of the American Nazi party changed everything.

> And then the Nazis came. Fifty uniformed . . . jack-booted, goose-stepping, stupid people. The vets made a ring between the rest of the demonstrators and the Nazis—arm to arm. . . . The fifty Nazis were going to take the stage. One of the vets was on the stage making announcements. . . . This stupid Nazi picks up a wooden folding chair . . . and hits Steve across the face. . . . Danny . . . picks up the same chair and hits the Nazi. . . . We then put four vets on each Nazi, one on each limb, and just carried them out of the community. It was so dramatic. At this point this community, which was not only working class but fairly Jewish, suddenly opened up. Like we drowned in chicken soup for two days. . . .

> We were going to the Democratic Convention the next night. We're all really tense. One lady, she said, "What can we do for you? Anything for you guys!" . . . and I made the stupid mistake of saying, "Well they like beer." Fifty cases of beer a day. It was the only time I ever saw VVAW have enough beer. When we came back for the Republican Convention it was like old home week. The police were real confused because all of a sudden the community was on our side. [61]

If the political parties had not been turned around, at least one community had been touched.

At the Republican Convention the antiwar veterans were not only barred from attending, but their demonstrations were the target of police tear gas. Still they fought for the right to speak at the convention. In scenes popularized by Oliver Stone's cinematic interpretation of Kovic's *Born on the Fourth of July*, a small group of veterans managed to enter the hall. Slipping through security and confronting antagonistic conventioneers, three disabled veterans, Kovic, Bobby Muller, and Bill Wienman, lined up on the convention floor. As Nixon approached the podium a wild ovation filled the convention hall.

> President Nixon began to speak and all three of us took a deep breath and shouted at the top of our lungs, "Stop the bombing; stop the war" . . . as loud and as hard as we could. . . . The security agents immediately threw up their arms, trying to hide us from the cameras and the president. For an instant Cronkite looked down, then turned his head away. . . . They're going to try and hide us like they did in the hospitals. Hundreds of people around us began to clap and shout "Four more years," trying to drown out our protest. . . . We continued shouting, interrupting Nixon again and again until Secret Service agents grabbed our chairs . . . and began pulling us backward as fast as they could out of the convention hall. [62]

Four years later Kovic's speech at the Democratic Convention capped a rhetorical success for antiwar veterans; their efforts to be heard in the arena of national party politics had paid off. Kovic's speech was given in nomination of Fritz Efaw for vice-president of the United States. Efaw had been a draft resister and a VVAW member, and had lived in exile for seven years. Efaw's nomination was intended to highlight the veterans' campaign for full amnesty for draft and military resisters. Kovic's speech offered a concise summary of the antiwar veterans' experience.

> I . . . joined the United States Marines. I wanted to serve my country. I wanted to be a good American. . . .
>
> I cried when I saw them burning draft cards and demonstrating in the streets. I was angry and called them 'traitors' for refusing to fight and die for what I believed in.

I continued to go out on patrol until . . . I was shot . . . and . . . permanently paralyzed. . . . I was sent back to VA hospitals that were like slums, with incredibly poor conditions where paralyzed men cried to be treated like human beings. They became the forgotten wounded. . . . The ones we didn't want to talk about—because they so much expressed the truth of the war. . . .

When students were killed at Kent State . . . I too began to speak out against the war. . . . And once, in front of the Re-elect Nixon Headquarters in Los Angeles in 1972, I was thrown out of my wheelchair—my medals torn off my chest—and kicked and beaten by police. I was arrested numerous other times with other Vietnam veterans. . . . I was cursed at, spat at, threatened, and called a traitor.[63]

Kovic's appearance at the convention reflected the rise of peace sentiment within the Democratic party and the nation as a whole. For a brief historical moment during the 1970s, a new consensus had been reached. Although their reasons for believing differed, a majority of Americans came to understand that the war in Vietnam was wrong. The common phrases, "We should have never been there in the first place," and "No more Vietnams" best captured the sentiment of the time.

The second inauguration of President Richard Nixon in 1973 was the occasion for the last of the massive antiwar demonstrations of the Vietnam era. The diversity of the inauguration protest showed how far the peace movement had come. Representing a broad cross section of the American people, hundreds of thousands marched once more for peace. It was also one of the last mass public displays of the veterans' antiwar movement. Five thousand veterans assembled and marched through the streets of the capital to protest the war in Vietnam.

Particularly during the Nixon years, the VVAW was often forced to make its own legal defense a political issue. As with the peace movement generally, the CIA, FBI, military intelligence, and local political police units called red squads spied on and harassed the veterans.[64] On July 7, 1972, twenty-two men and one woman, all VVAW members, were called to appear before a grand jury in Tallahassee, Florida, on allegations of conspiracy because of their role in the demonstrations at the conventions. Of the original twenty-three, eight of the primary organizers of the demonstrations were charged with conspiracy to promote, incite, and participate in a riot at the Republican Convention.[65] "The Gainesville Eight," as the veterans became known, were part of a general pattern of politically motivated grand juries and conspiracy trials against antiwar activists. The case against the veterans exposed a network of official spies and agent provocateurs, one of whom had encouraged defendant Scott Camil to purchase automatic weapons. The government offensive against the VVAW was later linked to persons involved in the Watergate scandal.[66]

The Gainesville defendants themselves represented the powerful political shifts of the 1960s. William Patterson was a highly decorated war hero, having been awarded a Distinguished Flying Cross, the Vietnamese Cross of Gallantry, the Purple Heart, three air medals, the Vietnamese Service Medal, the Combat Infantryman's Badge, the National Defense Medal, Aerial Crewmembers Wings, and other decorations. As a college student in El Paso Patterson protested the scapegoating of William Calley by turning himself into military authorities with a signed confession stating he had killed thirteen civilians on direct orders. Patterson went on to lead the VVAW in Texas.

Camil was the son of a policeman and gung-ho volunteer for the Marine Corps. The winner of nine service medals, a 1966 letter home to his parents was so stirring that a Miami newspaper featured it as an example of soldier patriotism. Later in college, while doing research using the *Pentagon Papers*, he came to the conclusion that "I had been tricked, deceived, used, and that my life had been made expendable for reasons that I didn't consider patriotic."[67]

Pete Mahoney came from a large Irish working-class family in Brooklyn. He was an exemplary student at a Catholic seminary, where he studied two years for the priesthood. As a boy Mahoney was one badge away from being an Eagle Scout. After the 1968 Tet offensive, Mahoney volunteered for military duty to help win the war and was awarded a Bronze Star. The ex-lieutenant settled in New Orleans after the war and was elected to national leadership in the VVAW.[68]

Two of the eight, Camil and John Kniffin, continually triggered the courtroom's metal detector when it read the shrapnel they carried in their bodies.

The VVAW responded by making the trials the center of a political campaign. Beginning in the Gainesville area, the VVAW organized a "Peoples Fair." Held at nearby Santa Fe Community College, four hundred people came out to meet the antiwar veterans. Later that week a rally of eight hundred people gathered to hear student leader Tom Hayden and musician Pete Seeger defend the veterans. Support demonstrations were also held in St. Louis, Denver, Chicago, San Francisco, Los Angeles, and Kansas City. The Gainesville Eight were found innocent of all charges.[69]

Reorganization and Decline

With the signing of the Paris Peace Accords in 1973, the military antiwar movement began to decline. Like many other peace organizations, the VVAW continued to oppose U.S. military aid to the Thieu and Lon Nol dictatorships. Searching for a means to continue the movement, the Winter Soldier Organization (WSO), an affiliated nonveteran organization, was formed in 1973. The VVAW–WSO was envisioned as an organization capable of leading the broader movement.

The WSO was the product of the many activities that the VVAW had conducted in local communities across the country. In many localities the VVAW was the primary representative of the movement for social change.

In some places the VVAW was the only game in town, the only antiwar group around. In other places we were the best around. Political coalitions tend to spend so much time on infighting, and we didn't. We went out and did things. We always reacted against being in the military . . . but . . . we also had a discipline—which in part came from being in the military— that other groups never had. That meant when something had to get done, we would do it. People appreciated that.[70]

Well into the mid 1970s VVAW–WSO was able to mount significant demonstrations. During the Fourth of July weekend 1974, five thousand VVAW–WSO members and supporters marched in Washington, D.C. demanding amnesty for all war resisters.[71]

By the mid 1970s Veterans' Day celebrations had became political campaigns. Built on earlier activities by local groups of antiwar soldiers and veterans, Veterans' Day was becoming a new tradition. In 1971, for example, over a hundred dissident GIs from Fort Hood were arrested for marching without a permit to celebrate Veterans' Day in Killeen, Texas.[72] Jim Pechin recalls Veterans' Day 1970 in Terre Haute, Indiana.

About twenty of us showed up to march in the parade and . . . there was a pecking order the way they lined up. . . . They put us at the end of the parade and there was one unit behind us . . . the black American Legion post. . . . We got real friendly with them during the parade . . . we ended up going down to their bar and drinking beer with them all day long. You got all these white college kid veterans and all these black World War II vets and they accepted us with open arms—they had some sense of what our experience had been.

For me, the highlight of the parade? Congressman John Meyers was on the reviewing stand with this general and . . . when we hit the reviewing stand we all took out kazoos and played the "Star-spangled Banner" . . . and gave the finger to the general—which they put a picture of in the newspaper. We were booed by most of the people who were watching.[73]

In 1974 the VVAW–WSO activities for Veterans' Day included hundreds of public appearances, media interviews, and speaking engagements. To underscore the injustice of President Ford's limited amnesty for war resisters and his full pardon of Richard Nixon, the Buffalo chapter organized a traveling forum on amnesty issues. In Columbus, Ohio, Burlington, Vermont, Philadelphia, and San Francisco, the VVAW–WSO were part of larger demonstrations against continued support for South Vietnam and the Ford amnesty program.[74]

On Veterans' Day 1974 the VVAW–WSO held demonstrations in eight major cities, involving nearly twenty local chapters of the organization. In many areas the veterans met with resistance or were flatly denied permission to march in official parades. The events of 1974 were typical of the ongoing official reaction

9 On the Fourth of July 1974 the VVAW organized five thousand demonstrators to call for full amnesty for all war resisters. Photograph by Rich Klein; courtesy of the VVAW.

to antiwar veterans. Long Beach, California, denied the VVAW the right to march because they were "unpatriotic." In Milwaukee, eighty-five dissident veterans, the only Vietnam veterans in the parade, were forced to march on the sidewalk after being expelled from the parade. Similarly, Columbus, Ohio, turned down VVAW organizers because they did not "follow the program." In Boston, Vietnam veterans were pushed out of the official parade by mounted police and had to find a place at the end of the line for their hundred-strong contingent.[75]

By the mid 1970s the declining power of the movements for social change raised real practical difficulties. Multi-issue organizing was becoming increasingly problematic, and most popular movements were heading toward single-issue constituencies.

> By 1975 or so the organization was splitting into two parts. One part of it tried to hold together briefly and couldn't do it because their interests were so different. A chapter here who is interested in housing . . . and a chapter in St. Louis whose focus is gay and lesbian issues. Well there's not a whole lot to hold them together.[76]

Social movements and organizations in decline tend toward a divisive and centrifugal dynamic. Like many other movements, the VVAW was fractured by internal disputes and struggles, particularly among the leadership. The Revolutionary Union, later named the Revolutionary Communist Party (RCP), was a Marxist-Leninist organization that had growing influence in the VVAW after 1973. The RCP was a major player in factional fighting and influenced the VVAW leadership until 1978. During this period the VVAW dwindled in size and effectiveness. In 1978 a final split created the VVAW–Anti-Imperialist (VVAW–AI) and ended the RCP's role in the VVAW.

Much more enduring and important than the VVAW's internal history, however, are the many subtle changes the military antiwar movement effected among everyday Americans.[77]

> We had about twenty-five thousand members at the end of Vietnam. Certainly not all these people are still active in progressive activity but . . . a lot of them are. We get letters from this incredible group, the Blackburn Coalition for Central America, a group of coal miners in some little town in West Virginia, which is run by a Vietnam Vet, an old VVAW member. They send us this newsletter once a month. It's this very literate, very remarkable thing out of some little town. . . . How many of these are there? I would guess literally hundreds.[78]

The Road Is Long

Although the Vietnam era came to a close, dissident veterans continued to be active in a variety of movements for peace, social justice, and veterans' benefits. The VVAW continues to oppose military adventures and to fight for veterans' benefits. Initiated by the Milwaukee chapter, the VVAW launched the "War on the VA." Demonstrating and lobbying, the VVAW fought the

Veterans' Administration to recognize Agent Orange poisoning and to improve medical care for all veterans.

The impact of veteran activism reached well beyond the antiwar movement. In the late 1970s, Bobby Muller, Jim Pechin, and other ex-VVAW activists organized the Vietnam Veterans of America. Initially focused on Agent Orange, the Vietnam Veterans of America grew to become the nation's largest organization of Vietnam veterans.[79]

Taking the name of the first Vietnam-era veterans peace organization, the Veterans for Peace (VFP), was organized in July 1985. Like its namesake from the 1960s and 1970s the VFP organizes antiwar veterans from all conflicts and periods.

The strident Cold War rhetoric and actual military interventions of the 1980s provoked renewed activity from America's antiwar veterans. Antiwar veterans centered in Utah formed an organization called Never Again and published *Common Sense*, an antiwar periodical. The Vietnam Veterans Peace Action Network responded to the threat of war in Central America.

The 1980s also saw the emergence of the gay veterans movement around the right to participate in Veterans' Day events. With Vietnam veterans playing leadership roles, the Gay Veterans' Association was founded in 1984 to fight discrimination and homophobia in the military.

In the 1990s, veteran organizations such as the Black Veterans for Social Justice, in Brooklyn; the Alliance of Atomic Veterans, out of Arizona; the Bill Motto post 5888 of the Veterans of Foreign Wars, in Santa Cruz; the Oklahoma Agent Orange Foundation; Swords to Plowshares, in San Francisco; the National Association of Black Veterans, headquartered in Milwaukee; and the Veterans' Vietnam Restoration Project, centered in Garberville, California, continue the fight for social justice at home and abroad. *Citizen–Soldier*, a newspaper founded by Vietnam-era activists, brings investigative reporting and dissenting viewpoints to today's servicemembers.

The VVAW and the VFP maintain dozens of chapters and are part of an extensive network of peace activists.[80] The antiwar veterans publish several newsletters, such as the VVAW's *DMZ*, written by the active Clarence Fitch Chapter in the New York–New Jersey area, and *Point*, published by the VFP's Smedley Butler Brigade in Boston. The VVAW national office in Chicago publishes *The Veteran*, and the Maine center of the VFP puts out a quarterly journal. In Kansas City, the Vietnam Veterans Radio Network broadcasts "history you can dance to." Celebrating twenty-five years of fighting for veterans, peace, and justice, hundreds of antiwar veterans and their supporters gathered in New York City for VVAW's 1992 silver anniversary.

In recent years the VVAW and VFP have sent delegations bearing medical and humanitarian aid to the Philippines, Nicaragua, El Salvador, Guatemala, Panama, Cuba, South Africa, Cambodia, and, of course, Vietnam. At the request of Dine and Hopi elders, the VVAW, VFP, and other veterans' groups organized the Veterans' Peace Convoy to Big Mountain, Arizona, to draw attention to the issue of forced relocation. In 1993 the VFP organized "Operation Angel" to evacuate wounded children from war-torn Bosnia to U.S. hospitals.

The peak of recent antiwar activity was reached during the Gulf conflict. Antiwar veterans emerged as leaders of protest groups and helped to organize demonstrations for a peace movement that was robust and diverse.[81] Vietnam veterans were on the front lines of the military counseling projects that helped serve the estimated twenty-five hundred conscientious objectors and thousands of other uncertain soldiers during the Gulf War.[82] Both the VVAW and the VFP grew rapidly during the conflict.

The VVAW and VFP continue to add dissenting voices to Memorial Day ceremonies, Fourth of July activities, and, of course, Veterans' Day observances. In their political and cultural activities these antiwar veterans continue to make a remarkable, if unheralded, contribution to American popular culture. These public ceremonies and the social movements from which they grew contain the germ of a potential American culture that is patriotic, peaceful, and just.

Military Resistance as a Social Movement

6

The most common charge leveled against the antiwar movement is that is was composed of cowards and draft dodgers. To have in it people who had served in the military . . . who were in fact patriots by the prowar folks' own definition, was a tremendous thing. VVAW in 1970 and 1971 was unlike almost anything I'd seen in terms of its impact on the public. . . .

We took away more and more of the symbolic and rhetorical tools available to the prowar folks—just gradually squeezed them into a corner. At some point Nixon had nothing left but to subvert the Constitution to maintain his ambition. . . . We took away little by little the reasons people had not to listen to the antiwar movement.

—BEN CHITTY, VIETNAM VETERAN

THE MILITARY ANTIWAR MOVEMENT occupied a special strategic position. As resistant soldiers they slowed the military machine. As "patriots" with deep ties to "the public" the new winter soldiers became the voice of their communities and helped to win a nation away from war. Ultimately the political genius of that movement was to reclaim the "symbolic and rhetorical tools" that justified war and transform them instead into the messengers of their antiwar appeal.

The Power of Protest

How effective were the soldier and veteran resistance movements? The thesis first put forward by David Cortright in *Soldiers in Revolt* seems convincing. Soldier resistance was a significant factor contributing to the American withdrawal from Vietnam. Ill-conceived from the outset, the American effort in Vietnam failed for many reasons. Given the demands of maintaining a vast network of foreign bases, the Vietnam War was an extraordinary drain on U.S. military personnel and material. The massive social disorders in American cities further diverted military resources. The fighting ability and commitment of the National Liberation Front (NLF) and North Vietnamese Army (NVA) ensured that the war would be long and costly. In *The Rise and Fall of an American Army: U.S. Ground Forces in Vietnam, 1965–1973*, Shelby Stanton thoroughly documents the exhaustion of American military capabilities. Stanton claims that by 1968, "clearly, the ability of the armed forces to react was being stretched to the breaking point."[1] Contrary to the image of America fighting with "one hand tied behind its back," the U.S. military was pushed to its utmost. Given these very real political and military constraints, the GI and veteran resistance sharply limited the possible responses of military and foreign-policy elites.

In a recent article, Cortright uses two government-contracted studies on soldier dissent to evaluate the extent of resistance. He claims that 37 percent of Vietnam-era servicepeople were involved in some form of disobedience or dissent, with 32 percent participating more than once.[2] In *Days of Decision*, Gerald Gioglio cites a 1980 Louis Harris study done for the Veterans Administration, in which 9 percent of the veterans questioned claimed to have attended an antiwar rally, participated in a demonstration, written letters to political representatives or the press, or helped aid draft resistance. Recognizing that these categories define only a small fraction of soldier and veteran resistance activities, Gioglio factors the 9 percent as a nine-hundred-thousand person minimum for military resistance.[3] Even a promilitary veterans group claimed that 15 percent of veterans identified themselves as radical in 1973.[4]

In *Bringing the War Home*, John Helmer cites a 1969 Nielson study of 244 veterans in which 47 percent responded that the war was a mistake, 40 percent felt the problem was essentially tactical, and only 10 percent strongly supported both the war and how it was fought.[5] On assignment in Vietnam during 1971, journalist Donald Kirk interviewed dozens of American soldiers. He claimed, "I found literally no young GIs in favor of the war."[6] Historian Gerald Gill claims that by 1970 a majority of African American soldiers thought that the war was a mistake, "hypocritical in intent and racist and imperialist by design."[7]

Between 1977 and 1979 Ellen Frey-Wouters and Robert S. Laufer conducted a nationwide survey of Vietnam-era males and published their findings in *Legacy of a War*. Of the 326 Vietnam veterans and 341 Vietnam-era veterans surveyed, "a majority . . . agreed that we should have stayed out of the conflict." Overall, *Legacy of a War* portrays Vietnam veterans as evenly divided over opposition to the war.[8]

Bobby Muller, founder of the Vietnam Veterans of America, reflecting on the cultural and political changes of the 1980s said, "Everyone in combat I found was against the war when we came back. It's a hard lesson to learn . . . that perhaps one third are like us, but a whole lot buy the conservative line."[9] In a 1980 poll of veterans between the ages of twenty-five and thirty-four, 64 percent agreed that they were glad to have served their country.[10] Yet in the same study 76 percent agreed that "our political leaders in Washington deliberately misled the American people about the way the war in Vietnam was going."[11] A recent in-depth study of twenty-five Chicano veterans from the Southwest claims that only two of the twenty-five never questioned the value of the war, "but they felt that almost every vet they knew sooner or later ended up being opposed to the war."[12] In Charley Trujillo's 1990 oral history *Soldados: Chicanos in Viet Nam*, five of the nineteen veterans he interviewed from Corcoran, California, voiced antiwar opinions.[13]

Fixing the precise size of the military peace movement is difficult. The often-amorphous nature of resistance and the ways in which protest was reported and suppressed hampers a precise statistical reconstruction of the movement. After summarizing the existing body of information and talking with a wide range of Vietnam veterans and observers of the war era, I can only conclude that the soldier and veteran movements were mass movements. A conservative estimate would claim that 20 to 25 percent of servicepeople were activists over a period of months or years. Perhaps more important, the activists articulated the sentiment of approximately half of all soldiers and veterans during the period itself. These figures take on greater meaning when one considers that they were roughly equivalent to the percentages of activists at the peak of the student movement and are much higher than the percentages of activists for all young people of the generation.[14]

The soldier and veteran protest had a direct effect upon the power of the U.S. military and ruling elites. The political and military dimensions of this resistance were remarkable and historically unprecedented. A significant minority of soldiers, sometimes led by antiwar officers, took the execution of the war into their own hands by declaring a grunts' ceasefire. Passive resistance, shamming, search-and-avoid missions, combat refusals, fraggings, and absenteeism were powerful forms of grassroots democratic diplomacy. In June 1971 a GI paper called *People's Press* ran an article claiming that NLF and NVA units were ordered not to open hostilities against U.S. troops displaying red bandannas or peace signs unless first fired upon.[15] In 1974, an anonymous U.S. Army colonel claimed:

> I had influence over an entire province. I put my men to work helping with the harvest. They put up buildings. Once the NVA understood what I was doing, they eased up. I'm talking to you about a de facto truce, you understand. The war stopped in most of the province. It's the kind of history that doesn't get recorded. Few people even know it happened, and no one will ever admit that it happened.[16]

The policymaking elites lost control of the ability to wage war to a degree unprecedented in recent American history. The top brass and the government viewed this democracy with horror. Commenting on the Movement for a Democratic Military (MDM), Marine Corps Commander General Chapman said, "MDM wants nothing less than democracy. I can think of no organization which is less democratic than the Marine Corps."[17]

The soldier and veteran revolt hobbled American intervention. Writing for the *Armed Forces Journal* in 1971, Colonel Robert D. Heinl, Jr., claimed, "The morale, discipline, and battle-worthiness of the U.S. armed forces are, with a few salient exceptions, lower and worse than at any time in this century and possibly in the history of the United States."[18] Heinl's claims, even if exaggerated, clearly portray a massive refusal of the armed forces to fight the war in Vietnam.

This policy of peace was executed by what had become the most democratic army in recent American history. The democratic upsurge created new command techniques called "working it out." Working it out consisted of negotiations between officers and men to determine orders. By 1970 democratic command was sufficiently widespread that reports of it were featured in popular periodicals. Low morale and high discontent had apparently convinced many officers that "you can't just hand out orders."[19] Indeed, the troops exercised control.

> The marines weren't so bad. You could make your own way. . . . The thing that worried them the most was losing control. If they were having trouble with the men, they would put in somewhere, give us a week's leave, or they would make up some reason why the mission had been canceled—even though everyone knew the real reason.[20]

When soldiers had power, "the marines weren't so bad." For a short but significant time this democratic upsurge altered the relationship between military institutions and civil society.

Military Democracy and American Society

The soldier and veteran movements brought American social values, such as democracy, into the military. Dissident soldiers and veterans became representatives of their communities within a major American institution. This new republican army had deep roots among the common people, their political traditions, and community values. Contrary to common images of the antiwar movement, ethnic, poor, and working-class communities held antiwar attitudes often greater than Americans in general did.[21]

The poor and politically weak have little access to the media, except as consumers, and few resources to communicate their opinions. When the antiwar attitudes of powerless communities conflicted with national policy, their views rarely registered in major media or the public debate. In addition, some elements within the diverse and complex antiwar movement rejected working-class struggles as a political legacy and repudiated workers as allies. In this they replicated an academic consensus that defined workers as deeply authoritarian and conservative.[22] The white, middle-class bias of the major media validated that definition and enforced ignorance of off-campus dissent.

The media's hawkish "hard hat" helped define mass perceptions of working-class attitudes. The notorious May 1970 attack by construction workers on antiwar demonstrators in New York City was the product of collaboration between union officials and the employers. Bosses suspended work and paid workers for participating. One contractor reportedly offered cash for attacks on protesters. Although the police had been warned about the possibility of violence, some witnesses claimed the police allowed assaults on antiwar demonstrators.[23] Among those attacked by the prowar rioters was a battle-wounded Vietnam veteran.

> I was right there when they had the Wall Street riots with the construction workers. . . . I found myself in the middle of all this mayhem, some construction worker beating up on a fourteen-year-old girl. . . . They were against people dying, and they were getting their asses kicked for it. . . . You got to take a side.
> I got into an argument with some construction worker who called me a draft-card-burning, welfare-collecting hippie. I freaked out and got into this whole mess with him. He knocked me down and I bounced up, and there were some police standing around laughing, and I went at them.[24]

A Harris survey suggested that labor was deeply divided over the so-called hard-hat demonstrations. Thirty-seven percent of union workers backed nonviolent counterdemonstrations, while 24 percent sided with the students, and 26 percent claimed neutrality. The general public, however, supported the hardhats by 40 percent, with 24 percent supporting the students. The majority of union members condemned the use of violence against student demonstrators.[25] Even though the general public was more prowar than the majority of union members, the hardhat functioned symbolically to legitimize conservative sentiment and hush working-class dissent.

The major exception to this was the massive soldier and veteran movements. The dissident GIs were aware of the systematic attempts to obscure their movement. Following a large GI antiwar demonstration, an article in *Fatigue Press* entitled "Media Lies" offered an insightful explanation of why an antiwar demonstration by soldiers was reported as just another "long-haired" demonstration.

> The Texas newspapers did us a job. This was no accident: the people who own the newspapers—both locally and nationally—have economic interests that stand in opposition to the welfare of the people as a whole. . . . They are members in good standing of an economic elite: a ruling class if you like. Moreover, every ruling class must construct an ideology—an ensemble of ideas, morals, rationalizations, etc., which serves to legitimize its authority and exploitive rule in the eyes of the people. . . .
> No movement in this country worries the ruling class more than the GI movement. Whether GIs move against racism, the war, or the fascistic conditions of their involuntary servitude, the result is the same: the army ceases to function effectively. And the army is the enforcer of the ruling class's foreign and domestic policies. . . . On the national level, the media have tried to black out news of the GI movement. On the local level . . . the media have contented themselves with flagrantly distorting the nature of these demonstrations. Thus, the hundreds of GIs who marched in

Killeen were transformed by the media into a handful of "long-haired," "students," "young people."[26]

The degree to which the history of the GI and veteran movements was lost, hidden, or marginalized demonstrates the ongoing power of dominant culture to impose definition on working-class and minority communities or protest movements. In a 1991 example, local historians were denied permission to show a collection of artifacts from the VVAW's 1971 Lexington, Massachusetts, Memorial Day march. The Cary Memorial Library decided that the Gulf War had made it "inappropriate to allow your exhibit to take place."[27] As historian Jackson Lears commented, "I feel like we've been air-brushed out of history."[28]

Because workers and veterans were often repelled by the outward appearances, tactics, and cultural differences of student protesters, they were often assumed to be prowar. Many in the student movement were perceived as rejecting educational opportunities that many workers failed to gain for their own children. But disdain for "hippies" or the student movement and prowar sentiment are simply not equivalent positions. Consider Andrew Levinson's report of a demonstration:

> Several thousand students slowly filed past the . . . downtown area. It was 1969, in a midwest city, and the issue was the war in Vietnam.
>
> My Nam vet neighbor from blue-collar Milwaukee was near the front, marching under the banner of the "Vietnam Veterans Against the War." A big young man . . . wearing paint-spattered overalls . . . was shouting at the passing demonstrators. . . . Screaming that he had "been there" and he knew the truth. . . .
>
> My neighbor walked right up. . . . "First Cav?" he asked. The guy looked for a moment and replied, "Yeah." "Me too, around Hue during Tet." "Yeah?" the guy said looking more closely. . . . "Look, we were over there—we know what was going on." "Damn right," the other replied. "Well, hell you know we should have never gotten in there in the first place—you know we didn't belong there." "Yeah," the other guy said dubiously. "Well, that's all we're saying," my friend replied.
>
> "Yeah, but I just can't take them damn kids who don't know what we went through, saying we're all a bunch of killers, and that the Viet Cong are all saints." . . . "But I just don't want anyone else killed in that mess." "I agree with you on that, but I just can't stand these hippies." "Well, maybe you'd like to join the vets against the war—we all were over there too."[29]

Antiwar attitudes must be read across class and cultural differences.[30] Dissent itself was often felt to be a privilege. In the eyes of working-class and African American observers, students often seemed to enjoy the connections and wealth needed to shield them from the violence and legal penalties that can often accompany protest.

E. E. LeMasters spent five years studying the attitudes of patrons in a blue-collar tavern called the Oasis. Vietnam periodically intruded on their world. As the funeral procession of a local soldier passed by the bar one man was compelled to speak.

> I'm damn sick and tired of watching these funerals go by. . . . I was in World War II and that was bad enough, but by God we at least knew what we were fighting for and who we were fighting against. But that poor kid they're burying today—what the hell chance did he have to know why he was sent halfway around the world to fight for a goddamn country he never heard of? It's a goddamn shame and I get sick to my stomach every time another one of our kids gets killed over there."[31]

LeMasters continued to document what he called "isolationist sentiment" by quoting another bar patron. "The trouble is, we're trying to be a policeman for the whole damn world and it's not working." In a footnote LeMasters added that prevailing sentiment usually went unchallenged and such statements were rarely objected to in his five-year study.[32] In a discussion of changes in younger workers LeMasters asserted, "I have never heard a young veteran of Vietnam say a good word for that war at the Oasis."[33]

Whenever direct empirical or political measurement of opinions were made, working-class districts registered considerable antiwar sentiment, often greater than that of their more affluent neighbors. Of six municipal referenda, three showed stronger working-class antiwar sentiment (Dearborn, Michigan, 1966 and 1968; San Francisco, 1967), two were roughly equivalent to middle-class sentiments (Beverly Hills, 1968; and Madison, Wisconsin, 1968), and only in one did working-class districts show less support for antiwar referenda (Cambridge, Massachusetts, 1968).[34]

By 1971, when labor was seen by the media as moving to the right, Harris surveys indicated that union workers were more antiwar than the public in general. Sixty-four percent of union workers favored withdrawal from Vietnam when the public figures were 61 percent in favor.[35] One analysis of the opinion polls of the war claimed that the strongest correlation between class and support for withdrawal from Vietnam occurred among poor and working-class respondents.[36] The military antiwar movement represented the sentiments of thousands of Vietnam-era soldiers and the communities from which they came. The GI and veteran movements stand as the most significant working-class antiwar movement in American history.[37]

As important as the working-class orientation of the soldier and veteran movements was its racial consciousness—expressed most powerfully as Black Power. Relying on a race-centered critique, African American soldiers created a black peace movement. When placed in the context of the urban rebellions of the late 1960s, the African American resistance was a powerful disruptive force. Although these somewhat spontaneous uprisings focused on urban and racial discontents, they also had an enormous impact in the military. In addition to the direct drain on military resources, the ghetto rebellions magnified injustices at home, undermined morale, and amplified black nationalism. By early 1970 an official military study of race relations concluded that "Negro soldiers seem to have lost faith in the Army."[38]

In the early war years, African American and Latino concerns were usually articulated in the language of the civil rights movement. Military duty was viewed as an important avenue to equality and full citizenship. In his memoirs, *The Courageous and the Proud*, veteran Samuel Vance wrote:

> Vietnam is a proving ground for many soldiers, especially black soldiers. We all have one common desire—to carry our load and bear our share of the responsibility so that when the war is over and we have finally all returned home the people in the United States will recognize that Negroes carried their responsibilities and shed their share of blood in Vietnam.[39]

After 1968 this civil rights ideology was increasingly transformed into a more nationalist perspective. The impact of Vietnam on race awareness offers some clues to the dynamic relationship between race consciousness and military experience. The civil rights movement predisposed many African American GIs toward resistance and change, but the life of African American soldiers in the military and Vietnam acted to crystallize dissent. For many the war and the military re-created an awareness of civil rights or race consciousness that before had been vague or peripheral. Racial identity, like class consciousness, is a dynamic phenomenon. When military planners used racial minorities and working-class people in ways demonstrably exploitative, then racial and class identities were strengthened.[40]

> We never could have gotten to Afrocentrism until after we had gone through the civil rights movement and . . . black pride . . . . I think the experience of Vietnam was a very powerful part of that for so many of us. . . . That no matter how good you are, race will always be a hindrance in terms of progress as far as the military's concerned. The military is only symbolic of the nation, but the military is an important test because one gives up their life . . . and that's the ultimate one can do in a society. So it was a very painful understanding.[41]

African Americans created political and cultural change that contained all the important elements of soldier transformation. The tension between the civil rights and Black Power movements created a realm of democracy and empowerment within the military. The process of working it out was sometimes shaped by the negotiations between diverse forces within the African American community. John Brown, an African American with a distinguished service record, served in Vietnam with the 25th Infantry Division, CRIP platoon (Central Reconnaissance Intelligence Platoon), attached to the 5th Group Special Forces, from October 1967 to January 1968. In December 1967 Brown and his platoon, all veterans of highly covert and sensitive combat missions, were sent on a peculiar operation to persuade mutinous American troops to return to combat.

> These five helicopters came in and they were bringing in guys from the line companies that refused to fight. Just so happens they all happen to be black. . . . We were assigned to take them to Long Binh jail, the LBJ, right outside Saigon. . . .
>
> I was a spokesman for the group that I was assigned to—they had a spokesman too. Him and I were given an hour to go off spend some time and try to work this out. This was not just—"Well, boy, you'll do this, that, and the other." This was a well-thought-out thing to try to keep down the animosity between the troops. We took a walk and were drinking and talking. Vietnam was a very strange experience.
>
> For one moment in my life I had to really back up and think about it. He said, "Look at you, you're fair in color, you're evidently fairly educated, you probably come from an integrated background, and you don't know too much about racism." And he was hitting the nail on the head.
>
> "Well most of us is just poor blacks. Most of us is referred to where we come from as just niggers. Most of us have people in the areas where the riots are going on and they have nowhere to go and no way out. Most of us are in line companies—line company is a sacrifice." . . .
>
> This guy was absolutely right. . . . So I said to him, "All you have to do is to tell the guys to go back. . . ." He said, "No man, the brothers out there . . . we'd rather go home whole . . . then go home—not have a home and be all fucked up." So I said, "At least I tried." He said, "Yea Bro, thank you." We did the five-step handshake. . . . It was sincere because he was right. The guy's name was Taylor.[42]

Vietnam soldiers Brown and Taylor relived one of the fundamental creative tensions of the African American experience. In *Crisis of the Negro Intellectual*, Harold Cruse identified a complex structure of conflict within African American history.[43] Much of African American history in the 1960s can be loosely organized around the struggle between integrationist and nationalist perspectives. Like the relationship between Frederick Douglass and Martin Delany, W. E. B. DuBois and Booker T. Washington, Martin Luther King and Malcolm X, the tensions that informed the cultural and political activities of black soldiers in Vietnam grew from the long legacy of Africans in America.

Although class and race consciousness are often viewed as opposing or conflicting ways of understanding politics, the white working-class and African

American opposition to the war progressed in tandem. The affinity between the wings was expressed by their appearance in the same historical moment, location, and shared anti–imperial attitude more than in their ability to work together. In ways more subtle and deeper than the explicitly proclaimed solidarity of movement activists, civil rights ideology and African American culture had significantly shaped the peace and youth movements that touched white working-class soldiers and veterans. It was, after all, the civil rights movement that legitimized dissent during the 1950s. The civil rights movement was the most direct conscious influence that changed political thinking and pushed the student, youth, women's, and antiwar movements into existence. Conversely, the overwhelming majority of black soldiers were working class, and many carried class-oriented traditions into black nationalist and civil rights organizations. The Black Panthers and the MDM never abandoned a class analysis of political events.

Like every social movement before them, the military antiwar movement could not fully overcome deeply ingrained racial animosities, mutual suspicions, and mistrust. Ongoing racism in the military from both the enlisted men and the brass demanded black organization for self-defense and empowerment.[44] Even among dissident soldiers the fundamental difference remained that the white wing tended to emphasize the class nature of the war while the black wing emphasized the racist aspects of the war. Although the two trends developed more or less separately, they were nonetheless parallel and complementary.

The strongest alliance between the diverse dissidents occurred under the conditions of combat or in the cultural upheaval that reshaped the buddy groups. In the field, survival demanded unity. In the rear, the heads and the brothers sometimes shared music, marijuana, and their youthful opposition to authority. The two trends coexisted in such a way that in practice both groups shared the common desire to stop the war and a vision of a more just society.

By the mid 1970s the soldier and veterans movements presented a contradictory picture. While declining in an organizational sense, they offered a look at the accumulated wisdom of a decade of social reform. Welding diverse influences from the women's, workers', youth, African American, Latino, American Indian, gay, solidarity, and environmental movements together, the veterans and their supporters created a perspective consciously historical and deeply American in character.[45]

This democratic upsurge took place not only in the material sense of combat refusals and demonstrations but ideologically as well. The symbolic power of the antiwar soldier and veteran shook the political, psychological, and cultural foundations of the American empire. The military resistance expressed a cultural rebirth, the deep strength of which flowed from a variety of sources: patriotism, black nationalism, working-class radicalism, and earlier veterans' movements. After 1968, the youth rebellion, the new environmental movement, and issues raised by feminism reworked the nature of the military antiwar movement. These diverse currents fused to produce a powerful anti–imperial impulse. By resisting empire, a contemporary version of American republicanism was recreated. This new patriotism represented an alternative understanding of American history, one that identified the social movements of the day with special moments in the American past. At a conference on women in the military, sponsored by the William Joiner Center, a Massachusetts research institute, a woman veteran embraced America's revolutionary history in her own call to action.

> I am reminded of the American history that it only took a few minutemen, in quotes, to get the revolution started and I think it only takes a handful of us to get women's rights recognized for veterans. . . . We can start with a sense of unity. We can start with a sense of sisterhood.[46]

For dissident soldiers and veterans of the Vietnam era this new historical consciousness centered on the reinvention and transformation of the American citizen–soldier ideal.

The Transformation of the Citizen-Soldier: War and Reconstruction

It wasn't fighting a war like we were taught to fight. . . .
You're losing guys to an unseen enemy. . . . It just seemed we were fucking over the people we were supposed to save. A ten-minute bombing sortie could wipe out whole villages. How's that saving them?
— JESS JESPERSON, MARINE VETERAN

Fuck it! It don't mean nothing.
— SOLDIER SLANG

I enter as a hawk, I come out as a phoenix in the morning.
— BOOK OF THE DEAD

The war against war is going to be no holiday excursion or camping party.
— WILLIAM JAMES

The Revolution was in the minds of the people.
— JOHN ADAMS

Nixon remember what happened to George III. We will make Kent State our Boston Massacre. The Continuing American Revolution is growing. The American Empire is falling. But like George III, Nixon will use force to stop the Revolution. The force is you—the GI. When the time comes will you be a Tory or a Patriot?
— TOM ROBERTS, ABOVEGROUND, MAY 1970

Imagine, they say, out of the embrace of memory a rewriting of the old dream of origin that might still find its flowering in the truest of new generations, a generation of peace.
— PHILIP D. BEIDLER, RE-WRITING AMERICA

THE VIETNAM WAR was a transforming event. A significant minority of American soldiers and veterans of that era committed themselves to a painful and prolonged process of change. Though intensely personal, the struggle to turn themselves from warriors into peacemakers also demanded that they transform symbols and ideas fundamental to American culture and identity. It began when soldiers were forced to confront incredibly confusing combat conditions.

For those who found themselves fighting a war disturbingly different from the way they "were taught to fight," or "wiping out whole villages" to "save" them, the war in Vietnam eroded a clear sense of mission among soldiers, destroying the potential for honorable combat. This symbolic and mortal vertigo, in which things "don't mean nothing," resulted in the dissolution of soldier identity.

Yet thousands of American GIs simultaneously transformed the very tradition of the soldier that the Vietnam War had destroyed. Consumed in fire by its own act, the "hawk" came "out as a phoenix," signifying renewal, if not the dawn of a new day. The antiwar soldier brought a transformed martial spirit to bear in "the war against war." This revolution "in the minds of the people" won the new winter soldiers entrance into a powerful tradition of cultural change dating back to 1776. In their struggle to stop the war and fight for justice, activist soldiers and veterans became part of the "Continuing American Revolution." The years 1966 to 1973, 1860 to 1865, and 1775 to 1781 were roughly equivalent historical moments—each produced the figure of the American citizen–soldier. Yet, to rewrite "the old dream of origin" the new winter soldiers had to transform the American citizen–soldier ideal itself.

Frag, Fragger, Fragged, Fragging, Fragments, Fragmentation

Vietnam introduced the word "fragging" into the English language. Derived from the fragmentation grenades used by rebellious soldiers to attack officers, fragging was the most extreme expression of soldier insurgency, for it signified the underlying collapse of cultural authority and meaning in Vietnam.[1] This collapse of meaning was the beginning of a process that resulted in the reconstruction and transformation of the soldier ideal. An inner civil war attended the soldiers' movement toward military resistance. The contradictory elements of the modern soldier ideal came to life as real people, real actions, and real alternatives. In boot camp, in combat, in contact with the local people, and in the experience of everyday life in Vietnam, the world the soldiers once knew began to unravel.

Elroy Schultz went to Vietnam expecting a "clear-cut" situation. His recollection of war typifies how the absence of the anticipated combat experience confounded him and thousands of GIs.

> In '67 the outlook was free-fire zone, you set up, you kill what moves—no matter what. Some of the kids were beat up, some of the older people where beat up. Before I went, I thought it would be clear cut—everyone would have a uniform. There'd be a line here—this is mine—that is yours. It didn't work that way. You'd take something, leave it for a night and come back and take it again. . . . Nobody was doing nothing the way it

should be done, not what you were taught. You just save your ass and get home. This ain't like John Wayne.[2]

Combat delivered a strident challenge to soldier's expectations and understandings. In the political context of the Vietnam War, combat created ideological crisis. Caught in the confusion between friend and enemy, front and rear, warrior and bureaucrat, good and evil, the foundations of honor and duty deteriorated.[3] Barry Romo, a combat veteran, offers a litany of lost expectations and disquieting surprises.

> The fact is that the Vietnamese didn't like us. . . . What became real apparent was that Vietnam seemed to be run by officer–bureaucrats. . . . People were getting promoted based upon body count. Body count never made sense to me. The disrespect for Vietnamese life never made sense to me. . . . Only 10 percent of GIs were combat and 90 percent were support and that didn't make sense. And the ARVN [Army of the Republic of Vietnam, South] never fought. . . . Meanwhile the Vietcong . . . they would engage you in combat and keep you engaged as long as they wanted. When we'd capture a local guerilla group, they'd fight to the death. They were brave, courageous, and bold. Our allies weren't. Why are we fighting for guys who wouldn't fight for themselves? Why are we fighting for generals to get promoted?[4]

So powerfully did Vietnam assault common assumptions that the ideals of the citizen–soldier threatened to collapse and disintegrate. As Schultz recalled his combat experience, "I didn't know why I was there. . . . No God, no flag, no country."[5] Many soldiers experienced a loss of meaning and direction.

> It was the last six months in 1969 . . . that really did me. . . . Building rage inside and hatred and I remember saying to myself, there better be a good fucking reason for this shit, man. There better be a good reason for me going through this. And there better be a good reason for me carrying these feelings. This better make some sense—when I get out of here.[6]

In this moment of moral vertigo, survival became the soldiers' most coherent imperative.

> I went to Vietnam at nineteen—went to Vietnam as an infantry platoon leader. After I was in country maybe two weeks the only things I cared about was getting as many men home alive—and didn't care about anything else because perceptually it didn't make sense. Went over with a teenager's anticommunist Catholic idealism, but the reality started to change me right away.[7]

Although most soldiers intended to fight honorably for freedom and democracy, Vietnam often acted as a powerful solvent upon these expectations. The classic heroic conflict must test the individual in a combat situation that adheres to certain characteristics understood by the soldier as honorable. Soldier must confront soldier and lock in mortal contest. The ideal soldier draws immortalizing energy from this combat ritual and the quest for glory it embodies. That glory must be a universal good such as freedom, truth, or democracy.[8] The citizen–soldier must experience the struggle to realize concretely the ideals that motivate heroic action. Only by fighting for freedom or democracy can the soldier enact the most sacred American traditions.

Instead of the citizen–soldier's struggle, the other coherent heroic soldier tradition Vietnam offered corresponded roughly to the needs of the fighter. The fighter confronts, not his equal, but victims or dehumanized evil and needs to dominate them. This rendition of the soldier ideal leaves only the possibility of survival or regeneration through violence. The basic dynamic of regeneration through violence connects the Vietnam fighter with a host of mythological and historical figures drawn from the American frontier experience.[9] Combat in Vietnam, particularly in areas with civilian populations, failed to fulfill soldiers' desire for what they understood as traditional combat action—unless they were prepared to become the fighter.

The transformation of the citizen–soldier occurred when the actual experience of combat rebounded upon the historical narrative of the soldier ideal. The collapse of military honor motivated revolutionary revisions in the way combatants understood war, history, and the tradition of the soldier. This inner struggle led to a series of developments in which antiwar soldiers and veterans created new and profoundly important cultural forms.

The New Winter Soldier and the New America

The appearance of new forms of the hero strongly suggests the possibility of remaking American culture. In the past, the figure of the citizen–soldier arose during the moments of American cultural creation and change, the Revolution and Civil War. The citizen–soldier who began to reshape American military culture during the Vietnam era was both cause and consequence of broader cultural changes.

The figure of the new winter soldier was embedded in the social movements representing political change during the late 1960s and early 1970s. The hero was remade by fusing the democratic and historical vision of the dissident soldiers to the political sensibilities of the new social movements. Ultimately, it is this new winter soldier, by invoking the broadest understandings of political community, who articulates the redefinition of nation initiated by the social movements.

As we have seen, the antiwar soldiers encountered conditions in Vietnam that either betrayed their sense of honor, duty, and justice or otherwise defied explanation. The loss of an honorable combat experience did not, however, result in a process of pure dissolution or rejection. The new worldview of the antiwar soldier was constructed from the shattered elements of the soldier ideal. A Vietnam volunteer talks through his moment of transition.

> I volunteered for the war out of Germany because I believed in it. And I also think that beliefs aren't worth a damn if you don't act on them. Now I'm opposed to the war. . . . I've got something now to grab hold of again—this opposition. At first it was the absence of . . . support for the war and belief in my country. It was a negative thing, it was a void and emptiness where something used to exist. Talking to other GIs . . . I'm beginning to find people like myself. . . . There's nothing wrong with me. . . . My opposition to the war . . . was . . . giving me back a life.[10]

For this soldier and many others, resistance to war replaced war as a means of articulating values and ideals.[11] Indeed, the antiwar soldiers found in their dissent the fulfillment of their greatest expectations as soldiers—that heroic act in which ideals became reality.

> I didn't just have ideals that I thought about, this was something that I had experienced myself. . . . My ideals became realities. It was my new idealism that was a reality for me.[12]

Under the special historical and cultural conditions of the Vietnam era, fragmentation and loss of meaning was only the first phase in a process of reconstruction.[13] This act of transformation entailed engagement with, not flight from, existing culture. The new winter soldiers started where they stood and transformed the military culture around them.

This process can be seen in the language and symbolism employed by the military antiwar movement. As pointed out by Harry W. Haines in his article "Soldiers against the War in Vietnam," the titles of underground newspapers and names of coffeehouses were often ironic reversals of military terminology.[14] These antiwar and antimilitary establishments transformed the everyday language of military culture. *Whack, Sound Off, Rough Draft, Right-on Post, Left Face, Fatigue Press,* and *All Hands Abandon Ship* are just a few of the newspapers that set military terminology against itself. The Oleo Strut coffeehouse took its name from a helicopter shock absorber and was itself created as a haven to absorb the shock of the military. The Shelter Half coffeehouse evoked collective action by choosing the name of an army-issued tent that required two soldiers to team-up for shelter.

The VVAW symbol itself was created from the official U.S. Military Assistance Command, Vietnam (MACV) logo. The VVAW explained, "We took the

UNDER THIS SYMBOL
55,000 AMERICAN SOLDIERS
HAVE DIED

UNDER THIS SYMBOL
MORE THAN 317,000
CAN BE BROUGHT HOME
ALIVE

10 The VVAW revised the MACV symbol for their own logo. (Photo reproduction, Aubrey Haynes.)

MACV patch as our own, replacing the sword with the upside-down rifle with helmet, the international symbol of soldiers killed in action."[15] Armed Forces Day became "Armed Farces Day" and was the occasion for the single greatest day of coordinated antiwar activities on military bases.

The new winter soldier's transformative impulse reached beyond the military to embrace traditional symbols. For example, the Statue of Liberty appeared in a host of forms in the GI and veteran press. While Liberty sometimes appeared in her traditional form, she was regularly depicted as betrayed, killed, revolted by, or an accomplice in the war effort. Most characteristic of the dynamic of transformation, Liberty appeared as a symbol of dissent. With torch replaced by power salute or peace sign, the statue symbolized traditional liberty fused with the new social movements to recapture and enlarge its original meaning. By occupying the Statue of Liberty itself in 1971 and again for the nation's bicentennial in 1976, the veterans reinvested meaning in America's most celebrated political icon. As with the citizen–soldier figure, Liberty appeared in traditional, deconstructed, and reconstructed versions, with the new forms being an elaboration and extension of the original symbolic meaning.

To continue the democratic, transformative, and immortalizing mission that was the classic American hero's charge, the new winter soldiers had to discover the moral equivalent of war. They found that equivalent in other projects full of the fascination and spirit that war had once held. Drawing upon a range of emerging alternative social worlds, the soldier ideal and its mission was revived and ultimately transformed.

The transformation of the citizen–soldier extended the redefinition of community that occurred in America in the late 1960s and early 1970s. The general affinity between the dissident soldiers and the new social movements suggests the degree to which these movements were coming to represent the nation and the republic. The social movements had created an array of historical narratives and social activities that made a renewed struggle for freedom and justice meaningful to the new winter soldiers. In that the GI and veteran antiwar movements related to the struggling communities of youth, race, class, sexuality, and gender they began to think like young rebels, African Americans, Chicanos, class-conscious workers, feminists, and new men.[16]

Cast adrift in Vietnam, soldiers found meaning and the potential to reestablish community in their racial identities. *Demand for Freedom,* an African American GI paper published in Okinawa, appealed to the principle of self-determination.

> Did you know that this Okinawan that you have so frequently related to as being a "gook," which is the same as being called a "nigger" in your so-called country, is your brother? . . . He's a victim of the same racism, fascism, and capitalism that oppresses us. The Okinawan people must struggle as black people . . . must struggle for self-determination.[17]

This African American consciousness was mobilized in Vietnam by the "brothers," or "bloods." Like the "heads," rebellious soldiers who identified with the youth culture, the brothers transformed the conventional buddy group into a stronghold of antiwar and antiracist sentiment. The brothers were the primary social group through which African American soldiers learned the meaning of national unity, black pride, and resistance against racism and war. Similarly, "la raza" appealed to the growing sense of Chicano and Latino identity.

The defiant attitudes of the heads were military versions of the anti-authoritarian and idealistic characteristics of their age cohort—attitudes that became increasingly pronounced in the late 1960s and early 1970s.[18] A medic with the 15th Medical Battalion in 1970, Dave Billingsley remembers the startling impact of the youth culture on his first days in Vietnam.

> They took us to Long Binh. . . . I saw this little club there called "Alice's Restaurant." Then, a helicopter flew over and it had a peace sign painted on it. It also had a speaker hanging out of it, and they were playing "Sgt. Pepper's Lonely Hearts Club Band." So, I went into Alice's Restaurant . . . and everywhere I looked there were dudes with peace signs around their necks, beads, headbands. And, I'm thinking to myself, "Where the fuck am I?"[19]

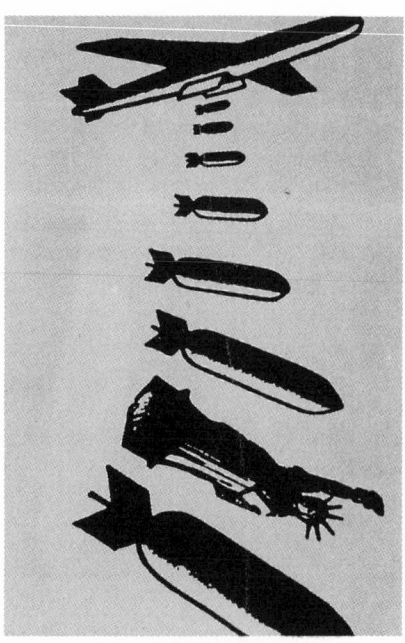

11 Liberty destroyed in war. This graphic appeared widely in the GI press. (Photo reproduction, Aubrey Haynes.)

12 Liberty terrorizing civilians. Signed by "Rodriguez," this graphic appeared in *Graffiti*. (Photo reproduction, Aubrey Haynes.)

13 Liberty reborn as a symbol of women's liberation. An illustration in the *Fatigue Press*. (Photo reproduction, Aubrey Haynes.)

14 The second VVAW occupation of the Statue of Liberty was in preparation for the July 4, 1976, bicentennial demonstration in Philadelphia. (Photograph courtesy of the VVAW.)

With an average age of nineteen, the antiwar soldiers expressed their kinship with their peers by breaking hair and dress regulations, wearing peace symbols, and most important, adopting the attitudes that shaped their generation. By embracing the cultural rebellion of working-class youth, the heads changed the conventional function of the military buddy group from motivating combat effectiveness to promoting rebellious and antiwar attitudes. For young white soldiers in particular the heads were the primary social group that encouraged resistance to the war and the development of alternative culture.[20] After 1967 the brothers, la raza, and the heads laid claim to the loyalties of significant numbers of American GIs.

The struggle against the war also sharpened class consciousness.[21] From every-day, spontaneous, shop-floor-style resistance to articulate class and revolutionary perspectives, young workers in uniform displayed class solidarity and resistance. Like other young workers, the GIs demanded a greater role in determining the terms and conditions of service. Some soldiers relied upon a class-based analysis through which they developed a critique of both the war and American society.

> A lot of people were becoming antiwar. I was becoming conscious of a class society. . . . You see who's doing the fighting and dying. It's the working-class white kids, the poor black kids, there was some Puerto Ricans too. You didn't see no rich kids. If they were—they were the officers.[22]

Working-class consciousness animated much of the debate of the soldier revolt and became an important position around which the new soldiers reorganized their democratic mission. The American Servicemen's Union, the Movement for a Democratic Military, and other organizations attempted to merge working-class and antiwar principles.

Most, if not all, of these re-created cultural worlds included and were structured around a revised sense of gender or sexual identity. Almost without exception, the women of the soldier and veteran antiwar movements identified themselves as feminists. Whether soldiers, nurses, or civilian supporters, the experience of war and military culture sharpened feminist thinking.

> I think that the real radicals were in the military. . . . My real political feelings for the war came when I was there. . . . That's when I really became feminized. . . . The military . . . made me feel equal.[23]

Particularly after 1969, a sexual analysis was used by nurses, female soldiers, gay soldiers, and movement activists to attack the sexist construction of the fighter.[24]

> My earliest reasons for being involved with the antiwar movement and gay activism was to stop the war . . . because of the military macho syn-

drome. . . . By proving that gay people . . . had fought in wars . . . this would help break down a myth that is related to causing wars.[25]

In criticizing machismo as the masculine ideal and model for the soldier, dissident GIs and veterans struck at the heart of military training and the fighter spirit.

Although it would be stretching the metaphor to call the men in the GI and veteran movements feminists, their notions of masculinity underwent important changes. In addition to the feminist ideas encountered in the antiwar movements, combat in Vietnam eroded their macho pretensions as fighters.[26] The aggressive soldier was often considered a danger by those around him.[27] Macho behavior and John Wayne–inspired heroics sometimes led to condemnation by peers, injury, or death. As soldiers moved from deference toward defiance, machismo became another suspect form of military discipline.

Certainly your machismo has always been equated. . . . In the army it's paratroopers and Delta Force, and Green Berets, and the crack shot—the guy that can shoot the best. This equates a person with their manhood. If you can't do this—then you're not much of a man. That's how they keep everybody lined up.[28]

For those who no longer wished to be "lined up," breaking ranks meant breaking machismo's hold.

In the military the whole sexual thing is like . . . if you don't cut it you're a pussy. . . . Vietnam and war calls that into question all the time. Before . . . war, war becomes the definition of being tough and manhood. Then there's a war and people find there's not any glory to it. . . . Historically veterans have always been used to convince the next generation to fight in the next war. Vietnam should make us question that and make a break. Vietnam is when all that history changed.[29]

Indeed, dissident veterans discovered the intimate connections between changing notions of masculinity and making history.

The newly redefined communities of resistance allowed or restored a vision of political power fundamental to citizenship. The oppositional nature of these communities in the upsurge of the 1960s and 1970s rekindled the democratic spirit. In this way, the appearance of the new winter soldier, resistance against the war, and the recognition of alternative communities were linked in the same process of transformation. The antiwar soldiers reaffirmed commitment to these communities and in so doing reestablished the democratic power of the citizen and their fidelity to universal values. This pragmatic multiculturalism and the self-determination of community it required was central to the transformation of the citizen–soldier.

Traditional community values renewed by the new social movements also became an important reference point for antiwar soldiers. The value of family as an ideal became identical with a critique of dominant culture, capitalism, and the war effort.

> I knew the people for the most part where I was and they were friendly enough, but they did not want us there. . . . They said, "We'll deal with our own problems. You got to stop intervening. You can't fight a unit like the Vietcong—they're family." They used to keep telling us they're Vietnamese family. We're not the world's saviors. We've never been good at that.[30]

The American reparations policy highlighted inequities within the family and between human life and property.

> If you blew a village up by mistake, you would pay reparation to the family. If you killed a child, it was 60 bucks; a mother was 90, and father of the family would get 120 dollars. That's how much you paid the family in reparations. If you destroyed . . . a Michelin tree, we would pay Michelin 600 dollars. So you think you're fighting for lives and blood, and you see your own people dying and you see kids lives are only worth 10 cents on the dollar to a rubber tree.[31]

A navy veteran court-martialed for antiwar activities came to understand her resistance to war as part of family values.

> My grandfather lived in San Francisco, and when the court-martial was over he called the *San Francisco Chronicle* and told them that the reason I did what I did was because my father had been a marine . . . killed in Guam, and I symbolically went back to take care of the men who were like my father. I remember laughing at it twenty-some-odd years ago. Now I think its probably fairly accurate.[32]

For some soldiers, Vietnamese family life offered an example of fairness, strength, and dignity. The example of family life sometimes caused a growing respect for Vietnamese culture and antiwar attitudes.

> When I was AWOL in Vietnam, I lived with a Vietnamese family. . . . Where the kids all had responsibility—never saw child abuse in Vietnam. . . . Never saw a kid talk back to a parent, but I never saw a parent beat a kid. . . . A lot of it had to do with the fact that they had strong family ties, a strong sense of their heritage, their culture.[33]

Although the military peace movement demonstrated that traditional values of community and family were conducive to cultural transformation, the precise content of these new forms is still emerging and is contested.[34]

The changes experienced by antiwar nurses suggest a similar transformation of conventional values.[35] At the core of the nursing tradition is the traditional feminine charge to heal and nurture. In the context of the women's movement and the cultural crisis of Vietnam these traditional values were transformed.

> I was undoing the damage that the military was doing overseas. . . . I was in fact reinforcing the war effort. I would patch the guys up, . . . and they'd be sent back to the front lines. If they didn't they would still be sent back to full duty. . . . It was wrong according to everything I really believed in, and I was a part of the system.[36]

> Coming from a background of very little sexism and walking into this rampant sexism . . . it never occurred to me it was anything other than a pathological aberration. The fact that it was suffered by 90 percent of the guys didn't make it any less . . . an illness. It's still sick. . . . Being a nurse with a rescue fantasy [the idea] was let's help cure it. Let's nurse it.[37]

In their untransformed state the values of healing, rescuing, and nursing were readily incorporated into the war machine as a necessary part of combat. Under the conditions of the Vietnam era however, the desire to nurture, heal, and rescue sometimes took on a critical and transformative potential.

The military itself was heralded as a melting pot where America's ethnic and racial tensions were overcome. The ideal of racial equality sometimes experienced in combat could become an important element in changing soldier attitudes. This 1967 letter by Dave Cline salvages universal ideals from the ambiguities of war and the experience of "foxhole democracy."

> Lately I've been thinking a lot about the problems America's got. . . . I've been reading about the riots in the cities. . . . Over here we don't have any racial tensions. . . . There's a few whites and colored guys who hate each other, but there's only a few of them.
>
> We're over here fighting for "freedom." Whether all of us believe this or support this war is doubtful. But when we come home everyone figures they gave their sweat and blood for whites and blacks. . . . When this thing ends either the cooperation and equality we have over here will go back with us or America will be a house on fire.[38]

The new winter soldier also drew on contemporary culture to create new notions of heroism. Aspects of the soldier ideal from popular culture remained as standards against which the real military was judged and found wanting.[39]

I guess if there is a revolution and someone asked me who I'd blame for causing the revolution, I'd have to say Walt Disney. He is the one who taught all of us to believe in the things that the country and the soldier is supposed to stand for, the Davy Crockett, Daniel Boone, George Washington image.[40]

Ideas from popular culture can also have a subversive effect. The ubiquity of John Wayne as a reference for Vietnam veterans indicates that popular culture informed consciousness with a powerful, truly sacred quality. Popular culture preserved the very notion of universal and transcendent heroism that was later recontextualized by the new winter soldiers. As veteran, author, and conscientious objector Gerald Gioglio argued, John Wayne was "an important role model not just for his patriotic swagger and hypermasculinity, but also for his portrayal of the honest person's quest for truth and justice."[41]

The fragmentation and reconstruction of the soldier ideal strongly suggests fundamental contradictions within all existing cultural strategies for creating soldiers. Although suitable for peacetime, the ways American culture imagined soldiering failed in combat in Vietnam. It seems as though war functioned as the arena of heroic action only as a metaphor in history, memory, myth, monument, film, fiction, and play, rather than in war itself.[42] Always more horrific than heroic, war could only be embraced as an ideal when embedded in the narrative traditions of the hero. The existing heroic narratives of film, literature, and history were unable to lend the appropriate meanings to the war in Vietnam. The citizen–soldier was unable to find the fight for freedom. Yet the universal values represented by heroic figures were appropriated by the new winter soldiers in their struggles for peace and justice. The new winter soldiers remade history.

When important organizing constructs of culture, such as the soldier ideal, become implausible or destructive, they must either collapse or be altered if they are to maintain their original meaning.[43] When the soldier ideal was shattered by the Vietnam experience, traditional community values and ideals from popular culture persisted, although in a new form. In this way the older values of the citizen–soldier were preserved within the new universe of meanings that the new winter soldier created. Nothing had been destroyed, and cultural continuity was maintained through dramatic cultural change.[44]

The New Ideal

Out of the experiences of the Vietnam era new and powerful reincarnations of the citizen–soldier emerged. Titanic inner conflict dissolved old ideals and refashioned new ones. These new ideals hold the potential for the renewal of American political culture by creating a model of civic duty through social action. The empowered and democratic citizen, the antiwar soldier, and the planet saver are the three faces of this new universal ideal.

This new citizenship was expressed by participation in community affairs and social movements, in neighborhoods, towns, churches, unions, and schools, or the peace, labor, women's, gay, environmental, youth, civil rights, and veterans movements. Taken together, the community and social movements constituted the ideal of a new republic worthy of an alternative patriotism. New patriotism was a demand for power that grows from the opposition to war, empire, and the blind patriotism that promotes it. As veteran Jim Pechin recalled, "We viewed stopping the war as the most patriotic thing that one could do."[45]

Vietnam-era veterans and American historians Jackson Lears and Mike Heaney typify the patriotism of peace grounded in opposition to imperial adventures and domination.

> You can be opposed to militarism and still be patriotic. . . . Policies that are wrapped in the flag are really policies that have nothing to do with the defense of the beloved homeland and everything to do with furthering the interests of bureaucratic elites and furthering investment opportunities overseas for multinational corporations. . . .
>
> The reflex of our . . . opinion makers is to equate patriotism with a kind of passive acceptance of duty, honor, country in an era when that kind of passivity is really just accepting the dictates of foreign-policy leaders who are anything but patriotic.[46]

> I love this country. . . . I have a lover's quarrel with it. . . . I view it as an experiment and a great one with great hope. . . .
>
> We have to realize that we can't—don't—dominate the world and we shouldn't. . . . We have to let other people find their own way more than we're doing now. That's what we did as a nation. That is what we pride ourselves on. Others want to do that too.[47]

The new patriots condemn a debased patriotism that relies on blind obedience and a lack of historical knowledge.

> I don't like . . . that knee-jerk, "My country right or wrong" and "You got to go fight because the president says so"—that's the kind [of patriotism] that bothers me. . . .
>
> I once got arrested for asking people to sign the Bill of Rights— Manhattan, 1967. We had a petition and we were asking people to sign the Bill of Rights. . . . The police didn't recognize it. These superpatriots who had just voted to be allowed to put the American flag patch on their uniforms and were rampantly patriotic gung-ho Americans thought the Bill of Rights was a communist document.[48]

New patriotism recognizes community activism and involvement with the social movements as the highest forms of civic honor and duty.

> To me a patriot is somebody who gets out in the street and demonstrates against military interventions. Somebody who could make a good living being a doctor or a lawyer . . . who chooses to work with the homeless—to me that's somebody who's patriotic.[49]

> I think patriotism is a commitment to your community. In that way I would say I'm very patriotic because I believe in my family. I believe in family values, in traditional values, and I believe in community. That's the reason I get involved. . . . You can wave the flag and say you're a patriot and look down at people because they're poor or homeless or look down on certain ethnic groups . . . then you're not a patriot.[50]

New patriotism enlarges its references by extending its reach into the communities that constitute America. New patriotism builds its moral power through a strong historical sense that demands allegiance to original American ideals.

> I define it [patriotism] by the principles behind it. . . . What do I have to do? Annunciate the Bill of Rights, the American Constitution? . . . I believe strongly in those freedoms. I grew up to believe in freedom of speech, religion, and democracy.[51]

> The kind of patriotism I'd like to see in this country is the kind that lives up to the Bill of Rights. That remembers the Constitution. . . . It's important to have patriotism mean something. If it means—do I believe in the Constitution?—like a religion. That's my religion! But don't ask me to fight for capitalism![52]

Anchored to universal ideals and a painful awareness of empire and blind patriotism, this new patriotism reveres an America that stands for and symbolizes freedom and democracy.

> The key to me seems to be democracy. If you have a genuinely democratic commonweal then the patriotism that reflects that . . . is a good thing. One thing that became clear to me in the military . . . was that the United States was not a democracy. . . . Ordinary people . . . did not control their government.[53]

Democracy is what matters. The America that dominates the world because it is number one, the chosen, the richest, or feared as the most powerful has fallen from grace for the new citizens.[54]

In the past, the citizen–soldier went to war for the freedom and cultural immortality represented in the historical saga of the people or nation. In our time, war can only mean total war in either counterinsurgency or nuclear conflict. Total war unleashes destructive and nihilistic forces, not creative or visionary struggle. Total war threatens the survival of humanity itself. Even limited imperial interventions can only reproduce the existing relations of power and domination. Be it total war, cold war, or limited war—war making restricts liberties, inhibits free debate, and centralizes power. War and the warrior are no longer able to create good.[55]

Given these conditions the citizen–soldier became the antiwar soldier—the peacemaker. The peacemaker draws honor and glory from the same principled search for immortality that once moved the citizen–soldier. Also indivisible from the citizen, the peacemaker sees peace as a path to social and economic justice and survival itself.

> We have to look at war as a way of not being able to survive anymore. We have to do away with it. We have to do away with racism . . . with poverty, with classism . . . if we want to survive on this planet.[56]

> Like Martin Luther King said in his speech opposing the war in Vietnam—your radical revolution of values is to overcome the . . . triplets of militarism, racism, and economic exploitation. . . . And Vietnam helped promote that. . . . See, war actually is obsolete at this point in history, with the development of nuclear weapons. But we haven't figured that out as a nation or as a world—yet.[57]

> I came to the conclusion that it didn't do any good to end the war if we don't end the cause of it. The cause of U.S. involvement in Vietnam was the kind of society we live in. . . . Millions and millions of dollars are made from military contracts. . . . From that standpoint the capitalist system needs war. . . .
> I came away . . . with a belief in people. . . . And if you can't believe in people, then you can't believe in anything.[58]

For the peacemaker the desire for peace follows Martin Luther King's powerful insight: peace is not simply the absence of conflict but the presence of justice.

In the transformation from citizen–soldier to new soldier, the moral core of the classic hero was enlarged to encompass not just community, nation, and peace, but earth. The new winter soldier appeared in a historical moment that was a time to struggle for peace and power, and also, a "time to care for and nurture each other and our planet."[59]

> One major commitment is for becoming militant soldiers for the environment. . . . From Agent Orange . . . and the devastating environmental

effects that the war had in Vietnam I became automatically more tuned in to environmental stuff.[60]

For American Indian antiwar veterans, honoring earth came from both their military experience and values at the center of their culture.

> The military really does a lot of things that destroy the earth. . . . What they call national sacrifice areas for . . . nuclear testing. They destroy sacred sites as well as common sites. . . .
> We have a saying in the Algonquin language . . . "ho mitique ousin" and that means that we're all related. . . . Not just all the people—all the fish, all the insects, birds in the sky, and the four-leggeds—we're all "ho mitique ousin." We're all related to the rivers, and mountains, and trees—even the air that we breathe. . . . We need to get back to thinking like that—the military does too.[61]

The new winter soldiers struggled for peace, power, and a whole earth. These three faces of the new hero are essentially indivisible.

> There are just not any separable things anymore. . . . The environmental movement, and the peace . . . movement, and making safe work places for American workers, that too. They should not be separate things—they should be integral things. . . . They have to be the same thing now.[62]

Veteran and poet Lamont Steptoe powerfully articulates the new values he shares with other winter soldiers.

> It is not a time to make excuses. It is a time to get involved . . . to organize. To interact with people of all backgrounds and to create a more human world. Vietnam did that for me. It left me feeling that we all can change things . . . and not tomorrow but now. . . . We can't depend on or wait for a leader. We have to become leaders ourselves. . . .
> The far right . . . would like to believe that they're the patriots and those of us on the left are something else. But all of these feelings of anger and rage come out of a sense of love for what I was taught America or the world could be about . . . justice—justice and peace. Creating a society, a democratic society for all people. . . . Woman, children, men, gay people, straight people, bi, everyone.
> The powers that be are racists, sexist, homophobic, and greedy—antilife. How can you not be antilife if you're making profits to the degree that it affects the very planet. You're cutting down the Amazon to make more hamburgers.
> All of these things have to be halted. Definitely for those people who

are in most jeopardy, which is people of color, and for the survival of the planet itself. The people that are in power continue to build nuclear bombs. You don't make these weapons and not use them. . . . It's to stop these people who are antilife. This is what the people that I define as warriors are fighting for.[63]

Although the new winter soldier created a universal heroic figure, it was by no means a departure from other particular identities. This new American identity is the universal version of the new racial or ethnic, working-class, peace, new masculine, feminist, and environmental consciousness. The new winter soldier figure draws on the deep roots of the many American cultures to create new universal forms. Marine veteran Joe Cross melds a traditional version of the warrior with the modern winter soldier to transform warrior consciousness.

There is a version of the warrior that has survived centuries past. . . . The Lakota people . . . they have a war shirt. . . . But more precisely these shirts really represent . . . they represented the people. That's why they were called shirt-wearers. . . . A warrior has much more to do with the values representing your family, speaking well, and not violating your family codes, or your tribal codes, or your mother's code, or your sister's codes of honor.
We think of a warrior as a Rambo—doesn't have a family. You don't see them going home and changing diapers, or packing the kids off to school. . . .
VVAW embraces those types of values that are more community-based and appealing to causes where there are injustices. You're not going to . . . just support any old militaristic venture. . . .
That's why I like the VVAW. They really did aspire to this. . . . I couldn't see another group that closely embraced those real warrior values.[64]

In weaving together different worlds and different times, Cross hints at the deep structures of thought fueling the transformation of the citizen–soldier. At the core of the new winter soldier lies the dynamo of a dual consciousness—an awareness of "two Americas." In the epilogue to *New Soldiers*, a book produced by the VVAW, John Kerry announced a most important discovery of the antiwar soldiers.

I think that, more than anything, the New Soldier is trying to point out how there are two Americas—the one the speeches are about and the one we really are. Rhetoric has blinded us so much that we are unable to see the realities that exist in this country.[65]

Whether expressed in terms of betrayal, dual consciousness, the gap between rhetoric and reality, or an awareness of multiple histories, it is the tension of living in the two Americas that produced the new winter soldier as citizen, earth saver, and peacemaker.

In his pioneering book, *The Souls of Black Folk*, W.E.B. DuBois's idea of double consciousness speaks to the African American condition but also offers us insight into the dual identity of the new winter soldier. Perhaps most important, DuBois allows us to enter into the conflicted world of American identity itself. The citizen–soldier and the fighter were produced by the cultural opposition between empire and republic—between the myth of the American Frontier and the myth of the American Revolution. Is America a republic or an empire? Are Americans the heirs of the citizen–soldier or the Indian fighter? Indeed, "it is a peculiar sensation, this double-consciousness. . . . One ever feels . . . two-ness . . . two souls, two thoughts, two unreconciled strivings, two warring ideals."[66] Much of American political culture was produced by the conflict between the "warring ideals" of empire and republic. This divided consciousness structures the American character itself.

The crisis of Vietnam extruded these dual Americas from what had been largely understood as a common past. Dual consciousness requires a perspective that recognized the existence of alternative and multiple histories. Once the protean quality of the past was understood, the present and future also became open to change.

The possibilities for historical change exist in the unfinished nature of alternative histories. The stories of African Americans, Latinos, American Indians, workers, youth, women, and gays all share the lack of narrative conclusion; that is to say, their positions have yet to be fully constructed and articulated. The struggle to empower subordinate communities and to tell the history of those struggles is central to a new American history. This kind of historical consciousness is perhaps the single-most important quality that distinguishes alternative culture from the ahistoricism, amnesia, and end-of-history assumptions of dominant culture.[67]

The military antiwar movement looked to numerous historical events to help refashion its understanding of America. Earlier episodes of the veterans movement were central to constructing the Vietnam veterans' vision. The history of the giant "Bring 'em Home" movement after World War II was mobilized to provide a historical context for the American withdrawal from Vietnam and to show the collective power of the veteran.[68] The Lincoln Brigade's fight against fascism during the Spanish Civil War emboldened the veterans' own democratic struggles and sense of tradition.

> In January we were having a demonstration against the war in the Gulf. . . . There was a group of Abraham Lincoln Brigade fellows right behind us and one of the people turned to them and said, "You know I really appreciate what you people have done for us. It was you Abraham Lincoln Brigade people who raised my consciousness and got me started in VVAW in the 1960s."

> Two hours later a group of young people about twenty years old walked up to . . . a group of us holding a VVAW banner, and said almost the damned identical thing—so we have a long tradition.[69]

In a public letter celebrating the twentieth anniversary of Dewey Canyon III, veteran Ed D'Amoto wrote, "Dewey Canyon III will go down in history along with Shays's Rebellion and the Bonus March as a demonstration of the power of the veterans' voice."[70] Shays's Rebellion and the Bonus Army were frequently cited as the historical parallel to the veterans struggle for decent benefits and economic justice.[71] Eugene Debs and the IWW were models of working-class antiwar resistance cited by dissident soldiers.[72] A few remembered the revolutionary actions of the mutinous Russian army and navy after World War I.[73] Mark Twain and other anti-imperialists who opposed the American war in the Philippines created a rhetoric that resonated with the antiwar soldiers' sensibilities. In the opening statement to *The Winter Soldier Investigation*, William Crandell evoked Twain to communicate the veterans' discontent.

> We are here to bear witness not against America but against those policy makers who are perverting America. We echo Mark Twain's indictment of the war crimes committed during the Philippine insurrection: "We have invited our clean young men to shoulder a discredited musket and do bandit's work under a flag which bandits have been accustomed to fear, not to follow."[74]

The frontier was a common source of references to help explain the meaning of Vietnam.[75] An ex-marine tells the story of his Vietnam experience through a new, more critical, understanding of history.

> The way it's sold is not unlike a book I read on women's diaries of the westward journey, about how people got suckered into going West. It's supposed to be this giant human dynamic unique to being American—the kind of people who came to America. . . . If you read it—they got hoodwinked, man! They saw these posters—it was Madison Avenue at its birth. . . .
>
> In this book women are writing: we're fucked, we don't have enough food to go back. We don't know where we're going. Everything's falling apart. We don't have enough of anything. It's hotter than hell. The locusts are eating us. The Indians are fucking with us, but not hurting us. Our super-dooper scout made off with the dough and here we are. . . . That predominantly seems to be the mode.[76]

By offering a critique of frontier mythology and by including women in history, this veteran gives evidence of the alternative structure of remembrance characteristic of the new winter soldiers. A Seminole veteran returns to the Indian wars in search of a parallel to Vietnam, but also for "something good."

> If you took the Vietnamese War . . . and compared it to the Indian wars a hundred years ago, it would be the same thing. All the massacres were the same. Nowadays they use chemical warfare; back then they put smallpox in the blankets and gave them to the Indians. . . .
>
> A lot of Indian people are . . . thinking about the old ways. You can take any culture . . . and if you look back into it deep, they had something good. Way back, they had it.[77]

The Civil War and abolitionism were important historical references for dissident soldiers. *The Abolitionist* evoked the struggle against slavery. The African American GI press frequently printed writings by recognized African American leaders. In the excerpt below from the GI paper *Black Unity*, Huey Newton returned to the unfinished revolution of the 1860s.

> I would like to backtrack a little to the period of 1863, 1865, after the Emancipation Proclamation and the so-called Reconstruction. The Freedman's Bureau was established during the Reconstruction in order . . . that Blacks be allotted forty acres and a mule. Because without the land it was realized that there would be no freedom. But this did not occur. . . . The Hayes Compromise of 1877 devastated the whole Reconstruction period and the few crumbs that we'd gained during that period. . . .
>
> The only way that we can now get freedom is to change that system that led us into slavery. We were brought into slavery because of the profit for the slave driver and the capitalist. So we question the very system.[78]

Lincoln was also used by the GI press to help symbolize the American Revolutionary tradition. One issue of the *Last Harass* from Fort Gordon, Georgia, carried on its cover a drawing of the American eagle clutching an American GI in one talon and a Vietnamese peasant in the other. Beneath the symbol of America-run-amok the soldiers quoted Lincoln's first inaugural address.

> This country, with its institutions, belongs to the people who inhabit it. Whenever they shall grow weary of the existing government, they can exercise their constitutional right of amending it, or their revolutionary right to dismember or overthrow it.[79]

Even the proximity of the Vietnam and Lincoln memorials in Washington, D.C., suggest a connection not lost on antiwar veterans.

> I go to "the Wall" a lot . . . and I find it a real special place . . . every time I go. . . . I also go to the Lincoln Memorial and I read the entire Gettys-

burg Address. It's just one of the most amazing documents. . . . It puts some . . . sense of order back into the world again.[80]

Like the revolutionary values it so eloquently recast, the Gettysburg Address acts as a historic touchstone creating a new "sense of order."

Reaching further back in time OM treated its readership to stories of "Los Patricios." During the Mexican–American War the Irish Catholic St. Patrick's battalion of the U.S. Army became Mexican national heroes. Infuriated by the desecration of churches and other anti-Catholic conduct, "Los Patricios" mutinied and crossed over into the Mexican Army.[81] In 1971 antiwar veterans in Texas occupied the Alamo to publicize their antiwar views.

A few veterans went back to the colonial roots of American freedom. In a call for action put out by the VVAW in Connecticut, the veterans echoed back over three hundred years to understand their choice of West Rock monument in New Haven as a site for their demonstration.

In the spring of 1661 three judges . . . members of Parliament who had stood against the tyranny of Charles I and the abridgement of British liberty, took sanctuary in . . . a cave high atop West Rock.[82]

The demonstration intended to focus "the attention of America on the new patriots—the Winter Soldiers of the Vietnam War." The leaflet concludes with the revolutionary Christian credo of colonial America, "Opposition to tyranny is obedience to God."[83]

Of all historical periods one stands out as the primary historical reference point for the new winter soldiers—the American Revolution. The Revolution provided a critical metaphor that measured how far America had strayed from its original traditions.

My first sort of raw analysis was that this was a civil war and we were sort of like Hessian troops—in reality we were more the aggressor. There wouldn't have been another force if we weren't there.[84]

We had hired house girls who did our laundry and our boots. . . . I'm laying in the hootch and they were crying. I said, "Tell me what's wrong," "Oh, Ho Chi Minh died." So I said, "Big deal, he's a fucking communist, so who gives a shit."

Then this girl, Than, gives me this whole rap about George Washington. "You know who George Washington is—he's the father of your country. That's what Ho Chi Minh is to us."

This kind of shocked me . . . actually viewing things from a different country's perspective . . . you realize these people are fighting for something rather than just communism in the abstract. . . . That stayed in my mind for a long time.[85]

Black and Latino soldiers also referred to the tradition of the American Revolution to understand the great urban rebellions, the civil rights movement, and war resistance.

> I think white America has demonstrated time and time again that they hold no genuine desire to grant us our humanity and our dignity. In the early days of this nation, the colonists were the victims of the same crime against humanity by England. In other words, I say that this is similar to the relationship between the white power structure in America and the colonized black people. [86]

> Hell yes, I'd riot. The white man had his goddam Boston Tea Party, so why can't we have our riots, and the white students their marches? Is there any difference? Check it. Is there any difference? [87]

> I have three just wars: the Revolutionary War, the Civil War, and the Second World War. I think in every other war those that went to jail are the true heroes—those that refused to fight. [88]

The Revolution was the principal historical context for the new winter soldiers. Perhaps most important the values of the Revolution became a project yet to be achieved.

> My spiritual beliefs—how I understand that I am my brother's keeper? The golden rule, the Bill of Rights, the Constitution. . . . All the values I put forward came out of those documents. . . . That everyone has the right to life, liberty, and the pursuit of happiness.
>
> Yes, we know that a bunch of slave-holding white males wrote this, that they didn't define Africans as people but property. But in their own words they put it down and now they have to be taken to task for it and their ancestors taken to task for it. [89]

> The kind of Revolution that I believe in . . . sort of going back to the principles of the Declaration of Independence and the Constitution. . . . I think that's pointed out by the fact that the North Vietnamese use almost the same document. . . . I think just to return to the principles of Thomas Paine is really revolutionary. I think we never reached the level of Thomas Paine and I think it's about time we did. [90]

Typical of the new winter soldiers' historical outlook, the tension between the historical limitations of the American Revolution and its great promise worked to produce a demand for empowerment and justice. Dissident GI newspapers like *The First Amendment, Common Sense,* and *1776—Right to Revolution* struggled to live up to their namesakes. A paper from the Philippines called the *Whig* was

15 "Rebellion to Tyrants Is Obedience to God." This seal ran regularly in the *Fatigue Press.* (Photo reproduction, Aubrey Haynes.)

edited by soldiers who adopted the pen names Tom Paine and Sam Adams.[91] As a regular feature, the *Fatigue Press* carried the proposed seal for the early U.S. government, whose motto was "Rebellion to tyrants is obedience to God."[92] *Shakedown's* masthead periodically included the silhouette of a GI offering a raised fist salute to a statue of a minuteman. The VVAW's *Winter Soldier* carried the traditional coiled rattlesnake and warned "Don't Tread on Me."

The Declaration of Independence became a model of revolutionary discourse and a call to action. As veteran James Credel suggests, the Declaration of Independence is "something we can envision as being potential."[93]

In an article titled "Equality, Equality," published in *Where It's At*, GI journalists juxtaposed the Vietnamese and American declarations of independence. Bracketed between the preambles of the two documents, the dissident soldier historians quoted Sam and John Adams, Patrick Henry, Tom Paine, Thomas Jefferson, and others to amplify the political, class, and democratic qualities of the American Revolutionary army. In the Vietnamese revolution some new soldiers found that "the Spirit of '76 lives on."

> Is it merely an accident that Ho Chi Minh modeled the Declaration of Independence of Vietnam after our own Declaration of Independence? . . .
> It is difficult not to compare the NLF [National Liberation Front] with the people's revolutionary organizations of the American Revolution. . . .
> You can imagine how the professional British troops felt when that ragged band of American farmers and shopkeepers proved a match for them. The British were not bad men. . . . But they were on the wrong side of history because the American Revolution was "an idea whose time had come," which excited its followers to enthusiasm, sacrifice, and dedication.[94]

This historical comparison demanded that solidarity with, not opposition to, the Vietnamese revolution was the truly American response.

The new soldiers often referred to the Revolutionary army as a source of alternatives to the existing military machine. *Bragg Briefs'* statement of purpose claimed that mission.

> Published in the spirit of the Declaration of Independence and the Constitution of the United States. It is a free press published by active-duty GIs stationed at Ft. Bragg, North Carolina, dedicated to establishing responsible alternatives to the current military system.[95]

A series of remarkable articles published in *The Ally* relied upon the military experience of the American Revolution to make an argument for a return to "an Army of the People." Like many other manifestos of the GI movement, the authors employed the same tension between decline, crisis, and renewal that forms the structure of the Declaration of Independence. According to the soldier–historians, the "Army of the People" can come into existence only in "the free society Madison proposed."

> The liberties that GIs are pledged to defend arose out of a resistance to tyranny. The Constitution, born out of the American Revolution, was meant to be the guarantee that liberty and equality be preserved. . . . Nowadays freedom and equality stand opposed to a military–industrial–political dictatorship. . . . The American military is the most important tool of that creeping despotism. . . . A standing military force of 3.5 million is the opposite of the free society Madison proposed: "The only way to provide for a standing army is to make them unnecessary." The militia is the alternative to the oppressive and illegitimate military we now have.[96]

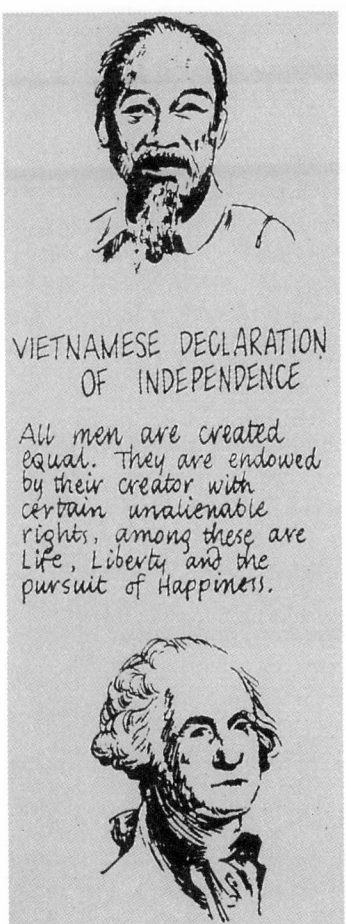

VIETNAMESE DECLARATION
OF INDEPENDENCE

All men are created equal. They are endowed by their creator with certain unalienable rights, among these are Life, Liberty and the pursuit of Happiness.

16 For antiwar soldiers the Vietnamese Declaration of Independence raised fundamental questions about the justice of the American war effort. This graphic from *Bragg Briefs* equates the American and Vietnamese revolutions. (Photo reproduction, Aubrey Haynes.)

A local dissident group called the Black Liberation party was founded at Fort Dix on September 3, 1969. An article titled "Long Overdue" from its first paper again reproduced the form of America's original revolutionary document. Beginning with the preamble to the Declaration of Independence, a litany of war and racial grievances was followed by a call for change.

Open your eyes, brother, and see this society for what it is. Unite and become one. Realize the potential warrior you are; no longer suppress your people. Riot control is not your bag. Read the Declaration of Independence; it clearly states that after a long period of time when you have attempted to bring change . . . and no change comes. IT IS YOUR DUTY TO DESTROY THAT GOVERNMENT. ALL POWER TO THE PEOPLE.[97]

African American dissenters suggested that "the civil rights struggle is no more than an extension of the American Revolution of 1776."[98] Indeed, the perspectives of the new winter soldiers produced a new patriotic spirit calling for revolution in "the American Way." The last issue of *Aboveground* featured an editorial written by Vietnam veteran Tom Roberts. After including portions of the Declaration of Independence and the ways in which the Vietnam War violated its spirit, Roberts issued the following call:

Nixon, remember what happened to George III. We will make Kent State our Boston Massacre. The Continuing American Revolution is growing. The American Empire is falling. But like George III, Nixon will use force to stop the Revolution. The force is you—the GI. When the time comes will you be a Tory or a Patriot?[99]

In their choices of demonstrations and antiwar activities the new winter soldiers looked to their citizen–soldier heritage. The Fourth of July always stirred the new citizens to action. Demonstrations for veteran benefits in Washington and other cities and an annual antiwar picnic in Wisconsin contested the meaning of Independence Day. The 1976 bicentennial demonstration in Philadelphia was cosponsored by the VVAW. Prior to the demonstration the VVAW again occupied the Statue of Liberty to protest cuts in veterans' benefits. In 1971 a dozen GIs from Fort Lewis were arrested on base for distributing the Declaration of Independence on the Fourth of July.[100] The same year six marines were arrested by military authorities in Iwakuni, Japan, for distributing copies of the same piece of unauthorized literature.[101] The previous year in Iwakuni, marines acted on the Fourth of July to protest brig conditions and their lack of constitutional rights by staging a fourteen-hour prison riot.[102] The largest demonstration of American soldiers in Europe occurred on the Fourth of July, 1970 when one thousand African American GIs gathered to protest war and racism. That same year other soldiers in Germany held a Fourth of July "Peace Picnic."[103]

These self-defined winter soldiers lived out Paine's vision of republican virtue. The VVAW's first national action laid claim to America's revolutionary heritage by hiking Washington's route from Jockey Hollow to Valley Forge. In Massachusetts the route of Paul Revere's ride was marched to awaken the citizens to the new tyranny. The veterans returned again to Valley Forge in the winter of 1971 to plan peaceful missions to occupy and liberate the national symbols. From the symbolic home of the first revolutionary army, the new soldiers staged demonstrations at the Statue of Liberty, the Lincoln Memorial, Independence Hall, and the Betsy Ross house. Perhaps the most dramatic and influential moment of the antiwar movement came when two thousand veterans collectively returned their war regalia on the steps of the United States Capitol during Dewey Canyon III.[104]

Even today, after long years of activism and struggle, the Revolution remains a potent inspiration.

> I work with Agent Orange victims, and I watch them die and their children suffer from birth defects. There is no medical care and they are abandoned. . . . When I burn out I take every opportunity to go to the Lexington Green and the Old North Bridge. Not only physically be there but allow yourself to become idealistic again. . . . It's almost like a pilgrimage. It allows you to get back to basics—in this country it's the Bill of Rights. It allows you to start over again.[105]

The movement of dissident soldiers and veterans was anything but a repudiation of American traditions. The vision of the new republic was born in the crisis of Vietnam and refashioned from elements of traditional community, contemporary culture, and American history.

Again the editors of *The Ally* returned to Madison for inspiration.

> Madison was very clear about the correct response to an illegitimate military despotism. He said: "If there be a principle that ought not to be questioned within the United States, it is that every nation has the right to abolish an old government and establish a new one. This principle is not only recorded in every public archive, written in every American heart, and sealed with the blood of a host of American martyrs, but it is the only lawful tenure by which the United States holds their existence as a nation."
>
> The government and the military are guilty of undermining our Constitution and as Madison said, they "prepare the way for a revolution, by a repetition of these infractions, until the people are aroused to appear in the majesty of their strength."[106]

If, as Madison claims, the right to revolution is "written in every American heart," then the new winter soldiers have struck upon an indigenous American principle with sweeping historical possibilities.

Here we find the greatest contribution of the new winter soldiers. In reworking the sacred terrain of American mythology and history they have demonstrated the continuing potential of American culture to create the conditions of human liberation.

The frontier and the ideas it promotes no longer need to hold sway over American consciousness. Instead, the new traditions, although young and fragile, draw strength from a different mythology, a different history, a different mission. The new America is grounded in our most uniquely characteristic history that is also our most creative myth: America is the story of a revolutionary and democratic republic, the first republic to put the promise of freedom, equality, and justice on the agenda of human history.

Only such a republic can include the contradictions stated so insightfully by W.E.B. DuBois. There are dual identities for all struggling groups and dual identities for America—yet, only in one America can we possibly reconcile "two souls, two thoughts . . . two warring ideals." It is not empire but only the "greater ideals of the American Republic" that can embrace the struggles and vision of the new winter soldiers. [107]

The figure of the new winter soldier truly transcends the older soldier ideal. [108] Although the old spirit of war is contained within it, the new expression of heroism runs deeper and wider. The new hero is more heroic. Blood and war, once the price for immortality and cultural rebirth, can now be paid in the struggle for peace, power, and earth. The new ideal still demands sacrifice but bestows honor greater than that found on the battlefields of empire.

The new soldier may be a model citizen for a new American republic. Citizenship must still be defined by duties and rights, but now that duty is to fight for social justice, and the right is to political power and self-determination. Unlike past reincarnations of the soldier ideal, the new hero must struggle for peace and include all those once excluded from the democratic process. Without community there is no way to establish the moral equivalent of war that the new soldier needs.

The ways in which the new soldiers completed William James's search for a moral equivalent of war suggests that a new republic could not be created by setting aside differences but may be constructed on the basis of differences— differences that have been fully articulated and empowered. Dissident Vietnam veterans collectively demonstrated the genius of a dual consciousness, both rending and fusing particulars and universals. Their path to the new universal ideals ran through the cultural cores of particular communities. In this way the social movements and other struggles for community, taken together, could be construed as the emerging moves of a new American republic. The new patriotism then, is a communal feeling, a collective consciousness that compels no singular identity. It holds the prospect of unity without uniformity.

This new historical consciousness does not repudiate the original vision of America but transforms it into a different sense of history and citizenship. [109] In the crisis of empire represented by Vietnam, a military and civic culture embodied by the classic American citizen–soldier evolved into the new winter soldier. The revolution of values that occurred in Vietnam found its roots in the American Revolution and the republican vision of the citizen–soldier. The figure of the new winter soldier is a universal form that may pertain to all.

Like the changes wrought by the first citizen–soldiers, the new winter soldiers also unleashed a "shot heard 'round the world." How should we interpret the echoes? It is a peculiar characteristic of the Vietnam era and our own that the desire to maintain cultural continuity with our most cherished values requires change of the most dramatic, revolutionary, and transformative kind.

Notes

Introduction

1 Books and articles written from a variety of political positions draw on the idea of decline and fragmentation. See, for example, Richard Boyle, *The Flower of the Dragon: The Breakdown of the U.S. Army during the Vietnam Era* (San Francisco: Ramparts, 1972); Stuart H. Loory, *Defeated: Inside America's Military Machine* (New York: Random House, 1973); Shelby L. Stanton, *The Rise and Fall of an American Army: U.S. Ground Forces in Vietnam, 1965–1973* (Novato, Calif.: Presidio Press, 1985); Cincinnatus, *Self-destruction: The Disintegration and Decay of the U.S. Army during the Vietnam Era* (New York: Norton, 1981); Robert D. Heinl, Jr., "The Collapse of the Armed Forces," *Armed Forces Journal* (June 1971): 34–45; and Eugene Linden, "The Demoralization of the Army: Fragging and Other Withdrawal Symptoms," *Saturday Review*, Jan. 8, 1972, p. 12 et passim. I would certainly agree that the draft, the long, slow American withdrawal, and the sheer price in blood and treasure motivated antiwar dissent among some soldiers. However, any approach that imagines antiwar motivation to be a purely practical and therefore momentary response to the dire conditions of war cannot explain the enduring impact of the military antiwar movements on veterans, their long and tenacious struggle against war, or the transformation of military culture, all the very things that constitute this book's primary objects of study.

2 Antonio Gramsci, *Prison Notebooks* (New York: International Publishers, 1971), p. 323. The focus on collective consciousness draws my analysis toward symbol, history, culture, and myth, and away from a detailed or sociological investigation of the motivations of individual soldiers. The precise or immediate causes that motivated the participants of the military antiwar movement, like causes of the war itself, are complex, tangled, and overabundant. According to Jan Barry, cofounder of the Vietnam Veterans Against the War, "We used to say that for every five guys who joined the VVAW there were six reasons" (phone conversation with author, May 5, 1994).

3 This new memory was endorsed by Ronald Reagan, who was the main proponent of Vietnam as a noble cause. Howell Raines, "Reagan Calls Arms Race Essential to Avoid a 'Surrender' or 'Defeat,' " *New York Times*, Aug. 19, 1980, pp. 2, D17. For a more detailed argument about memory and Vietnam amnesia, see Richard Moser, "Talking the Vietnam Blues: Vietnam Oral History and Our Popular Memory of War," in *The Legacy: Vietnam and the American Imagination*, ed. Michael Shafer (Boston: Beacon Press, 1990), pp. 104–21; Harry W. Haines, " 'They Were Called and They Went': The Political Rehabilitation of the Vietnam Veteran," in *From Hanoi to Hollywood: The Vietnam War in American Film*, ed. Linda Dittmar and Gene Michaud (New Brunswick, N.J.: Rutgers University Press, 1990); Rick Berg, "Losing the War: Covering the War in an

Age of Technology," in Dittmar and Michaud, *From Hanoi to Hollywood*; Michael Klein, "Historical Memory, Film, and the Vietnam Era," in Dittmar and Michaud, *From Hanoi to Hollywood*; Leo Cawley, "The War About the War: Vietnam Films and American Myth," in Dittmar and Michaud, *From Hanoi to Hollywood*; Walter LeFeber, "The Last War, the Next War and the New Revisionists," *Democracy* (Jan. 1981): 93–109; Robert A. Divine, "Historiography: Vietnam Reconsidered," *Diplomatic History* 12 (Winter 1988): 79–93; and Marilyn Young, "Revisionists Revised: The Case of Vietnam," *Society for Historians for American Foreign Relations Newsletter*, no. 10, 1979.

4 William F. Crandell, "They Moved the Town: Organizing the VVAW," in *Give Peace a Chance: Exploring the Anti-war movement*, ed. Melvin Small and William D. Hoover (Syracuse, N.Y.: Syracuse University Press, 1992), p. 142.

5 Steve Tice appears in "A Program for Vietnam Vets and Everyone Else Who Cares" (Chicago: WTTW Chicago in association with the Office of the Dean of Students, University of Wisconsin at Madison). Video.

6 See George Bush's statements and media commentary during and after the Gulf conflict of 1991 in Evan Thomas, John Barry, Ann McDaniel, and Douglas Woller, "This Will Not Be Another Vietnam," *Newsweek*, Dec. 10, 1990, p. 24 et passim. For journalistic treatments of the Vietnam syndrome and the Gulf War, see Edwin Chen and Paul Richter, "U.S. Shakes Off Torment of Vietnam," *Los Angeles Times*, Mar. 2, 1991, pp. 1, 14; Harry G. Summers, Jr., "Putting the Vietnam Syndrome to Rest," *Los Angeles Times*, Mar. 2, 1991, pp. 6, 15; E. J. Dionne, Jr., "Kicking the Vietnam Syndrome" *Washington Post*, Mar. 4, 1991, p. 1; Richard Slotkin, *Gunfighter Nation: The Myth of the Frontier in Twentieth-Century America* (New York: HarperPerennial, 1992), p. 652; and Betty Jean Craige, "Multiculturalism and the Vietnam Syndrome," *Chronicle of Higher Education* (Jan. 12, 1994): B3. See also Lorenzo M. Crowell, "The Lessons and Ghosts of Vietnam," in *Looking Back on the Vietnam War: A 1990s Perspective on the Decisions, Combat, and Legacies* ed. William Head and Lawrence E. Grinter (Westport, Conn.: Praeger, 1993), pp. 229–40.

7 The symbolic label John F. Kennedy chose for his administration and policies was the "New Frontier." Although U.S. involvement in Vietnam cannot be solely attributed to Kennedy, the New Frontier captures the spirit and élan of American intervention. The myth of the frontier in American history has been thoroughly investigated by Richard Slotkin in his remarkable trilogy: *Regeneration through Violence: The Mythology of the American Frontier, 1600–1860* (Middletown, Conn.: Wesleyan University Press, 1973); *The Fatal Environment: The Myth of the Frontier in the Age of Industrialization, 1800–1890* (New York: Atheneum Press, 1985); and *Gunfighter Nation*.

8 Dave Cline, interview by author, Jersey City, N.J., Mar. 1, 1988.

9 The cultural developments that gave rise to armed right-wing extremism has been perceptively analyzed by James William Gibson in *Warrior Dreams: Paramilitary Culture in Post-Vietnam America* (New York: Hill and Wang, 1994).

10 Thomas Myers, *Walking Point: American Narratives of Vietnam* (New York: Oxford University Press, 1988); John Hellman, *American Myth and the Legacy of Vietnam* (New York: Columbia University Press, 1986); and Lloyd Lewis, *The Tainted War: Culture and Identity in Vietnam Narratives* (Westport, Conn.: Greenwood Press, 1985).

11 Charles DeBenedetti and Charles Chatfield, *An American Ordeal: The Antiwar Movement of the Vietnam Era* (Syracuse, N.Y.: Syracuse University Press, 1990); Sara Evans, *Personal Politics: The Roots of Women's Liberation in the Civil Rights Movement and the New Left* (New York: Vintage, 1979); Clayborne Carson, *In Struggle: SNCC and the Black Awakening of the 1960's* (Cambridge, Mass.: Harvard University Press, 1981); Ron Grele, in *1968: A Student Generation in Revolt*, ed. Ronald Fraser (New York: Pantheon Books, 1988); Wini Breines, *Community and Organization in the New Left, 1962–1968: The Great Refusal* (New Brunswick, N.J.: Rutgers University Press, 1989); and Todd Gitlin, *The Sixties: Years of Hope, Days of Rage* (New York: Bantam, 1987).

12 Norman Podhoretz, *Why We Were in Vietnam* (New York: Simon and Schuster, 1982); and Guenther Lewy, *America in Vietnam* (New York: Oxford University Press, 1978).

13 Haines, " 'They Were Called and They Went,' " p. 86. Haines states, "Guenther Lewy's *America in Vietnam* is a classic revisionist interpretation of the war and has influenced subsequent attempts to discount the soldiers' experience of ideological crisis in Vietnam" (p. 86). See also Jeffrey Kimball, "The Stab-in-the-Back Legend and the Vietnam War," *Armed Forces and Society* 14, no. 3 (1988): 433–58.

1 Happy Veterans' Day

1 Audio recording of radio broadcast on WORT, Madison, Wis. Fifth annual broadcast of the Veterans Day memorial service, Nov. 11, 1989.

2 Ibid.

3 See Tom M. Holm, "American Indian Veterans and the Vietnam War," in *The Vietnam Reader*, ed. Walter Capps (New York: Routledge, 1991), pp. 200–201. Holm claims that many Indian ceremonies focus on honoring the warrior rather than war itself and that these ceremonies may possibly function as a "social absorption of combat-related trauma."

4 The text of the letter can be found in Lynda Van Devanter, *Home before Morning* (New York: Beaufort Books, 1983), pp. 174–75.

5 The full text can be found in John Kerry and the VVAW, *New Soldiers* (New York: Collier Books, 1971), pp. 158–66.

6 Ibid.

7 Ibid.

8 Brendan O'Mara, "Vietnam Vets Celebrate Peace, Push for Rights," *Daily Cardinal* (Madison, Wis.) Nov. 12, 1992, p. 4.

9 Audio recording of radio broadcast on WORT, Madison, Wis.

10 Ibid.

11 Morgan Whiteagle, interview by author, Nov. 11, 1993, Madison, Wis.

12 Linda Jameson, interview by author, Nov. 13, 1993, Madison, Wis.

13 Ron Arm, interview by author, Nov. 13, 1993, Madison, Wis.

14 Dennis Kroll, interview by author, Mar. 25, 1990, Madison, Wis.

15 See John Whiteclay Chambers II, *To Raise an Army: The Draft Comes to Modern America* (New York: Free Press, 1987), pp. 2, 4, 9, 19–23. See also Lawrence D.

Cress, *Citizens in Arms: The Army and the Militia in American Society to the War of 1812* (Chapel Hill: University of North Carolina Press, 1982).

16 Alexander Hamilton, James Madison, and John Jay, *The Federalist Papers* (New York: Mentor, 1961), no. 46.

2 The Soldier Ideal

1 Robert Jay Lifton, *Home from the War: Neither Victims nor Executioners* (New York: Simon and Schuster, 1973), pp. 25–31. Lifton uses the notion of the soldier ideal in its universal version to help explain the psychological transformation of Vietnam veterans. See also Erich Neumann, *The Origins and History of Consciousness* (New York: Pantheon Books, 1970), p. 366. Neumann suggests that the soldier ideal is unparalleled in its ability to radically alter the way in which consciousness and actions are organized.

> The transformation of a petty office clerk into the responsible leader of a death-dealing bomber squadron is probably one of the most radical psychic transformations that can be demanded of modern man. This metamorphosis of the normal peace-loving citizen into a fighter is, even today, only possible with the help of symbols. Such a transformation of personality is achieved by invoking the symbols of God, King, Fatherland, Freedom, the "most sacred good of the nation," and by dedicatory acts steeped in symbolism.

2 Lifton, *Home from the War*, p. 27.

3 Richard Slotkin, *Regeneration through Violence: The Mythology of the American Frontier, 1600–1860* (Middletown, Conn.: Wesleyan University Press, 1973), p. 7; and Neumann, *Origins and History of Consciousness*, p. 70. For an excellent and concise presentation of the role of myth and military culture, see William J. Gibson, "Paramilitary Fantasy Culture and the Cosmogonic Mythology of Primeval Chaos and Order," *Vietnam Generation* 1, no. 3–4 (Summer–Fall 1989): 12–15.

4 Friedrich Nietzsche, "The Birth of Tragedy," in *The Complete Works of Friedrich Nietzsche*, vol. 1, ed. Oscar Levy (New York: Russell and Russell, 1964), p. 181.

5 Ali A. Mazrui, "Gandhi, Marx and the Warrior Tradition: Toward Androgynous Liberation," in *The Warrior Tradition in Modern Africa* (Leiden, The Netherlands: E. J. Brill, 1977), pp. 182–83. And as discussed in Chapter Two, African American Marines used the Mau Mau as the name for their own organizations.

6 Abraham Lincoln, first inaugural address, March 4, 1861. See also Marcus Cunliffe, *Soldiers and Civilians: The Martial Spirit in America, 1775–1865* (Boston: Little, Brown, 1968), p. 393.

7 Molefi Asante, *Afrocentricity* (Trenton, N.J.: Africa World Press, 1988), pp. 122–23.

8 Elise Boulding, "Warriors and Saints: Dilemmas in the History of Men, Women and War," in *Women and the Military System*, ed. Eva Isaksson, (New York: St. Martin's Press, 1988), p. 226.

9 Richard Shy, *A People Numerous and Armed: Reflections on the Military Struggle for American Independence* (Ann Arbor: University of Michigan Press, 1990), pp. 160–61. For a clear description of the citizen–soldier, see Manfred Berg, "Soldiers and Citizens: War and Voting Rights in American History," German Historical Institute, Washington, D.C., unpublished article, 1993. See also Chilton Williamson, *American Suffrage: From Property to Democracy, 1760–1860* (Princeton, N.J.: Princeton University Press, 1960).

10 For an excellent general discussion, see John Whiteclay Chambers II, *To Raise an Army: The Draft Comes to Modern America* (New York: Free Press, 1987), pp. 1–39. The twin military legacies of the Revolution are clearly presented by Russell F. Weigley, "The Dual Military Legacy of the Revolution," in *Towards an American Army: Military Thought from Washington to Marshall*, ed. Russell F. Weigley (Westport, Conn.: Greenwood Press, 1962), pp. 1–9.

11 As the most militant elements in anti-impressment, antitax, and anti-imperial mobs, "a motley crew" of seamen, young boys, Africans, and Irish escalated the level of revolutionary thought and action. For example, the Knowles riot of 1747 was the largest mass opposition to British authority prior to those precipitated by the Stamp Act. Mobs of rebellious Bostonians resisted impressment by the British Navy and inspired revolutionary thinking. As their political defense, the Knowles rioters used, for the first time in America, the notion of natural rights instead of the rights of Englishmen to justify resistance to authority. See John Lax and William Pencak, "The Knowles Riot and the Crisis of the 1740's in Massachusetts," in *Perspectives in American History*, ed. Donald Fleming and Bernard Bailyn (Cambridge, Mass.: Charles Warren Center for Studies in American History, 1976), pp. 203–6, 214. For the role of seamen and sailors, see Jesse Lemish, "Jack Tar in the Streets," *William and Mary Quarterly* 25 (1968): 390, 407.

12 Steven Rosswurm, *Arms, Country and Class: The Philadelphia Militia and the "Lower Sort"* (New Brunswick, N.J.: Rutgers University Press, 1987), p. 31. See also Peter Linebaugh and Marcus Rediker, "The Many-headed Hydra: Sailors, Slaves and the Atlantic Working Class in the Eighteenth Century," *Journal of Historical Sociology* 3, no. 3 (Sept. 1990): 235; and Marcus Rediker, *Between the Devil and the Deep Blue Sea: Merchant Seamen, Pirates, and the Anglo-American Maritime World, 1700–1750* (Cambridge: Cambridge University Press, 1975), p. 252–53.

13 W.E.B. DuBois, *Black Reconstruction in America* (New York: Russell and Russell, 1963), p. 112.

14 Mary Berry, *Military Necessity and Civil Rights Policy* (Port Washington, N.Y.: Kennikat Press, 1977), esp. p. 94; and Thomas W. Higginson, *Army Life in a Black Regiment* (Lansing: Michigan State University Press, 1960), pp. 197–98.

15 DuBois, *Black Reconstruction in America*, p. 104. This is a central theme for Eric Foner, *Reconstruction: America's Unfinished Revolution* (New York: Harper and Row, 1988), pp. xxiv–xxv, xxvii, 3–11. See also Abraham Lincoln's quote on black soldiers in James M. McPherson, *Battle Cry of Freedom: The Civil War Era* (New York: Oxford University Press, 1988), p. 769. For additional research on African American soldiers, see Gary A. Donaldson, *The History of African-Americans in the Military* (Malabar, Fla.: Krieger, 1991), pp. 46–47; and Jack Foner, *Blacks and the Military in American History* (New York: Praeger, 1974), p. 51.

16   Benjamin Quarles, *Black Abolitionists* (London: Oxford University Press, 1969), pp. 248–49.

17   Cited in Cynthia Enloe, *Does Khaki Become You?* (Boston: South End Press, 1983), p. 122. See also Linda Grant Depauw, "Women in Combat," *Armed Forces and Society* 2, no. 21 (Winter 1981): 209; Paul Engle, *Women in the American Revolution* (Chicago: Follett, 1976), pp. 1–26; and Sally Smith Booth, *The Women of 76* (New York: Hastings House, 1973).

18   Depauw, "Women in Combat," 218.

19   Berry, *Military Necessity*, p. 79; DuBois, *Black Reconstruction in America*, p. 104; and Benjamin Quarles, *The Negro in the American Revolution* (Chapel Hill: University of North Carolina Press, 1961), p. vii. See also Alfred F. Young, "George Robert Twelve Hewes (1742–1840): A Boston Shoemaker and the Memory of the American Revolution," *William and Mary Quarterly* 38 (1981): 590; Thomas Slaughter, *The Whiskey Rebellion: Frontier Epilogue to the American Revolution* (New York: Oxford University Press, 1986), pp. 48, 128, 137, 227; Richard Severo and Lewis Milford, *The Wages of War: When American Soldiers Came Home—from Valley Forge to Vietnam* (New York: Simon and Schuster, 1989), pp. 51–79; and Cunliffe, *Soldiers and Civilians*, p. 43.

20   Shy, *People Numerous and Armed*, pp. 222–24; Rosswurm, *Arms, Country and Class*, p. 251; DuBois, *Black Reconstruction in America*, pp. 84–126; Linebaugh and Rediker, "The Many-headed Hydra," p. 233; and Higginson, *Army Life in a Black Regiment*, p. 193.

21   Cited in Peter Barnes, *Pawns: The Plight of the Citizen–Soldier* (New York: Knopf, 1972), pp. 15–16; and Alexander Hamilton, James Madison, and John Jay, *The Federalist Papers* (New York: Mentor, 1961), p. 299.

22   J.G.A. Pocock, *The Machiavellian Moment: Florentine Political Thought and the Atlantic Republican Tradition* (Princeton, N.J.: Princeton University Press, 1975), pp. 89–90, 202–3; Michael Walzer, *Obligations: Essays on Disobedience, War and Citizenship* (New York: Simon and Schuster, 1971), p. 49; and Gordon Wood, *The Creation of the American Republic* (New York: Norton, 1972), pp. 65–70.

23   Eliot A. Cohen, *Citizens and Soldiers: The Dilemmas of Military Service* (New York: Cornell University Press, 1985), p. 123.

24   Russell F. Weigley, "The Long Death of the Indian-fighting Army," in *Soldiers and Civilians: The U.S. Army and the American People*, ed. Garry D. Ryan and Timothy K. Nenninger (Washington, D.C.: National Archives and Records Administration, 1987), p. 27.

25   Robert M. Utley, *Frontier Regulars: The United States Army and the Indian, 1866–1891* (New York: Macmillan, 1973), p. xiii; and Robert F. Berkhofer, Jr., *The White Man's Indian: Images of the American Indian from Columbus to the Present* (New York: Knopf, 1978), pp. 91, 97–98.

26   Berkhofer, *White Man's Indian*, pp. 168–69.

27   Ibid., p. 186; Utley, *Frontier Regulars*, pp. 396, 401; and Brian Dippie, *The Vanishing American* (Middletown, Conn.: Wesleyan University Press, 1982), p. 146.

28   Utley, *Frontier Regulars*, p. 51.

29   Russell F. Weigley, *The American Way of War* (New York: Macmillan, 1973), pp. 153–63.

30 Robert Utley, *Life in Custer's Cavalry* (New Haven, Conn.: Yale University Press, 1977), p. 274; and Utley, *Frontier Regulars*, pp. 51–52.

31 For a more exhaustive and insightful treatment of frontier ideology, see Richard Slotkin's trilogy, *Regeneration through Violence; The Fatal Environment: The Myth of the Frontier in the Age of Industrialization, 1800–1890* (New York: Atheneum Press, 1985); and *Gunfighter Nation: The Myth of the Frontier in Twentieth-Century America* (New York: Harper Perennial, 1992).

32 Cunliffe, *Soldiers and Civilians*, pp. 402–3.

33 Ibid., p. 417.

34 Weigley, "Long Death of the Indian-fighting Army," p. 32.

35 For evidence of the fighter mentality, see Stuart Creighton Miller, *Benevolent Assimilation: The American Conquest of the Philippines, 1899–1903* (New Haven, Conn.: Yale University Press, 1982), pp. 179, 188, 189, 241.

36 Ibid., pp. 139, 241. See also Slotkin, *Gunfighter Nation*, chap. 3.

37 The popular legacy of World War II included an array of strong democratizing influences that, among other consequences, stimulated the emerging civil rights movement and led to the dismissal of white supremacy as a scientific theory and fascism as a political system. Working-class people began to attend college in numbers for the first time, and women moved into the military and previously male-dominated sectors of the workforce. New standards of justice such as those produced by the Nuremberg trials also gained legitimacy.

38 For a discussion of "national security" and its impact on American power and politics, see Daniel Yergin, *Shattered Peace: The Origins of the Cold War and the National Security State* (Boston: Houghton Mifflin, 1977); and Melvyn P. Leffler, *A Preponderance of Power: National Security, the Truman Administration, and the Cold War* (Stanford, Calif.: Stanford University Press, 1992). For total war, see F. J. P. Veale, *Advance to Barbarism: The Development of Total War from Serajevo to Hiroshima* (New York: Devin-Adair, 1968); Peter Calvocoressi and Gut Wint, *Total War: The Story of WWII* (New York: Pantheon Books, 1972); Gordon Wright, *The Ordeal of Total War, 1939–1945* (New York: Harper and Row, 1968); and Raymond Aron, *The Century of Total War* (Boston: Beacon Press, 1954).

　　From the time of the American Revolution, the separation between civilian life and military action had begun to erode. Indeed, the citizen-soldier figure that fused the civilian and military spheres appeared during that time. The tendency toward total war evolved as industrialization, mass politics, and imperial expansion gained ground. The Civil War, the Indian wars, the Philippine-American War, and World War I all contributed to the evolution of total war. By the end of World War II, however, total war became the dominant, if not the only possible, form of warfare.

39 Morris Janowitz, *Professional Soldier* (Glencoe, Ill.: Free Press, 1960), p. 35.

40 Samuel Huntington, *The Soldier and the State* (Cambridge, Mass.: Belknap Press of Harvard University Press, 1957), p. 61.

41 Ibid., pp. 17, 63–64.

42 Janowitz, *Professional Soldier*, p. 32.

43 Jack Klein, interview by author, Milwaukee, Wis., Mar. 20, 1990. For an enlightening description of boot camp, see W. D. Ehrhart, *Vietnam—Perkasie: A Combat Marine Memoir* (Jefferson, N.C.: McFarland, 1983), chap. 3.

44   John Lindquist, interview by author, Milwaukee, Wis., Mar. 22, 1990.

45   William Davis, interview by author, Chicago, Ill., Mar. 18, 1990. See also Matthew Dandridge, interview by Sam Cameron, Fisk University Library, Black Oral History Program, Nashville, Tenn., Jan. 25, 1973.

46   See also Lifton, *Home from the War*, p. 242.

47   Vince Muscari, interview by Pacer Smith, New York, N.Y., June 25, 1994.

48   Jess Jesperson, interview by author, Milwaukee, Wis., Mar. 21, 1990.

49   Wilhelm Reich, *Mass Psychology of Fascism* (New York: Farrar, Straus and Giroux, 1970), p. 31. See also Evelyn Yoshimuta, "GI's and Asian Women," *GI News and Discussion Bulletin* 3, (Mar. 1971): 25.

50   Joel Greenberg, interview by author, Chicago, Ill., Mar. 17, 1990.

51   See Peter Gabriel Filene, *Him/Her Self: Sex Roles in Modern America* (New York: Harcourt Brace Jovanovich, 1974), chap. 3. In different terms, William James discusses the need to fuse action or manhood to ideals in "What Makes a Life Significant," in *The Writings of William James: A Comprehensive Edition*, ed. John J. McDermot (Chicago: University of Chicago Press, 1978), pp. 657–58. See also Mark Gerson, *A Choice of Heroes: The Changing Faces of American Manhood* (Boston: Houghton Mifflin, 1982).

52   For an exhaustive discussion of sexism, masculinity, and the production of soldiers, see Klaus Theweleit, *Male Fantasies* (Minneapolis: University of Minnesota Press, 1989); Susan Jeffords, *The Remasculinization of America: Gender and the Vietnam War* (Bloomington: Indiana University Press, 1989); and Betty A. Reardon, *Sexism and the War System* (New York: Teachers College Press, Columbia University, 1985).

53   Yoshimuta, "GI's and Asian Women," p. 25; See also Reich, *Mass Psychology of Fascism*, pp. 24–33.

54   Scott Shimabukaro, quoted in Vietnam Veterans against the War, *The Winter Soldier Investigation: An Inquiry into American War Crimes* (Boston: Beacon Press, 1972), p. 152.

55   Enloe, *Does Khaki Become You?* pp. 14–15. See also Jacqueline E. Lawson, " 'She's a Pretty Woman . . . for a Gook': The Misogyny of the Vietnam War," *Journal of American Culture* 2, no. 3 (Fall 1989): 55–65.

56   Elroy Schultz, interview by author, Two Rivers, Wis., Mar. 21, 1990.

57   Jess Jesperson, interview. For additional testimony, see quote from Scott Camil, in John Kerry and the VVAW, *The New Soldier* (New York: Collier Books, 1971), p. 148.

58   See John Clark Pratt's preface to W. D. Ehrhart, *Unaccustomed Mercy: Soldier-Poets of the Vietnam War* (Lubbock: Texas Tech University Press, 1989), p. vii. For more oral history evidence of the impact of filmic images, see Danny Friedman's oral history in Joan Morrison and Robert K. Morrison, *From Camelot to Kent State: The Sixties Experience in the Words of Those Who Lived It* (New York: Times Books, 1987), p. 85.

59   Joel Greenberg, interview.

60   Jack Klein, interview.

61   The Indian fighter in particular populated innumerable cinematic, literary, and historical accounts of American history during the 1950s. The dramatic tension with the quintessential 1950s western is more or less constructed around the

violent conflict between the Indian fighter and the "wild Indian." From childhood's "cowboys and indians" to the "Injun country" of Vietnam, the Indian-fighter figure was influential and ubiquitous. For an interpretation of western film genre relative to imperial culture, see Slotkin, *Gunfighter Nation.*

62 Myra Jehlen, "New World Epic: The Novel and the Middle Class in America," *Salmugundi* 36 (1977): 49–68. Jehlen discusses the centrality of the family drama to literary and, I suggest, cinematic forms. More fundamentally, Jehlen identifies in the novel a basic characteristic of dominant culture. Characters struggle through an individual repudiation of or separation from family or society only to make an eventual return to the fold.

For a related analysis of *The Sands of Iwo Jima*, see William J. Gibson, "Paramilitary Fantasy Culture and the Cosmogonic Mythology of Primeval Chaos and Order," *Vietnam Generation* 1, no. 3–4, (Summer–Fall 1989): 12–32.

The Flying Leathernecks, also starring Wayne, has a similar plot line with a single political statement narrated at the film's introduction.

63 *The Sands of Iwo Jima*, dir. Allen Dwan (Republic, 1949).

64 For a related discussion of how family ideology and Cold War politics fused during the 1950s, see Elaine Tyler May, *Homeward Bound: American Families in the Cold War Era* (New York: Basic Books, 1988), pp. 14–15, 135, 145–46, 160–61, 176.

65 Steve Shuey, interview by author, Somerset, N.J., Jan. 14, 1988.

66 Although many elements of the Hollywood hero were the moral opposite of the qualities of the citizen–soldier, the cinematic hero nonetheless restored the very concept of heroism that had weakened after World War I. See Filene, *Him/Her Self*, p. 157; and Theodore L. Gross, *The Heroic Ideal in American Literature* (New York: Free Press, 1971), p. xi. See also Thomas Myers, *Walking Point: American Narratives of Vietnam* (New York: Oxford University Press, 1988), p. 17. In his preface to Ehrhart, *Unaccustomed Mercy* (p. vii), John Clark Pratt suggests that John Wayne unwittingly portrayed the archetypal warrior created by the figures of Hector and Achilles from Greek mythology.

67 John Lindquist, interview.

68 Ron Arm, interview by author, Madison, Wis., Nov. 12, 1993.

69 Tom Holm, "Forgotten Warriors: American Indian Service Men in Vietnam," *Vietnam Generation* 1, no. 2 (Spring 1989): 61. Holm's study also suggests the complex interaction between dominant and alternative figures of the soldier. He points out that a few tribes "have syncretized service in the American armed forces with their own tribal customs" (pp. 60–61).

70 Lea Ybarra, "Perceptions of Race and Class among Chicano Vietnam Veterans," *Vietnam Generation* 1, no. 2 (Spring 1989): 85. See also Douglas Martinez and Manuel Gomez, "Chicanos and Vietnam," in *The Vietnam Reader*, ed. Walter Capps (New York: Routledge, 1991), p. 186. This notion is also referred to in George Mariscal, " 'Our Kids Don't Have Blue Eyes, but They Go Overseas to Die': Chicanos in Vietnam" (Paper presented at America and Vietnam: From War to Peace, Notre Dame University, Dec. 4, 1993).

71 D. A., cited in Ybarra, "Race and Class Among Chicano Veterans," p. 86.

72 R. C., cited in ibid., p. 87.

73 Kerry and the VVAW, *New Soldier*, p. 172; and Gerald R. Gioglio, *Days of Decision: An Oral History of Conscientious Objectors in the Military during the Vietnam War* (Trenton, N.J.: Broken Rifle Press, 1989). Gioglio also found that the overwhelming majority of objectors he interviewed had come from backgrounds they identified as conservative.

74 Ben Chitty, interview by author, New York, N.Y., Jan. 5, 1994.

75 For other evidence that antiwar veterans were raised with traditional values or in subordinate communities, see Gioglio, *Days of Decision*, particularly pp. 21, 27, 37, 42, 115, 130; Willa Seidenberg and William Short, *A Matter of Conscience: GI Resistance during the Vietnam War* (Andover, Mass.: Addison Gallery of American Art, 1992), p. 4, passim; and Nora Sayre, *Sixties Going on Seventies* (New York: Arbor House, 1973), pp. 93–94.

76. Annie Bailey, interview by author, Milwaukee, Wis., Mar. 21, 1990.

77 Greg Payton, interview by author, Irvington, N.J., Dec. 1, 1989.

78 Joel Greenberg, interview.

79 Paul Atwood, cited in Seidenberg and Short, *Matter of Conscience*, p. 4.

80 For a collection of letters that powerfully document the impact of World War II on black soldiers and popular civil rights thought, see Phillip McGuire, ed., *Taps for a Jim Crow Army: Letters from Black Soldiers in World War II* (Lexington: University Press of Kentucky, 1993).

81 Clarence Fitch, cited in Seidenberg and Short, *Matter of Conscience*, p. 10.

82 Greg Payton, interview.

83 Robert Townsend, interview by author, Highland Park, N.J., July 10, 1985.

84 William Davis, interview.

85 Dave Cline, interview by author, Jersey City, N.J., Mar. 1, 1988.

86 For other oral history evidence of this militant patriotism, see Bill Short, "A Matter of Conscience," *Vietnam Generation* 2, no. 1 (1990): 82, quote by Steve Fournier. See also Gioglio, *Days of Decision*, p. 19.

87 Joe Urgo, interview by author, New York, N.Y., July 2, 1985.

88 Robert Muller, cited in Kerry and VVAW, *New Soldier*, p. 96.

89 Stephen A. Howard, cited in Wallace Terry II, *Bloods: An Oral History of the Vietnam War* (New York: Random House, 1984), p. 123.

90 Jan Barry, interview by author, Montclair, N.J., June 5, 1985.

91 In Kerry and VVAW, *New Soldier*, the VVAW documents the fact that the majority of veteran activists were volunteers, not draftees, see p. 172.

92 Thomas S. Kuhn, *The Structure of Scientific Revolutions* (Chicago: University of Chicago Press, 1962), pp. 64–65. Kuhn's description of the role of belief in, and knowledge of, the existing paradigm in the shift to new ideas is strikingly similar to the process experienced by many antiwar veterans. For additional evidence of the transformation of traditional beliefs held by dissident soldiers, see the discussion on nurse Joan Furey in Laura Palmer, "The Nurses of Vietnam, Still Wounded: Only Now Are They Healing Themselves," *New York Times Magazine*, Nov. 7, 1993, p. 36, passim. See also Kenneth Fred Emerick, *War Resisters Canada: The World of the American Military–Political Refugees* (Knox, Pa.: Pennsylvania Free Press, 1972), chap. 7; Lifton, *Home from the War*, pp. 143, 156; and Roger Neville Williams, *The New Exiles: American War Resisters in Canada* (New York: Liveright Press, 1971), pp. 272–307.

3   GI Dissent in Vietnam

1   Indicators of soldier unrest such as desertion and application for conscientious objector status rose considerably by 1967. The first major base riot of American soldiers also occurred in 1967. In the same year a working-class antiwar organization called the American Servicemen's Union was founded, and African American soldiers began to express their sympathy for and solidarity with the urban rebellions. Indeed, by that time soldiers began to associate themselves with both the Black Power movement and the youth counterculture—associations that would eventually lead many to dissent.

As early as 1965 American veterans of World War II and Korea began public dissent against the war and the next year officially formed the Veterans for Peace in Vietnam. In 1966 *RITA Notes* (Resisters inside the Army) became the first underground GI publication. By 1967 *The Bond, Veterans Stars and Stripes for Peace,* and *Vietnam GI* began publishing the dissenting views of American soldiers and veterans. The Vietnam Veterans Against the War, perhaps the only antiwar organization born in that period and still in existence, was founded in 1967.

2   The literature on Tet is contentious and considerable. See Peter Braestrup, *Big Story* (Boulder, Colo.: Westview Press, 1977); Gabriel Kolko, *Anatomy of a War: Vietnam, the United States, and Modern Historical Experience* (New York: Pantheon, 1985); Andrew F. Krepinevich, *The Army and Vietnam* (Baltimore, Md.: Johns Hopkins University Press, 1986); Don Oberdorfer, *Tet! The Turning Point in the Vietnam War* (Garden City, N.Y.: Doubleday, 1971); and Harry G. Summers, Jr., *On Strategy: A Critical Analysis of the Vietnam War* (New York: Dell, 1982).

3   For resistance in the U.S. military after the Vietnam era, see David Cortright and Max Watts, *Left Face: Soldier Unions and Resistance Movements in Modern Armies* (New York: Greenwood Press, 1991).

4   For an exhaustive look at the social control techniques used by the military during this period, see Lawrence B. Radine, *The Taming of the Troops: Social Control in the U.S. Army* (Westport, Conn.: Greenwood Press, 1977). See also Robert Sherrill, *Military Justice Is to Justice as Military Music Is to Music* (New York: Harper and Row, 1969); and idem, "Must the Citizen Give Up His Civil Liberties When He Joins the Army?" *New York Times Magazine,* May 18, 1969, pp. 25–26, 120–125.

5   David Cortright, *Soldiers in Revolt: The American Military Today* (Garden City, N.Y.: Anchor Press, Doubleday, 1975), p. 51. For a well-researched short account, see Terry Anderson, "The GI Movement and Response from the Brass," in *Give Peace a Chance: Exploring the Vietnam Antiwar Movement,* ed. Melvin Small and William D. Hoover (Syracuse, N.Y.: Syracuse University Press, 1992), pp. 93–115. See also Matthew Rinaldi, "The Olive Drab Rebels: Military Organizing during the Vietnam War," *Radical America* (May–June 1974): 17–51; and James R. Hayes, "The Dialectics of Resistance: An Analysis of the GI Movement," *Journal of Social Issues* 31, no. 4 (1975): 125–39. For more journalistic evidence, see the excerpts from Georgie Anne Geyer's *Chicago Daily News* articles, in Virginia Elwood-Akers, *Woman War Correspondents in the Vietnam War, 1961–1975* Metuchen, N.J.: Scarecrow Press, 1988), pp. 164–77.

6 Jan Barry, interview by author, Montclair, N.J., June 5, 1985.

7 Donald Duncan, "The Whole Thing Was a Lie," *Ramparts* 13 (Feb. 1966): 12–24. See also Duncan, *The New Legions* (New York: Random House, 1967). For other evidence of early opposition by special forces, see "U.S. Officer Guilty; Refused Jungle Post," *New York Times*, June 26, 1965, p. 1; and "Two Freed G.I.'s Say U.S. Should Quit Vietnam," *New York Times*, Dec. 1, 1965, p. 1, 5.

8 Duncan, "Whole Thing Was a Lie," p.23.

9 Duncan, *New Legions*, pp. 79–82.

10 "U.S. Officer Guilty," pp. 1, 5.

11 R. W. Apple, Jr., "G.I. Who Refused to Bear Arms in Vietnam Gets Year," *New York Times*, June 12, 1966, p. 1.

12 William Wilders to James F. Wilders, Phuoc Binh, RVN, Oct. 6, 1966.

13 Nancy Zaroulis and Gerald Sullivan, *Who Spoke Up? American Protests against the War in Vietnam, 1963–1975* (Garden City, N.Y.: Doubleday, 1984), p. 366.

14 Charley Trujillo, *Soldados: Chicanos in Viet Nam* (San Jose, Calif: Chusma House, 1990), p. 64.

15 Rinaldi, "Olive Drab Rebels," p. 29.

16 *As You Were* 7 (Aug. 1969). New York University, Tamiment Library (hereafter cited as TL).

17 Myra MacPherson, *Long Time Passing: Vietnam and the Haunted Generation* (Garden City, N.Y.: Doubleday, 1984), p. 512; Richard Boyle, *The Flower of the Dragon: The Breakdown of the U.S. Army during the Vietnam Era* (San Francisco: Ramparts, 1972), pp. 87–88; and Horst Faas and Peter Arnett, "Told to Move Again on 6th Deathly Day, Company A Refuses," *New York Times*, Aug. 26, 1969, p. 1, 3.

18 *Up Against the Bulkhead* 1, No. 2 (May 15, 1970), TL.

19 Cortright, *Soldiers in Revolt*, p. 37.

20 Dennis Kroll, interview by author, Madison, Wis., Mar. 25, 1990.

21 Shelby L. Stanton, *The Rise and Fall of an American Army: U.S. Ground Forces in Vietnam, 1965–1973* (Novato, Calif.: Presidio Press, 1985), p. 349.

22 "Vietnam Mutiny," *Fatigue Press* (May, 1971). Private collection of David Cline, copy in posession of author (hereafter cited as DCPC).

23 Boyle, *Flower of the Dragon*, p. 228; and "Company Removed from Base After Soldiers Balk at Patrol," *Chicago Tribune*, Oct. 12, 1971.

24 Cortright, *Soldiers in Revolt*, p. 41.

25 *Congressional Record* 92d Cong. 1st sess., Oct. 28, 1971, p 38082.

26 Cortright, *Soldiers in Revolt*, p. 38. For other evidence of combat refusals, see Thomas Stallworth, interview by Sam Cameron ad Sam Fustukjian, Fisk University Library, Black Oral History Program, Nashville, Tenn., Dec. 7, 1972 (hereafter cited as FUBOP); and Freddie Smith, interview by Sam Cameron and Sam Fustukjian, Oct. 30, 1972, FUBOP.

27 Colonel Tom Ware, "The U.S. Soldier in Vietnam at the Beginning, the Middle and the Ending" (Paper cited in BDM Corporation, *A Study of Strategic Lessons Learned in Vietnam*, Vol. 4, [Defense Logistics Agency, Alexandria, Virginia, 1979], pp. 4–22). Microfilm published by Scholarly Resources Inc. and Navy Historical Library, Washington, D.C.

28 Charley Trujillo, *Soldados*, pp. 153–58.

29 "B-52 Commander Applies for CO," *Camp News* 4, no. 2 (Jan. 15, 1973).

Indiana University, Underground Newspaper Collection, Bloomington, Microfilm AN 123, reel 95 (hereafter cited as UNCIUB); and Cortright, *Soldiers in Revolt, p. 135.*

30 *Camp News* 4, no. 1 (Jan. 15, 1973), UNCIUB.

31 Report cited in Cortright, *Soldiers in Revolt,* p. 125.

32 Everett R. Holles, "130 Refuse to Join Ship; Most Reassigned by Navy," *New York Times,* Nov. 10, 1972; p. 1. Henry P. Leifermann, "The *Constellation* Incident," *New York Times Magazine,* Feb. 18, 1973, p. 17 et passim; and Cortright, *Soldiers in Revolt,* pp. 121–22. For the most complete description of Vietnam-era naval mutinies, see Leonard F. Guttridge, *Mutiny: A History of Naval Insurrection* (Annapolis, Md.: U.S. Naval Institute, 1992).

33 Cortright, *Soldiers in Revolt,* p. 23.

34 Pete Seeger, "King Henry," in *Dangerous Songs,* 1965.

35 Richard A. Gabriel and Paul L. Savage, *Crisis in Command: Mismanagement in the Army* (New York: Hill and Wang, 1978), table 3, p. 182; and Richard Holmes, *Acts of War: The Behavior of Men in Battle* (New York: Free Press, 1985), pp. 329–30.

36 Cortright, *Soldiers in Revolt,* p. 43.

37 Congressional Quarterly, "Problems in the Ranks: Vietnam Disenchantment, Drug Addiction, Racism Contribute to Declining Morale," in *The Power of the Pentagon,* (Washington, D.C.: Congressional Quarterly, 1972), p. 22.

38 Cincinnatus, *Self-destruction: The Disintegration and Decay of the U.S. Army during the Vietnam Era* (New York: Norton, 1981), p. 66.

39 Eugene Linden, "The Demoralization of the Army: Fragging and Other Withdrawal Symptoms," *Saturday Review,* Jan. 8, 1972, p. 12.

40 Cincinnatus, *Self-Destruction,* pp. 65–66; Stanton, *Rise and Fall,* p. 301; and Robert Townsend, interview with author, July 10, 1985, Highland Park, N.J.

41 Barry Romo, interview by author, Chicago, Ill., Mar. 18, 1990.

42 Lamont Steptoe, interview by author, Philadelphia, Pa., Feb. 23, 1989.

43 Ibid.

44 "Free Billy Smith," *Fatigue Press* (Apr. 1972), DCPC.

45 Linden, "Demoralization of the Army," p. 13.

46 Boyle, *Flower of the Dragon,* p. 187.

47 Ed Sowders, interview by author, New Brunswick, N.J., Apr. 4, 1991, and June 1, 1989.

48 Linden, "Demoralization of the Army," p. 12.

49 John Lindquist, interview by author, Milwaukee, Wis., Mar. 22, 1990.

50 Stanton, *Rise and Fall,* p. 357.

51 Charles J. Levy, *Spoils of War* (Boston: Houghton Mifflin, 1974), pp. 34–36.

52 William L. Hauser, *America's Army in Crisis: A Study in Civil–Military Relations* (Baltimore, Md.: Johns Hopkins University Press, 1973), p. 77.

53 Joan Crowell, *Fort Dix Stockade: Our Prison Camp Next Door* (New York: Links Books, 1974), p. 138.

54 Greg Payton, interview by author, Irvington, N.J., Dec. 1, 1989.

55 Ibid.

56 Ibid.

57 Ibid.

58 Clarence Fitch, cited in Joan Morrison and Robert K. Morrison, *From Camelot*

to Kent State: The Sixties Experience in the Words of Those Who Lived It (New York: Times Books, 1987), pp. 79–80.

59 For the best short history of African American soldiers and their attitudes on the war, see Gerald Gill, "Black Soldiers' Perspectives on the War," in *The Vietnam Reader*, ed. Walter Capps (New York: Routledge, 1991), pp. 173–85. See also David Cortright, "Black GI Resistance during the Vietnam War," *Vietnam Generation* 2, no. 1 (1990): 51–64.

60 Pete Zastrow, interview by author, Chicago, Ill., Mar. 16, 1990.

61 Ibid.

62 Greg Payton, interview. For other comments on perceptions of Vietnamese identification with African Americans, see Freddie Smith, interview.

63 John Lindquist, interview.

64 Ibid.

65 "Slow Down, You Move Too Fast," *All Hands Abandon Ship* 3, no. 4 (Sept, 1974), TL.

66 Jack Klein, interview by author, Milwaukee, Wis., Mar. 20, 1990.

67 Marc Leepson, interview by author, South Bend, Ind., Dec. 4, 1993.

68 Thomas Bradley, interview by author, Asbury Park, N.J., May 24, 1985.

69 Boyle, *Flower of the Dragon*, pp. 171–73.

70 "GI's Rebel in Vietnam," *Shakedown* 1, no. 10 (Oct. 4, 1969), TL.

71 Lamont Steptoe, interview.

72 Richard Boyle, *GI Revolts: The Breakdown of the U.S. Army in Vietnam* (San Francisco: United Front Press, 1973), p. 11; Cortright, *Soldiers in Revolt*, p. 33; Hal Wingo, "From GIs in Vietnam, Unexpected Cheers," *Life*, Oct. 24, 1969, p. 36 et passim; and "Some G.I.s in Vietnam Join Protest," *New York Times*, Oct. 16, 1969, p. 22.

73 Wingo, "GIs in Vietnam," p. 36.

74 Dave Blalock, cited in Willa Seidenberg and William Short, *A Matter of Conscience: GI Resistance during the Vietnam War* (Andover, Mass.: Addison Gallery of American Art, 1992), p. 30.

75 Lynda Van Devanter, *Home before Morning* (New York: Beaufort Books, 1983), p. 159.

76 *The Bond* 5, no. 1 (Jan. 20, 1971), TL.

77 *Ally*, no. 38 (Nov. 1971), TL.

78 Cortwright, *Soldiers in Revolt*, p. 34.

79 Ibid.

80 Henry Kamm, "Army Is Checking Antiwar Petition," *New York Times*, Nov. 21, 1969, p. 10; and Cortright, *Soldiers in Revolt*, p. 33.

81 For examples of antiwar letters from Vietnam soldiers, see Steve Rees, "A Questioning Spirit: GIs Against the War," in *They Should Have Served That Cup of Coffee*, ed. Dick Cluster (Boston: South End Press, 1979), pp. 149–80; and Cortright, *Soldiers in Revolt*, p. 23.

82 William Davis, interview by author, Chicago, Ill., Mar. 18, 1990.

83 *Task Force*, Box 1, State Historical Society of Wisconsin, Social Action Collections.

84 David J. DeRose, "Soldados Razos: Issues of Race in Vietnam War Drama," *Vietnam Generation* 1, no. 2 (Spring 1989): 40–55. See also Wallace Terry II, "Bringing the War Home," in *Vietnam and Black America: An Anthology of Protest*

and Resistance, ed. Clyde Taylor (Garden City, N.Y.: Anchor Press, Doubleday, 1973), p. 214, originally in *Black Scholar* 23 (Nov. 1970): 6–18; Gerald Gill, "Black Soldiers' Perspectives"; and Robert Sanders Stanley, *Brothers: Black Soldiers in the Nam* (Novato, Calif.: Presidio Press, 1982).

85 Freddie Smith, interview.

86 Wallace Terry II, "Bringing the War Home" (*Black Scholar*), p. 6. In addition, Terry presents considerable data on other attitudes among African American troops, including substantial support for student antiwar protest.

87 National Archives, Suitland Reference Branch, Washington, D.C., Record Group 472, "USARV Inspector General Report of Investigation, no. 72–11." Summary of testimony given by Andrew L. Love, Roy Guillard, Bruce Gilmore, and Edward L. Johnson. See similar comments by Matthew Dandridge, Ulysses Wilks, and Sam Cameron in FUBOP.

88 "Black GIs Tell of 'Mutiny' Case," *Pacific Stars and Stripes* (Oct. 17, 1971). National Archives, Suitland Reference Branch, Washington, D.C., Record Group 472, USARV Inspector General Report of Investigation no. 72–11.

89 National Archives, Suitland Reference Branch, Washington, D.C., Record Group 472, "USARV Inspector General Report of Investigation nno. 72–11." Summary of investigation and conclusions, Inspector General Colonel Glifford H. Ford, Jan. 19, 1972, p. 83.

90 Ibid. Testimony of Captain Wade E. Gano. See also testimony of Sergeant Robert F. Hose, Roy Gillard, and Jerry Williams.

91 Ibid. Summary of investigation and conclusions, pp. 68, 69, 89.

92 Ibid. Testimony of Kenneth C. McManus.

93 Ibid. Summary of investigation, report of inquiry concerning racial tensions in United States Army support command, Cam Ranh Bay and 35th Engineer Group, Phan Thiet, p. 66.

94 Ibid., p. 70.

95 Samuel Stouffer, A. A. Lumsdaine, M. H. Lumsdaine, R. M. Williams, Jr., M. B. Smith, I. L. Janis, S. A. Star, and L. S. Cottrell, Jr., *The American Soldier: Combat and Its Aftermath,* vol. 2 (Princeton, N.J.: Princeton University Press, 1949), pp. 108, 135–49.

96 For a discussion of the "heads," see John Helmer, *Bring the War Home: The American Soldier in Vietnam and After* (New York: Free Press, 1974), esp. pp. 190–98.

97 Dave Cline, interview by author, Jersey City, N.J., Mar. 1, 1988.

98 Ibid.

99 Jack Klein, interview. For other testimony, see Lifton, *Home from the War: Neither Victims nor Executioners* (New York: Basic Books, 1973), p. 174.

100 John Helmer argues for the centrality of the heads to the white working-class resistance (*Bringing the War Home,* pp. 199, 296; and *The Deadly Simple Mechanics of Society* [New York: Seabury Press, 1974], p. 219).

101 David L. Terry photograph in Donald Kirk, "Who Wants to Be the Last American Killed in Vietnam?" *New York Times Magazine,* Sept. 19, 1971, p. 9. See also *Where Are We?* (May 1971), TL.

102 Gill, "Black Soldiers' Perspectives." For more evidence, see Donald Kirk, *Tell It to the Dead: Memories of a War* (Chicago: Nelson-Hall, 1975), p. 80.

103 Leslie Whitfield, taped interview, Dec. 14, 1972, FUBOP

104 Lamont Steptoe, interview.
105 Ibid.
106 Ibid.
107 Trujillo, *Soldados*, pp. 34–35.
108 Ibid., p. 35.
109 Helmer, *Bringing the War Home*, p. 221.
110 Steve Shuey, interview by author, Somerset, N.J., July 12 and 15, 1985, and Jan. 14, 1988.
111 Cincinnatus, *Self-destruction of the U.S. Army*, p. 71. Also see Stuart H. Loory, *Defeated: Inside America's Military Machine* (New York: Random House, 1973).
112 Clarence Fitch, cited in Morrison and Morrison, *From Camelot to Kent State*, p. 77. See similar comments by Ulysses Wilks in FUBOP.

4   The GI Movement in the U.S.

1 For a journalistic overview, see Douglass E. Kneeland, "War Stirs More Dissent Among G.I.'s," *New York Times*, June 21, 1970, p. 1; B. Drummond Ayres, Jr., "Army Is Shaken by Crisis in Morale and Discipline," *New York Times*, Sept. 5, 1971, p. 1; Ben A. Franklin, "Army Is Worried over Increase in Aggressive Antiwar Militancy by Soldiers," *New York Times*, Apr. 6, 1969, p. 3.
2 Cortright, *Soldiers in Revolt: The American Military Today* (Garden City, N.Y.: Anchor Press, Doubleday, 1975), p. 52. For other examples of early dissent, see Michael Biddy, "Fragging the Chains of Command: GI Resistance Poetry and Mutilation," *Journal of American Culture* 16, no. 3 (Fall 1993): 29; and Roger Neville Williams, *The New Exiles: American War Resisters in Canada* (New York: Liveright, 1971), pp. 90–95.
3 Alice Lynd, *We Won't Go: Personal Accounts of War Objectors* (Boston: Beacon Press: 1968), pp. 184–85.
4 "War Stimulates Dissent and Politics," *Congressional Quarterly Almanac*, vol. 23, 90th Cong., 1st sess., 1967, p. 936. Perhaps the best account of the Fort Hood Three is in Fred Halstead, *Out Now: A Participant's Account of the Movement in the U.S. against the Vietnam War* (New York: Pathfinder Press, 1991), pp. 174–86.
5 "GI Asia War Foe Guilty of Balking," *New York Times*, Nov. 14, 1967, p. 4.
6 "Kangaroo Court," *The Graffiti*, no. 3 (undated Special Moratorium Issue), New York University, Tamiment Library (hereafter cited as TL; and Fred P. Graham, "Two Marines Test Right of Dissent," *New York Times*, Mar. 7, 1969, p. 11.
7 *About Face*, no. 2 (Apr. 1968), TL; *The Graffiti*, no. 3, TL.
8 Joanne Grant, *Black Protest: History Documents and Analysis* (New York: St. Martin's Press, 1968), pp. 415–16. The only other reference to the 1965 hunger striker calls him "Private Oval" (Williams, *New Exiles*, p. 92).
9 Grant, *Black Protest*, pp. 415–16. For other documentation of civil rights and Black Power resistance to the war, see Robert W. Mullen, *Blacks and Vietnam* (Washington, D.C.: University Press of America, 1971), pp. 65, 66; William L. Van Deburg, *New Day in Babylon: The Black Power Movement and American Culture, 1965–1975* (Chicago: University of Chicago Press, 1992), pp. 97–107; Clyde Taylor, *Vietnam and Black America: An Anthology of Protest and Resistance*

(Garden City, N.Y.: Anchor Press, 1973); and Peter Levy, "Blacks and the Vietnam War," in *The Legacy: Vietnam in the American Imagination*, ed. D. Michael Shafer (Boston: Beacon Press, 1990), pp. 209–32.

10 Lynd, *We Won't Go*, p. 146. For other discussions of antiwar sentiment in the Latino community, see Carlos Ornelas and Michael Gonzales, "The Chicano and the War: An Opinion Survey in Santa Barbara," *Aztlan* 2, no. 1 (Spring 1971): 27–32. See also Lea Ybarra, "Perceptions of Race and Class among Chicano Vietnam Veterans," *Vietnam Generation* 1, no. 2 (Spring 1989): 69–93; Douglas Martinez and Manuel Gomez, "Chicanos and Vietnam," in *The Vietnam Reader*, ed. Walter Capps (New York: Routledge, 1991), pp. 186–90; and George Mariscal, " 'Our Kids Don't Have Blue Eyes, but They Go Overseas to Die': Chicanos in Vietnam," (Paper presented at America and Vietnam: From War to Peace, Notre Dame University, Dec. 4, 1993).

11 See Richard Perrin's account of early ASU activities, in Williams, *New Exiles*, pp. 156–70.

12 House Committee on Internal Security, *"Investigations of Attempts to Subvert the U.S. Armed Services," Hearings before the Committee on Internal Security*, 92d Cong., 2d sess., 1972, p. 6542. For an account of the ASU that emphasizes the influence of the New Left, see Edward F. Sherman, "Dissenters and Deserters: Antiwar Agitation in the Military," *New Republic*, Jan. 6, 1968, pp. 23–26.

13 Andy Stapp, *Up Against the Brass* (New York: Simon and Schuster, 1970), pp. 104, 187; and Willa Seidenberg and William Short, *A Matter of Conscience: GI Resistance during the Vietnam War* (Andover, Mass.: Addison Gallery of Art, 1992), p. 32.

14 For a highly documented account of antiwar efforts among labor unions, see Philip S. Foner, *U.S. Labor and the Vietnam War* (New York: International Publishers, 1989).

15 Peter B. Levy, "The New Left, Labor and the Vietnam War," *Peace and Change* 15, no. 1 (Jan. 1, 1990): 49.

16 Levy, "New Left," p. 57.

17 E. W. Kenworthy, "523 Union Chiefs Assail U.S. on War," *New York Times*, Nov. 13, 1967, p. 9.

18 For a good description of pre-1967 soldier antiwar attitudes, see Daniel Land, *Patriotism without Flags* (New York: Norton, 1974), chap. 3. See also Murray Polner, *No Victory Parades: The Return of the Vietnam Veteran* (New York: Holt, Rinehart and Winston, 1971), pp. 46–93.

19 Alan Klein, cited in Seidenberg and Short, *Matter of Conscience*, p. 28.

20 Ibid.

21 David Brown, cited in Gerald Gioglio, *Days of Decision: An Oral History of Conscientious Objectors in the Military during the Vietnam War* (Trenton, N.J.: Broken Rifle Press, 1989), p. 232. The CCCO is the Central Committee for Conscientious Objectors.

22 Fred Gardner, *The Unlawful Concert: An Account of the Presidio Mutiny Case* (New York: Viking Press, 1970); and Gerry Nicosia, "The Presidio 27," *Vietnam Generation* 2, no. 1 (1990): 65–80. Linden Blake's account can be found in Williams, *New Exiles*, pp. 213–33. For another description of brig conditions, see Jack Fincler, "In a Marine Corps Prison: The Hog-tied Brig Rats of Camp Pendleton," *Life*, Oct. 10, 1969, pp. 32–37.

23 Seidenberg and Short, *Matter of Conscience*, p. 35.

24 Bruce Borrus, "Thousands March on Fort Dix; Military Police Gas Protestors," *Rutgers Targum*, Oct. 13, 1969. Rutgers University Archives.

25 For a description of a smaller prison riot at Fort Bragg in 1970, see Nora Sayre, *Sixties Going on Seventies* (New York: Arbor House, 1973), pp. 98–99.

26 A brief listing of prison uprisings appears in Joan Crowell, *Fort Dix Stockade: Our Prison Camp Next Door* (New York: Links Books, 1974), pp. 138–39.

27 Jack Klein, inverview by author, Milwaukee, Wis., Mar. 20, 1990.

28 Ibid.

29 Ibid.

30 *The Bond* (Nov. 3, 1967), quoted in Larry G. Waterhouse and Mariann G. Wizard, *Turning the Guns Around: Notes on the GI Movement* (New York: Praeger, 1971), p. 64; and Stapp, *Up Against the Brass*, p. 97.

31 Elaine Elinson, "The Story Behind the Travis Air Force Base Explosion," *Task Force*, Box 1, State Historical Society of Wisconsin, Social Action Collections (hereafter cited as SHSW).

32 *Fatigue Press*, no. 31 (July 1971), Private collection of David Cline (hereafter cited as DCPC). Copy in possession of author.

33 Ibid.

34 Stuart H. Loory, *Defeated: Inside America's Military Machine* (New York: Random House, 1973), p. 153. See also William L. Hauser, *America'a Army in Crisis: A Study in Civil–Military Relations* (Baltimore, Md.: Johns Hopkins University Press, 1973), p. 76.

35 Loory, *Defeated*, p. 154.

36 Cortright, *Soldiers in Revolt*, pp. 12–13; and John Kifner, " 'Underground Railroad' Aids Deserters to Canada," *New York Times*, Oct. 5, 1969, p. 1.

37 Richard DeCamp, "The GI Movement in Asia," *Bulletin of Concerned Asian Scholars* 4, no. 1 (Winter 1972): 110.

38 Robert Trumbull, "Japanese Pacifists Report 4 Deserted a U.S. Carrier in War Protest," *New York Times*, Nov 14, 1967, p. 1. See also Bill Kovack "Sailor Back from Exile a Symbol of Deserters' Plight," *New York Times*, Dec. 27, 1971, p. 1.

39 "Anti-War 'Chain Gang' Goes to Church Here," *San Francisco Examiner*, July, 16, 1968.

40 See Buffy Parry's account in Williams, *New Exiles*, pp. 181–95.

41 Lawrence Baskir and William Strauss, *Chance and Circumstance: The Draft, the War and the Vietnam Generation* (New York: Random House, 1978), p. 148; and Terry Whitmore, *Memphis-Nam-Sweden: The Autobiography of a Black American Exile* (Garden City, N.Y.: Doubleday, 1971). See also, Bill Kovach, "Sailor Back from Exile"; and "G.I. Who Deserted from Vietnam Gets 4 years," *New York Times*, Mar. 7, 1969, p. 10.

42 Ed Sowders, interview by author, New Brunswick, N.J., Apr. 4, 1991, and June 1, 1989.

43 *The Ally*, no. 9 (Sept. 1968), TL.

44 "Green Beret Deserter Still Free and Fighting for Amnesty," *Amex-Canada* 5, no. 4, whole no. 43, (May–June 1975), SHSW.

45 *Winter Soldier* 5, no. 3 (Mar. 1975), DCPC.

46 See Devi Prasad, *They Love It but Leave It: American Deserters* (London: Farmer and Sons, 1971).

47 Baskir and Strauss, *Chance and Circumstance*, p. 122; and Richard A. Gabriel and Paul L. Savage, *Crisis in Command: Mismanagement in the Army* (New York: Hill and Wang, 1978), table 1, p. 181.

48 Cortright, *Soldiers in Revolt*, p. 11.

49 Ibid., pp. 11–14.

50 Ibid, p. 122.

51 *Fatigue Press*, no. 32 (Aug. 1971), DCPC; and *Travesty* 1, no. 2 (no date), TL.

52 "9 Miss Sailing, Held Deserters, *Washington Post*, Oct. 2, 1971, p A6.; "9 Deserters Flown Back to Carrier," *Chicago Tribune*, Oct. 3, 1971, p. 6.

53 Williams, *New Exiles*, p. 114.

54 Ibid., p. 116.

55 Cortright, *Soldiers in Revolt*, p. 15.

56 Myra MacPherson, *Long Time Passing: Vietnam and the Haunted Generation* (Garden City, N.Y.: Doubleday, 1984), p. 335. Given the cultural, ethnic, and linguistic distance between most American soldiers and the Vietnamese, desertion in Vietnam posed considerable obstacles.

57 House Appropriations Committee, *Hearings before a Subcommittee of the Committee on House Appropriations*, Department of Defense, pt. 9, 92d Cong., 2d sess., 1972, p. 587; and Cortright, *Soldiers in Revolt*, pp. 10–11.

58 Baskir and Strauss, *Chance and Circumstance*, p. 122.

59 "The U.S.S. *Hollister* in Vancouver," *Yankee Refugee*, reprinted in *The American Exile in Canada* 1, no. 14 (Apr. 24, 1969): 3, SHSW. See also Williams, *New Exiles*. For a good description of the deserter community in Sweden, including the motivation of deserters, see Lang, *Patriotism without Flags*, chap. 2.

60 John Kifner, " ' Underground Railroad.' ", p. 1.

61 Ed Sowders, interview.

62 Ibid. For Sowders's surrender, see "Amnesty Panel Hears Deserter, Who Then Surrender to Police", *New York Times*, May 25, 1973, p. 9.

63 Annie Bailey, interview by author, Milwaukee, Wis., Mar. 18, 1990.

64 Baskir and Strauss, *Chance and Circumstance*, pp. 115, 155.

65 The political nature of these discharges is suggested by the fact that African Americans and other people of color were disproportionately represented. *Amex-Canada* claimed that in 1972 at the height of the resistance, African Americans made up approximately 12 percent of the service yet received 33 percent of the dishonorable discharges, 20 percent of the bad conduct discharges, 17 percent of the undesirable discharges, 20 percent of the general, and only 9 percent of the honorable discharges ("Universal Unconditional Amnesty," *Amex-Canada* 5, no. 6 [Oct.–Nov. 1976], SHSW).

66 Ben Chitty, interview by author, New York, N.Y., Jan. 5, 1994.

67 Ibid.

68 Although soldiers had marched in antiwar demonstrations before, the GI-Veteran March for Peace was the first predominantly military march. See Donna Mickleson, "GIs to March out of Step," *San Francisco Express Times*, Aug. 21, 1968, p. 1; *Task Force* (Aug. 10, 1968), TL; and "First GI March Successful Despite Obstacles," *Veterans Stars and Stripes* (Oct. 1968), in Waterhouse and Wizard, *Turning the Guns Around*, pp. 73–74.

69 Susan Schnall, interview by author, New York, N.Y., Oct. 25, 1990.

70 Ibid.

71 Ben A. Franklin, "Army Is Worried over Increase in Aggressive Antiwar Militancy by Soldiers," *New York Times*, Apr. 6, 1969, p. 3.

72 Halstead, *Out Now*, p. 478.

73 "GI's Lead Struggle," *Shakedown* (Nov. 24, 1969), Rutgers University Special Collections, New Brunswick, N.J.

74 Dave Cline, interview by author, Jersey City, N.J., Mar. 1, 1988.

75 "43 Arrested at Ft. Hood," *Vietnam GI* (Sept. 1986), p. 1, TL; "No Riot Duty for the Ft. Hood 43," *San Francisco Chronicle*, Aug. 26, 1968.

76 *Camp News* 4, no. 2 (Feb. 15, 1973), Indiana University, Newspaper Collection, Bloomington, microfilm AN 123, reel 94, Underground (hereafter cited as UNCIUB).

77 *Fatigue Press*, no. 23 (May 1970), DCPC.

78 Cortright, *Soldiers in Revolt*, p. 82.

79 *About Face*, 2, no. 4 (June 1972), TL.

80 *Shakedown* 2, no. 2 (Apr. 24, 1970), TL. For examples of other Armed Forces Day demands, see "Armed Farces Day," VVAW leaflet, unprocessed material, SHSW; and *Fatigue Press*, no. 23 (May 1970), DCPC.

81 Cortright, *Soldiers in Revolt*, p. 94.

82 Hauser, *America's Army in Crisis*, p. 80.

83 Ibid., p. 78.

84 For example, see Anthony Ripley, "2 Airmen Cleared of Distributing Peace Leaflets at Idaho Base," *New York Times*, Dec. 10, 1971, p. 49.

85 *Up against the Bulkhead* 1, no. 11 (May 1972), TL.

86 *Congressional Record*, 92d Cong. 1st sess., Oct. 28, 1971, 38083.

87 "Carrier Revolt Brewing," *Ally*, no. 38 (Nov. 1971), TL; and "Protest Viet Duty," *Chicago Tribune*, Oct. 12, 1971.

88 *Up from the Bottom* 2, no. 6 (Dec. 15, 1972), TL.

89 Jon Oplinger, *Quang Tri Cadence: Memoir of a Rifle Platoon Leader in the Mountains of Vietnam* (Jefferson, N.C.: McFarland, 1993), p. 116.

90 "How to FTA," *Aboveground* Mar. 1970), TL.

91 "How to FTA."

92 Ed Sowders, interview.

93 Cortright, *Soldiers in Revolt*, pp. 123–25.

94 *Attitude Check* 2, no. 2 (Mar. 20, 1969), TL.

95 *Right-on Post* 1, no. 4 (Aug. 1970). Reproduced in House Committee on Internal Security, "Investigation of Attempts to Subvert the United States Armed Services," *Hearings Before the Committee on Internal Security, pt. 3, 92d Cong., 2d sess., 1972, committee exhibit 11-B, p. 6776.

96 Charles C. Moskos, Jr., "The American Combat Soldier in Vietnam," *Journal of Social Issues* 34, no. 4 (1975): 36.

97 Andrew Kopkind, "Captain Levy I: Doctors Plot" and "The Trial of Captain Levy:II," in *Trials of the Resistance* (New York: New York Review, 1970), pp. 14–42; and "Capt. Levy Is Refused a Hearing by Supreme Court," *New York Times*, Nov. 14, 1967, p. 8.

98 Lynd, *We Won't Go*, p. 265.

99 Michael Sutton, interview by author, Chicago, Ill., Mar. 15, 1990.

100 Loory, *Defeated*, pp. 241–42.

101 Hauser, *America's Army in Crisis*, pp. 84–86.

102 Ibid., p. 87.

103 Jackson Lears, interview by author, New Brunswick, N.J., Sept. 14, 1988.

104 *Congressional Record*, 92d Cong., 1st sess., Oct. 28, 1971, 38084.

105 Lynd, *We Won't Go*, pp. 127–45.

106 Jackson Lears, interview.

107 Pacific Counseling Service, pamphlet (San Francisco: Pacific Counseling Service, 1970), p. 10, reproduced in House Internal Security Committee, "Investigation of Attempts to Subvert the United States Armed Services," *Hearings before the Committee on Internal Security*, 92d Cong., 1st sess., 1971, pt. 1, 6664. USSF, *The New Army* (1971), DCPC.

108 Jackson Lears, interview.

109 Cortright, *Soldiers in Revolt*, p. 16. For an overview of conscientious objection, see Gerald R. Gioglio, "In the Belly of the Beast," in *Sights on the Sixties*, ed. Barbara L. Tischler (New Brunswick, N.J.: Rutgers University Press, 1992), pp. 211–25.

110 In 1967 COs made up only 8 percent of the number inducted, yet by 1971 COs had become 43 percent of the total. In 1972 the ratio of CO classifications surged to a historically unprecedented 131 percent; that is, more young Americans were granted CO status than were actually drafted. This rapid increase also included the legal expansion of CO status to include secular objections. See John W. Chambers II, "Conscientious Objectors and the American State from Colonial Times to the Present," in *The New Conscientious Objection: The Secularization of Objection to Military Service*, ed. Charles C. Moskos and John W. Chambers II (New York: Oxford University Press, 1993), p. 42.

111 *GI News and Discussion Bulletin*, no. 8 (Aug. 1971), SHSW.

112 James T. Wooten, "500 G.I.'s at Debut of Antiwar Show," *New York Times*, Mar. 15, 1971, p. 9; Mel Gussow, "Anti-Army 'F.T.A. Show,'" *New York Times*, Nov. 23, 1971, p. 55; and Dick Brukenfeld, "Where There's Hope, There's Fonda," *Village Voice*, Nov. 25, 1971.

113 G. Louis Heath, ed., *Mutiny Does Not Happen Lightly: The Literature of the American Resistance to the Vietnam War* (Metuchen, N.J.: Scarecrow Press, 1976), pp. 406–7; and Ben A. Franklin, "The Private and the General: War Foe's Petition Poses Challenge," *New York Times*, May 12, 1969, p. 4.

114 Fred Halstead, *GIs Speak Out against the War: The Case of the Ft. Jackson 8* (New York: Pathfinder Press, 1970). GIs United against the War seems to have been the only major GI project of the SWP. For other activity of the YSA, see Tom Wells, *The War Within: America's Battle over Vietnam* (Berkeley: University of California Press, 1994), p. 196.

115 Fred Halstead, *Out Now*, pp. 170–73, 425ff., 675.

116 Homer Bigart, "Antiwar Soldiers Face Army Trials," *New York Times*, Jan. 25, 1970, p. 8.

117 *Vietnam GI* (Jan. 1969), TL.

118 *Camp News* 4, no. 6 (June 15, 1973), UNCIUB.

119 "Waves Face Repression," *Navy Times Are a Changin'* 3, no. 1 (Apr. 1972), TL.

120 "Queer Fear," *All Hands Abandon Ship* 3, no. 4, (Sept. 1972), TL. For other sexual analyses, see *Shakedown* 2, no. 2 (Apr. 24, 1970), TL; and "Forward Macho," *Hansen Free Press* 2, no. 1 (Mar. 15, 1973), TL.

121 *Fed Up* (Dec. 1970), TL.

122 *GI News and Discussion Bulletin,* no. 4 (Apr. 1971), SHSW.

123 Harry W. Haines, "Soldiers against the War in Vietnam: The Story of *Aboveground,*" *Serials Review,* 17, no. 1 (Spring 1991): 81; and Ronald Sullivan, "Fort Dix Soldiers Publish Newspaper Opposing War," *New York Times,* Apr. 6, 1969, p. 3.

124 Haines, "Soldiers Against the War," p. 78.

125 House Committee on Internal Security, "Investigations of Attempts to Subvert the Armed Forces," *Hearings before the Committee on Internal Security,* 92d Cong., 2d sess. pt. 3, 1972, p. 7082.

126 "MDM Statement," *Right-On Post* 1, no. 4 (Aug. 1970), House Committee on Internal Security, "Investigations of Attempts to Subvert the Armed Forces," *Hearings before the Committee on Internal Security,* 92d Cong., 2d sess., pt. 3, 1972, committee exhibit 11-B, p. 6776.

127 Editorial, *People's Press* 1, no. c (June 1971): 4, TL.

128 For the most complete existing discussion of women and the GI press, and military antiwar movement generally, see Barbara Tischler, "Voices of Protest: Women and the GI Antiwar Press," *Sights on the Sixties* (New Brunswick, N.J.: Rutgers University Press, 1992), pp. 197–209; and *Women's Newsletter* (Aug. 1970), USSF file, Box 5, SHSW.

129 Military women struggled against pervasive stereotyping that, in its most common expressions, categorized then as either lesbians or whores. This stereotype of women soldiers resulted from the way the military attempted to create soldiers. The military embraced a macho ideal for soldiers to which conventional femininity was the mutually exclusive opposite. Women soldiers did not fit this model, so their femininity or sexuality could be understood only in unconventional terms. See the discussion of sexuality in Chapter Two. See also *GI News and Discussion Bulletin* (June 1971), SHSW. For another analysis of sexism in the military see "Forward Macho," *Hansen Free Press* 2, no. 1 (Mar. 15, 1973), TL.

130 *Fatigue Press* (Oct. 25, 1971), DCPC.

131 "Elect Your Own Officers," *The Ally,* no. 24 (Mar. 1970), TL.

132 *Attitude Check* (Nov. 1969), TL.

133 *Fatigue Press,* no. 35 (Nov. 1971), DCPC. For many more examples of the American Revolution in the military antiwar movement, see Chapter Seven.

134 United States Servicemen Fund, *New Army* (1971): 5, DCPC; Cortright, *Soldiers in Revolt,* p. 53; and Halstead, *Out Now,* p. 425.

135 Robert D. Heinl, Jr., "The Collapse of the Armed Forces," *Armed Forces Journal* (June 1971): 32.

136 Dave Cline, interview.

137 Ibid.

138 Haines, "Soldiers against the War," p. 77.

139 The *Women's Newsletter* printed a speech entitled "Remember Mother Jones," given by Terry Davis at the Oleo Strut coffeehouse in Texas on International Women's Day, 1970. Davis recalled the history of International Women's Day and called for women to lead the movement (*Women's Newsletter* (Aug. 1970), USSF file, Box 5, SHSW).

140 Sayre, *Sixties Going on Seventies,* p. 101.

141 *Fatigue Press,* Riot Control Issue (no date), DCPC. See also Martin Dreyer,

"War and Peace at the Oleo Strut," *Houston Chronicle Texas Magazine*, July 12, 1970, pp. 7–16.

142 See, for example, *Camp News* 4, no. 8 (Aug. 15, 1973), UNCIUB, for a report of an uprising of two thousand soldiers at Fort Bragg in July 1973. See also *Winter Soldier* 5, no. 2 (Feb. 1975), DCPC; and David Cortright and Max Watts, *Left Face: Soldier Unions and Resistance Movements in Modern Armies* (New York: Greenwood Press, 1991).

143 "Navy Purge," *Camp News* 4, no. 2 (Feb. 15, 1972), UNCIUB.

144 *Camp News* 4, no. 5 (May 15, 1973, UNCIUB.

145 Ybarra, "Perceptions of Race and Class," pp. 87–88.

146 Seymour Hersh, "GIs from Vietnam Protest Harshness," *Washington Star*, Nov. 1, 1970; *The Ally*, no. 32 (Nov.–Dec. 1970), TL.

5 The Veterans' Antiwar Movement

1 Although African American, Latino, Asian, and American Indian veterans played, and continue to play, important roles in the VVAW, Veterans for Peace, and other veteran movements, the self-described antiwar veterans movement I am treating in this chapter was more white working-class than the general soldier resistance in Vietnam or the United States. See Gerald Gill, "Black Soldiers' Perspectives on the War," in *The Vietnam Reader*, ed. Walter Capps (New York: Routledge, 1991), pp. 181–82; and Thomas A. Johnson, "Negro Veteran Is Confused and Bitter," *New York Times*, July 29, 1968, p. 1.

2 Chuck Noell and Gary Wood, *We Are All POW's* (Philadelphia, Fortress Press, 1975).

3 This account of the veterans movement is a brief overview of the highlights of veteran protest. Any detailed history would include thousands of events in the United States, Europe, and Vietnam and would involve dozens of issues beyond the questions of war and peace. For an excellent short account by a participant–historian, see William F. Crandell, "They Moved the Town: Organizing the VVAW," in *Give Peace a Chance: Exploring the Vietnam Antiwar Movement*, ed. Melvin Small and William D. Hoover (Syracuse, N.Y.: Syracuse University Press, 1992), pp. 141–54.

4 Andy Stapp, *Up against the Brass* (New York: Simon and Schuster, 1970), p. 97; David Cortright, *Soldiers in Revolt: The American Military Today* (Garden City, N.Y.: Anchor Press, Doubleday, 1975), p. 56; and Barbara L. Tischler, "Breaking the Ranks," *Vietnam Generation* 2, no. 1 (1990): 21.

5 *Veterans Stars and Stripes for Peace* 1, no. 2 (Oct. 1967), New York University, Tamiment Library (hereafter cited as TL).

6 Ibid.

7 Jan Barry, interview by author, Montclair, N.J., June 5, 1985.

8 Ibid.

9 Ibid.; and VVAW, "Viet-Nam Veterans Speak Out," *New York Times*, Nov. 19, 1967, p. E7.

10 VVAW, "Viet-Nam Veterans Speak Out," p. E7.

11 VVAW, "Vietnam Vet's Statement of Principle," unprocessed material, State

Historical Society of Wisconsin, Social Actions Collections (hereafter cited as SHSW). Copy in possession of author.

12 "What's Being Done," leaflet, Veterans for Peace in Vietnam, Box 1, SHSW, For evidence of VFP participation in later demonstrations, see Michael Stern "87,000 March in War Protests Here," *New York Times* Apr. 28, p. 1, 72, and "March in San Francisco," *New York Times, Apr. 28, 1968, p. 72.*

13 Robert Buzzanco, "Division, Dilemma, and Dissent: Military Recognition of the Peril of War in Viet Nam," *Vietnam Generation* (undated, informed dissent issue): 9–37.

14 "Vets Demand Viet Peace," leaflet, Veterans for Peace in Vietnam, Box 2, SHSW. Copy in possession of author.

15 David Shoup, quoted in "Military Opposition to the War," *Vietnam* (June 1994): 41.

16 David M. Shoup, "The New American Militarism," *Atlantic,* Apr. 1969, pp. 51–56.

17 Buzzanco, "Division, Dilemma, and Dissent," p. 27.

18 "Vets Demand Viet Peace."

19 David Curry, speech at twentieth anniversary of Dewey Canyon III, Washington, D.C., Apr. 24, 1991. Recorded by author.

20 John Helmer, *Bringing the War Home: The American Soldier in Vietnam and After* (New York: Free Press, 1974), p. 212.

21 Jesse Torres, interview by author, Milwaukee, Wis., Nov. 12, 1993.

22 Ibid.

23 Annie Bailey, interview by author, Milwaukee, Wis., Mar. 21, 1990.

24 William Davis, interview by author, Chicago, Ill., Mar. 18, 1990.

25 *Different Sons,* Jack Ofield, dir., and Arthur Littman, prod. (1970). Video.

26 Ibid.

27 Ibid.

28 Ibid.

29 Barry Romo, interview by author, Chicago, Ill., Mar. 18, 1990.

30 Tod Ensign, "Organizing Veterans through War Crimes Documentation," in *Nobody Gets off the Bus* (Woodbridge, Conn.: Vietnam Generation, 1994), pp. 145–47; and Elliot L. Meyrowitz and Kenneth J. Campbell, "Vietnam Veterans and War Crimes Hearings," in *Give Peace a Chance,* pp. 129–40.

31 VVAW, *The Winter Soldier Investigation: An Inquiry into American War Crimes* (Boston: Beacon Press, 1972), p. xiii.

32 VVAW, *Winter Soldier Investigation,* p. 1.

33 Helmer, *Bringing the War Home,* pp. 91, 252.

34 T. G., quoted in Lea Ybarra, "Perceptions of Race and Class among Chicano Vietnam Veterans," *Vietnam Generation* 1, no. 2 (Spring 1989): 84.

35 Guy Osmer, interview by author, June 21, 1985, Wanaque, N.J.

36 *Camp News* 4, no. 4 (Apr. 15, 1973), Indiana University, Underground Newspaper Collection, Bloomington, microfilm AN 123, reel 95 (hereafter cited as UNCIUB).

37 *The Veteran,* 17, no. 2, (Spring 1987). Private collection of Dave Cline (hereafter cited as DCPC). Copy in possession of author.

38 Jeffrey Antevil "Shoup, Viet Vets Set War Protest in D.C.," *New York Daily News,* Mar. 16, 1971, p. 1.

39 In Jan Barry, *Peace Is Our Profession: Poems and Passages of War Protest* (Montclair, N.J.: East River Anthology, 1981), p. 157.

40 Michael Roach, quoted in John Kerry and the VVAW, *The New Soldier* (New York: Collier Books, 1971), p. 118.

41 All of the above testimony comes from VVAW, "It's Only the Beginning," 1972, film. See also Art Goldberg, "Vietnam Vets: The Anti-War Army," *Ramparts* 10, no. 1 (July 1971): 10–17; and "Veterans Discard Medals in War Protest at Capitol," *New York Times*, Apr. 24, 1971, p. 1.

42 Kerry and the VVAW, *New Soldier*, p. 138.

43 John Upton, interview by author, Washington, D.C., Apr. 25, 1991.

44 Ibid.

45 Fred Halstead, *Out Now: A Participant's Account of the Movement in the U.S. against the Vietnam War* (New York: Pathfinder Press, 1991), p. 607.

46 Peter Zastrow, interview by author, Chicago, Ill., Mar. 16, 1990.

47 I am deeply indebted to Eugenia Kaledin for sharing this description of the Memorial Day events in Lexington. Eugenia Kaledin, "Lexington, Massachusetts: Memorial Day 1971" (Paper presented at America and Vietnam: From War to Peace, Notre Dame University, Dec. 4, 1993).

48 *The Veteran* 17, no. 2 (Spring 1987), DCPC.

49 Jesse Torres, interview by author, Milwaukee, Wis., Nov. 11, 1993.

50 Tom Holm, "Forgotten Warriors: American Indian Servicemen in Vietnam," *Vietnam Generation* 1, no. 2 (Spring 1989): 64.

61 Ann Hirschman, interview by author, Cranbury, N.J., May 8, 1991. See also *The Veteran* 23, no. 1, (Spring 1993), DCPC.

52 *Winter Soldier* 3, no. 3 (May 1973), DCPC.

53 Ibid.

54 "25 War Protesters Are Held After Seizing Betsy Ross House," *New York Times*, Dec. 28, 1971, p. 21.

55 Lou Pinchinson, interview by author, Highland Park, N.J., Feb. 4, 1990.

56 Lawrence Van Gelder, "War Foes Reject U.S. Plan to Reopen Statue of Liberty," *New York Times*, Dec. 28, 1971, p. 1. See also Robert D. McFadden, "War Foes Seize Statue of Liberty," *New York Times*, Dec. 27, 1971, p. 1.

57 Much of this description of Operation Peace on Earth is drawn from Mark S. Foley's private journal, excerpts of which were published in a special commemorative journal: VVAW, *25 Years Fighting for Veterans, Peace and Justice*, 1992, pp. 8–9.

58 The interpretation of data from public opinion polls is beyond the scope of this study. Although the first polls to produce pluralities against the war were taken in February 1968, this "antiwar" opinion often agreed with the official policy of Vietnamization or was sharply critical of the antiwar movement. By the fall of 1971 polls suggested that "general opposition to the war was greater than at any time in the previous decade" (Charles DeBenedetti and Charles Chatfield, *An American Ordeal: The Antiwar Movement of the Vietnam Era* [Syracuse, N.Y.: Syracuse University Press, 1990], p. 298.

59 Ron Kovic, *Born on the Fourth of July* (New York: McGraw-Hill, 1976), pp. 157–58.

60 Ann Hirschman, interview.

61 Ibid.

62 Kovic, *Born on the Fourth of July*, pp. 168–69.

63 Kovic's speech was reproduced in *Amex-Canada* 5, no. 6, whole no. 45 (Oct.–Nov. 19, 1976): 10, microfilm P71-948, SHSW.

64 Red Squad was a movement term for city, municipal, or campus police officers and operations that specialized in surveillance of political activism. For more evidence of repression against VVAW members, see the section on Scott Camil in Ruth Schultz and Bud Schultz, *It Did Happen Here: Recollections of Political Repression in America* (Berkeley: University of California Press, 1989), pp. 319–34. See also Nancy Zaroulis and Gerald Sullivan, *Who Spoke Up? American Protests against the War in Vietnam, 1963–1975* (Garden City, N.Y.: Doubleday, 1984), p. 415.

65 *Winter Soldier* 3, issue 2 (Apr. 1973), DCPC; Robert Sanford, "Tallahassee Eight—Warriors for Peace," *St. Louis Dispatch*, Oct. 29, 1972; and Shaun D. Mullen, "War Hero of 1967 Now Finds He's Become 'Political Criminal,' " *Evening Journal*, Wilmington, Del., Jan 5, 1973.

66 John Kifner, "Informer Appears Key to U.S. Case Against Antiwar Veterans," *New York Times*, Aug. 14, 1972, p. 16; Kifner, "Behind Antiwar Veterans' Trial: Watergate, Spies, and Break-ins," *New York Times*, Aug. 9, 1973, p. 24; and Jere Moore, Jr., "Mitchell Denies Gainesville 8 Bugging," *Mobile Register*, Apr. 26, 1973. For an account of political repression against veterans, see Schultz and Schultz, *It Did Happen Here*, pp. 319–33.

67 "Biographical sketch," Scott Camil, Vietnam Veterans Against the War, unprocessed material, SHSW.

68 Descriptions of the three defendants come from "Biographical Sketch," Scott Camil, William Patterson, Peter Paul Mahoney, Vietnam Veterans against the War, unprocessed material, SHSW.

69 *Winter Soldier* 3, no. 6, (Aug. 1973), DCPC; and *Winter Soldier* 3, no. 8 (Oct. 1973), DCPC.

70 Peter Zastrow, interview.

71 *Amex-Canada* 5, no. 1, whole no. 40 (Oct. 1974), microfilm P71-948, SHSW.

72 United States Servicemen's Fund, *The New Army*, 1971; and David Zieger, *The History of the Oleo Strut Coffeehouse: 1968–1972* manuscript, 1972, DCPC. Copy in possession of author.

73 Jim Pechin, interview by author, South Bend, Ind., Dec. 3, 1993.

74 *Winter Soldier* 4, no. 9 (Nov. 1974), DCPC.

75 *Winter Soldier* 4, no. 12 (Dec. 1974), DCPC. In Boston this situation continued until the late 1970s. For this and a good local account of the relationship between Vietnam veterans and conservative veterans organizations, see Paul Camacho, "The Future of the Veterans' Lobby and Its Potential Impact for Social Policy," in *The American War in Vietnam*, ed. Jayne Werner and David Hunt (Ithaca, New York: Cornell University, Southeast Asia Program, 1993), pp. 107–121.

76 Peter Zastro, interview.

77 The VVAW–AI seemed, in part, influenced by the political perspectives of the Revolutionary Union and its offshoot, the Revolutionary Communist party. See Crandell, "They Moved the Town," pp. 151–52.

78 Pete Zastrow, interview.

79   Wilbur J. Scott, *The Politics of Readjustment* (New York: Aldine De Gruyter, 1993), chap. 4.

80   The VFP claims four thousand members in seventy-eight chapters nationwide (Veterans for Peace membership letter from national office, P.O. Box 3881, Portland, Maine, 04104).

81   See, for example, Frances M. Beal and Ty Depass, "African American Opposition to War: Past and Present," *Crossroads: Contemporary Political Analysis and Left Dialogue* 7 (Feb. 1991): 4–8.

82   Willa Seidenberg and William Short, *A Matter of Conscience: GI Resistance during the Vietnam War* (Andover, Mass.: Addison Gallery of American Art, 1991), p. 69. See also "African American Youth Resist 'Operation Cannon Fodder,' " *Crossroads: Contemporary Political Analysis and Left Dialogue* 7 (Feb. 1991): 9–12. Organizations such as the War Resisters League, Citizen–Soldier, Central Committee for Conscientious Objectors, American Friends Service Committee, the Midwest Committee for Military Counseling, the Committee Opposed to Militarism and the Draft, and the Youth and Militarism Project are among the more than twenty such organizations nationwide and exemplify the impact of Vietnam-era military antiwar movements on current military politics.

6   Military Resistance

1   Shelby L. Stanton, *The Rise and Fall of an American Army: U.S. Ground Forces in Vietnam, 1965–1973* (Novato, Calif.: Presidio Press, 1985) p. 213; and David Cortright, "The Collapse of the U.S. Military in Vietnam," *Monthly Review* (Oct. 1988): 42–53. See also Robert D. Heinl, Jr., "The Collapse of the Armed Forces," *Armed Forces Journal* (June 1971): 38–45. For journalistic evidence, see B. Drummont Ayres, Jr., "Army Is Shaken by Crisis in Morale and Discipline," *New York Times*, Sept. 5, 1971, p. 1; idem, "War Disillusions Many G.I.'s in Vietnam," *New York Times*, Aug. 4, 1969, p. 3; and Fred Gardner, "War and G.I. Morale," *New York Times*, Nov. 21, 1970, p. 31.

2   David Cortright "GI Resistance during the Vietnam War," in *Give Peace a Chance: Exploring the Vietnam Antiwar Movement*, ed. Melvin Small and William D. Hoover (Syracuse, N.Y.: Syracuse University Press, 1992), pp. 116–28. The study Cortright used was H. Olson and R. William Rae, *The Determination of the Potential for Dissidence in the U.S. Army*, vol. 1, *Nature of Dissent* (McLean, Va.: Virginia Research Analysis Corporation, 1971), technical paper RAC-TP-410. See also David Cortright, "Black GI Resistance during the Vietnam War," *Vietnam Generation* 2, no. 1 (1990): 54; and David Cortright and Max Watts, *Left Face: Soldier Unions and Resistance Movements in Modern Armies* (New York: Greenwood Press, 1991), p. 20.

3   Gerald R. Gioglio, *Days of Decision: An Oral History of Conscientious Objectors in the Military during the Vietnam War* (Trenton, N.J.: Broken Rifle Press, 1989), pp. 320–21.

4   Myra MacPherson, *Long Time Passing: Vietnam and the Haunted Generation* (Garden City, N.Y.: Doubleday, 1984), p. 341.

5   John Helmer, *Bringing the War Home: The American Soldier in Vietnam and After* (New York: Free Press, 1974), p. 35.

6   Donald Kirk, "Who Wants to Be the Last American Killed in Vietnam?" *New York Times Magazine*, Sept. 19, 1971, p. 59.

7   Gerald Gill, "Black Soldiers' Perspectives on the War," in *The Vietnam Reader*, ed. Walter Capps (New York: Routledge, 1991), pp. 174, 181.

8   Ellen Frey-Wouters and Robert S. Laufer, *Legacy of a War: The American Soldier in Vietnam* (New York: M. E. Sharpe, 1986), pp. 83–94, 333.

9   MacPherson, *Long Time Passing*, p. 615.

10 Ibid., p. 544.

11 Ibid., p. 335.

12 Lea Ybarra, "Perceptions of Race and Class among Chicano Vietnam Veterans," *Vietnam Generation* 1, no. 2 (Spring 1989): 81–82.

13 Charley Trujillo, *Soldados: Chicanos in Viet Nam* (San Jose, Calif.: Chusma House, 1990).

14 Paul Lyons, "The Silent Majority Baby Boomers: Class of 1966 in a South Jersey Town," *Vietnam Generation* 1, no. 2 (Spring 1989): 140.

15 "This Paper May Save Your Life!" *People's Press*, no. 3, (June 1971), p. 2. New York University, Tamiment Library (hereafter cited as TL).

16 Cited in Harry W. Haines, "Hegemony and the GI Resistance: Introductory Notes," *Vietnam Generation* 2, no. 1 (Spring 1989): 3.

17 *Attitude Check* 2, no. 2 (Mar. 1970), TL.

18 Heinl, "Collapse of the Armed Forces," p. 38.

19 John Saar, "You Can't Just Hand Out Orders," *Life*, Oct. 23, 1970, pp. 30–38. For more evidence of this new democracy in the military, see Virginia Elwood-Akers, "Our New GI: He Asks Why," in *Woman War Correspondents in the Vietnam War, 1961–1975* (Metuchen, N.J.: Scarecrow Press, 1988), pp. 164–77. *The section uses excerpts from Georgie Anne Geyer's articles in the Chicago Daily News*, Jan. 13–17, 1969.

20 Thomas Bradley, interview by author, Asbury Park, N.J., May 24, 1985.

21 See Gerald Gill, "From Maternal Pacifism to Revolutionary Solidarity: African-American Women's Opposition to the Vietnam War," in *Sights on the Sixties*, ed. Barbara L. Tischler (New Brunswick, N.J.: Rutgers University Press, 1992), pp. 177–195. For evidence of Chicano war dissent and its centrality to the rise of Mexican American political consciousness, see Edward J. Escobar, "The Dialectics of Repression: The Los Angeles Police Department and the Chicano Movement, 1968–1971," *Journal of American History* 79, no. 4 (Mar. 1993): 1483–1514. For working-class dissent, see Philip S. Foner, *U.S. Labor and the Vietnam War* (New York: International Publishers, 1989); Harlan Hahn, "Dove Sentiments among Blue-Collar Workers," *Dissent* (May–June 1976): 202–5; Richard F. Hamilton, "A Research Note on the Mass Support for 'Tough' Military Initiatives," *American Sociological Review* (June 1969): 439–45; and Patricia Cayo Sexton and Brendan Sexton, *Blue Collars and Hard Hats* (New York: Vintage Books, 1971), p. 102.

22 For classism in the antiwar movement, see Christian G. Appy, *Working Class War: American Combat Soldiers and Vietnam* (Chapel Hill: University of North Carolina Press, 1993). On authoritarian workers, see Seymour Lipset, "Democracy and Working-Class Authoritarianism," *American Sociology Review* 24, no. 4 (Aug. 1959): 482–502.

23 Foner, U.S. Labor and the Vietnam War, pp. 104–6, cited in Jack Colhoun, "The Antiwar Movement They Don't Talk About," Amex-Canada 5, no. 6, whole no. 45 (Oct.–Nov. 1976). State Historical Society of Wisconsin, Social Actions Collections (hereafter cited as SHSW): Maurice Carroll, "Police Assailed by Mayor on Laxity at Peace Rally," New York Times, May 10, 1970, p. 1; and Michael T. Kaufman, "City Hall Directive Called 'Inconsistent' as Guide in Attack by Workers," New York Times, May 11, 1970, p. 1.

24 Danny Friedman, cited in Joan Morrison and Robert K. Morrison, From Camelot to Kent State: The Sixties Experience in the Words of Those Who Lived It (New York: Times Books, 1987), pp. 86–87.

25 Louis Harris, "Unions Top Public in Backing Pullout," Long Island Press, Mar. 4, 1971.

26 "Media Lies," Fatigue Press, no. 23 (May 1970), private collection (hereafter cited as DCPC). Copy in possession of author.

27 Eugenia Kaledin, "Lexington, Massachusetts: Memorial Day 1971" (Paper presented at America and Vietnam: From War to Peace, Notre Dame University, Dec. 4, 1993). This paper includes a copy of the letter from the Cary Memorial Library. Copy in possession of author.

28 Jackson Lears, interview by author, New Brunswick, N.J., Sept. 14, 1988.

29 Andrew Levinson, The Working Class Majority (New York: Coward, McCann and Geoghegan, 1974), pp. 156–58.

30 For an in-depth discussion of class in the context of the Vietnam War, see Appy, Working Class War, esp. chap. 9. For more evidence of working-class attitudes, see the discussion of auto workers in Louisville, Kentucky, in Sexton and Sexton, Blue Collars and Hard Hats, pp. 85–88.

31 E. E. LeMasters, Blue-Collar Aristocrats: Life Styles at a Working-Class Tavern (Madison: University of Wisconsin Press, 1975), pp. 172–73.

32 Ibid., p. 175.

33 Ibid., p. 194.

34 Hahn, "Dove Sentiments Among Blue-Collar Workers," p. 204; and Levinson, Working Class Majority, pp. 159–60; and Lawrence E. Davies, "War Vote Assayed in San Francisco," New York Times, Nov. 9, 1967, p. 34.

35 Harris, "Unions Top Public in Backing Pullout."

36 Helmer, Bringing the War Home, p. 249.

37 For an opposing view, see Iver Bernstein, The New York City Draft Riots (New York: Oxford University Press, 1990). Bernstein claims that the Civil War riots were the most important working-class antiwar movement, and he does a masterful job of elaborating the working-class character of the draft riots. Yet in addition to being antiwar, the GI and veteran movements were anti-imperialist, self-consciously democratic, and against racism and sexism. This has not been persuasively argued for the New York rioters.

38 Ralph Blumenthal, "Army Finds Rise of Racial Tension in Study of Bases," New York Times, Jan. 25, 1970, p. 1. Although the immediate issue that sparked urban uprisings was related to domestic racism, Vietnam was often an explicit consideration. See reports of unrest in Plainfield, New Jersey in "Forbearance Cools Plainfield Unrest," Courier News, July 15, 1967, p. 2.

39 Samuel Vance, The Courageous and the Proud (New York: Norton, 1970), p. 159.

40 Cynthia Enloe, Ethnic Soldiers: State Security in Divided Societies (Athens:

University of Georgia Press, 1980). This shift is also well documented in Gerald Gill, "Black Soldiers' Perspectives." See also William L. Van Deburg, *New Day in Babylon: The Black Power Movement and American Culture, 1965–1975* (Chicago: University of Chicago Press, 1992), pp. 97–107; Stanley Goff, Robert Sanders, and Clark Smith, *Brothers: Black Soldiers in the Nam* (Novato, Calif.: Presidio Press, 1982); and George Mariscal, " 'Our Kids Don't Have Blue Eyes, but They Go Overseas to Die': Chicanos in Vietnam" (paper presented at America and Vietnam: From War to Peace, Notre Dame University, Dec. 4, 1993). Mariscal argues for a three-part analysis for understanding Chicanos' relationship with the war. He claims that discourses of "assimilation," "identification," and "solidarity" helped to organize Chicano support for, questioning of, and opposition to the war.

41 James Credel, interview by author, Newark, N.J., July 1, 1992.

42 John Brown, interview by author, Lakewood, N.J., Feb. 1, 1990.

43 Harold Cruse, *The Crisis of the Negro Intellectual* (New York: Morrow, 1967), throughout, but see esp. parts V and VI.

44 For a discussion of Black Power in the military peace movement, see "Black Liberation and the Anti-War Movement," *As You Were*, no. 13 (Apr. 1970), TL.

45 The long-term effects of this movement are still at work despite their relative invisibility. The unprecedented antiwar movement during the 1991 Gulf War was granted little attention by major media. Yet the characteristics of that short-lived movement were strikingly similar to the antiwar movement of the 1970s. The newer antiwar movement was extremely diverse in terms of culture and class, with critical leadership by people of color. It was explicitly patriotic and willing to contest the meaning of patriotism, and therefore was massive in its appeal. One of the largest demonstrations, at least 250,000 strong, occurred in Washington, D.C., on January 26, 1991. Absent from any major media account of the demonstration was the fact that approximately four-thousand veterans, largely from the Vietnam era, led the march. Some twenty-five hundred soldiers applied for conscientious objector status between August 1990 and June of the following year. Papers such as *The Anti-WARrior* and *Citizen–Soldier* promoted the emerging movement of soldier dissent. For a recent discussion that presents striking similarities between Vietnam and Gulf War military resisters, see the interview with antiwar activist Yoland Huet-Vaughn in Marlene C. Piturro "Study War No More: Price of Conscience" *On the Issues* (Summer 1994): 26–28.

46 "Invisible Force: Women in the Military," Nov. 1985 (Based on a conference sponsored by the William Joiner Center). Video.

7 Transformation of the Citizen-Soldier

1 The literature documenting the collapse of meaning and accepted values in Vietnam is quite considerable. Jonathan Shay discusses the impact of combat trauma (*Achilles in Vietnam: Combat Trauma and the Undoing of Character* [New York: Atheneum, 1994]). Robert Jay Lifton discusses the psychological dimensions of fragmentation in terms of the "counterfeit universe" and the absurd.

(*Home from the War: Neither Victims nor Executioners* [New York: Simon and Schuster, 1973]). John Hellmann employs Vietnam literature to show a fundamental rupture between the American mythology of the frontier and the Vietnam experience. (*American Myth and the Legacy of Vietnam* [New York: Columbia University Press, 1986]). Thomas Meyers is concerned with the fragmentation and attempted reconstruction of meaning in narrative forms, including myth and fiction. On the fragmentation of meaning, see the Introduction and p. 143 in particular (*Walking Point: American Narratives of Vietnam* [New York: Oxford University Press, 1988]). Lloyd Lewis also documents the collapse of meanings as expressed in Vietnam literature. Lewis posits the assertion of the survival instinct as the organizing principle for combat soldiers (*The Tainted War: Culture and Identity in Vietnam Narratives* [Westport, Conn.: Greenwood Press, 1985]). The work of Tim O'Brien, particularly *The Things They Carried* (Boston: Houghton Mifflin, 1990), can be read as a literary exploration built on the ruins of the American war novel genre.

Two particularly concise expressions of this fragmentation are presented by W. D. Ehrhart. See "Learning the Hard Way," and "Soldier–Poets of the Vietnam War," particularly the final three pages of that essay, in *The Shadow of Vietnam: Essays, 1977–1991* (Jefferson, N.C.: McFarland, 1991). Ehrhart's other works, particularly *Passing Time: Memoir of a Vietnam Veteran against the War* (Jefferson, N.C.: McFarland, 1989) and *Vietnam-Perkasie: A Combat Marine Memoir* (Jefferson, N.C.: McFarland, 1983) are further literary evidence of the transformations in consciousness I am discussing. John Clark Pratt's preface to W. D. Ehrhart, *Unaccustomed Mercy: Soldier–Poets of the Vietnam War* (Lubbock: Texas Tech University Press, 1989), is a concise argument about the fragmentation of poetic traditions for soldier–poets. Pratt states, "The whole becomes lost in the parts" (p. viii). Other interesting articles are Michael Biddy, "Fragging the Chains of Command: GI Resistance Poetry and Mutilation"; and Vince Gotera, "The Fragging of Language: D. F. Brown's Vietnam-War Poetry"; both appear in *Journal of American Culture* 16, no. 3 (Fall 1993): 29–38 and 39–46, respectively.

For other oral history sources that convey the general sense of meaninglessness created by combat in Vietnam, see Al Santoli, *Everything We Had: An Oral History of the Vietnam War* (New York: Ballantine Books, 1985); and in connection with antiwar soldiers specifically, see Gerald Gioglio, *Days of Decision: An Oral History of Conscientious Objectors in the Military during the Vietnam War* (Trenton, N.J.: Broken Rifle Press, 1989), pp. 114, 122–23, 197.

For research on the reconstruction of meaning, see Philip D. Beidler, *Rewriting America: Vietnam Authors in Their Generation* (Athens: University of Georgia Press, 1991). See Ralph Mavis's concept of "troop culture" in " 'I'm Not a Murderer, nor Am I a Hero': Troop Culture Among Combat Veterans in Vietnam," manuscript, *Department of History, Rutgers University*, 1991; and Gioglio's *Days of Decision* and Lifton's *Home from the War* for other discussions of the reconstruction of cultural meanings.

2 Elroy Schultz, interview by author, Two Rivers, Wis., Mar. 21, 1990.

3 Hellmann, *American Myth and the Legacy of Vietnam*, p. 110.

4 Barry Romo, interview by author, Chicago, Ill., Mar. 18, 1990.

5 Elroy Schultz, interview.

6 Steve Shuey, interview by author, Somerset, N.J., Jan. 14, 1988.

7 Barry Romo, interview. For an additional sampling of veteran testimony regarding combat experience, see Ellen Frey-Wouters and Robert S. Laufer, *Legacy of a War: The American Soldier in Vietnam* (Armonk, N.Y.: M. E. Sharpe, 1986), pp. 87–95.

8 Lifton, *Home from the War*, p. 25.

9 See Richard Slotkin's trilogy on the mythology of the frontier: *Regeneration through Violence: The Mythology of the American Frontier, 1600–1860* (Middletown, Conn.: Wesleyan University Press, 1973); *The Fatal Environment: The Myth of the Frontier in the Age of Industrialization, 1800–1890* (New York: Atheneum Press, 1985); and *Gunfighter Nation: The Myth of the Frontier in Twentieth-Century America* (New York: Harper-Perennial, 1992). See also J. William Gibson, "Paramilitary Fantasy Culture and the Cosmogonic Mythology of Primeval Chaos and Order," *Vietnam Generation* 1, no. 3–4 (Summer–Fall 1989): 30. See Lifton, *Home from the War*, pp. 197–99, on the psychological contours of the logic of domination. For oral history testimony describing the fighter spirit in Vietnam, see Roger Neville Williams, *The New Exiles: American War Resisters in Canada* (New York: Liveright, 1971), pp. 272–83.

10 Ed Sowders, interview by author, New Brunswick, N.J., Apr. 4, 1991, and June 1, 1989.

11 Another interesting oral history expression of this can be found in Gioglio, *Days of Decision*, p. 286.

12 Ron Arm, interview by author, Madison, Wis., Nov. 12, 1993.

13 For poetic evidence of dissolution and reconstruction, see Steve Mason, *Warrior for Peace* (New York: Simon and Schuster, 1989), pp. 101–7.

14 Harry W. Haines, "Soldiers against the War in Vietnam: The Story of *Aboveground*," *Serials Review* 17, no. 1 (Spring 1991): 75–93.

15 *The Veteran* 23, no. 1 (Spring 1993): 11. Private collection of Dave Cline (hereafter cited as DCPC). Copy in possession of author.

16 Some readers may find this generalization overdrawn in social or political terms. This cultural analysis, which focuses on the cultural and symbolic affinity between antiwar soldiers and the new social movements, in not a glossing-over of the many tensions, difficulties, and differences that existed between dissident soldiers and the peace, women's, or black nationalist movements. It is a well-established matter of the historical record that conflicts and contradictions existed between and within every known social movement, political organization, or school of thought. Indeed, it may well be in "the richness of its confusions" that the social movements proved such a fertile source of new symbols, images, and ideas. See Lifton, *Home from the War*, p. 237; and Christian Appy, *Working Class War: American Combat Soldiers and Vietnam* (Chapel Hill: University of North Carolina Press, 1993).

17 Cited in Richard DeCamp, "The GI Movement in Asia," *Bulletin of Concerned Asian Scholars* 4, no. 1 (Winter 1972): 113.

18 David Cortright and Max Watts, *Left Face: Soldier Unions and Resistance Movements in Modern Armies* (New York: Greenwood Press, 1991), pp. 17–18, 247–50. Cortright's primary analytical approach is to relate soldier dissent to the category of youth in industrial societies. See also Lifton, *Home from the War*, p. 232ff.

19   Gioglio, *Days of Decision*, pp. 132–33.

20   John Helmer, *Bringing the War Home: The American Soldier in Vietnam and After* (New York: Free Press, 1974), pp. 198–99. See also Helmer, *The Deadly Simple Mechanics of Society* (New York: Seabury Press, 1974), chap. 5. Lifton discusses the relationship between the youth culture and antiwar veterans in *Home from the War*, pp. 227ff.

21   Stanley Aronowitz, *False Promises: The Shaping of American Working Class Consciousness* (New York: McGraw-Hill, 1973), pp. 85–86.

22   Robert Townsend, interview by author, Highland Park, N.J., July 10, 1985.

23   Olivia Mitchell, interview by author, Plainsboro, N.J., Dec. 27, 1993.

24   On the link between feminism and peace, see Betty A. Reardon, *Sexism and the War System* (New York: Teachers College Press, Columbia University, 1985), esp. chap. 5.

25   Vince Muscari, interview by Pacer Smith, New York, N.Y., June 25, 1994.

26   For other examples of gender analysis from the GI press, see *The Paper* 2, no. 1 (Dec. 1971), New York University, Tamiment Library (hereafter cited as TL); and *Shakedown* 2, no. 2 (Apr. 1970), TL. For examples of women's history, see *Omega Press* 11, no. 8 (Dec. 1973), TL; and *Rage* 3, no. 6 (Sept.–Oct. 1974), TL. Lifton discusses the shift in gender attitudes in *Home from the War*.

27   See Mavis, " 'I'm Not a Murderer,' " pp. 21, 32.

28   Greg Payton, interview by author, Irvington, N.J., Dec. 1, 1989.

29   David Cline, interview by author, Jersey City, N.J., Mar. 1, 1988.

30   Guy Osmer, interview by author, Wanaque, N.J., June 21, 1985. For other oral testimony on how family was used as a critical standard, see *Different Sons*, Jack Ofield, dir., and Arthur Littman, prod. (1970). Video.

31   Barry Romo, interview.

32   Susan Schnall, interview by author, New York, N.Y., Oct. 25, 1990.

33   Greg Payton, interview.

34   While this focus on family ideals reflects an awareness of the connections between empire, the fighter spirit, and the patriarchal family, the history of the family is beyond the scope of this study.

35   For more evidence of this change among nurses, see Laura Palmer, "The Nurses of Vietnam, Still Wounded: Only Now Are They Healing Themselves," *New York Times Magazine*, Nov. 7, 1993, pp. 34–43, 68, 72. See especially the discussion of Joan Furey. The cultural construction of nurses is a topic sufficiently rich and different from that of soldiers to require its own study. Florence Nightingale, for example, is a remarkably complex and powerful figure. Like John Wayne, Nightingale seems to unite diverse and contradictory images of nurses while absorbing and displacing earlier understandings. Clara Barton, the Civil War nurse, and Edith Cavell, the Canadian nurse who died in World War I, also play important roles in the conceptions of nursing. During the mid twentieth century, military sociologists developed images of nursing that parallel the bureaucratic rendition of soldiers discussed in Chapter Two. See Fred Davis, ed., *The Nursing Profession: Five Sociological Essays* (New York: Wiley, 1966).

36   Susan Schnall, interview.

37   Ann Hirschman, interview by author, Cranbury, N.J., May 8, 1991.

38   Dave Cline to his parents, Aug. 17, 1967. Copy in posession of author. See also Charles Clemens, cited in Willa Seidenberg and William Short, *A Matter of*

Conscience: GI Resistance during the Vietnam War (Andover, Mass.: Addison Gallery of American Art, 1992), p. 26.

39 Lifton, *Home from the War*. Lifton devotes most of chap. 8, esp. p. 251, to a discussion of the role that the "John Wayne thing" played in veteran psychology.

40 Jack Mallory, quoted in John Kerry and the VVAW, *The New Soldier* (New York: Collier Books, 1971), p. 106.

41 Gioglio, *Days of Decision*, p. 318.

42 Johan Huizinga, *Homo Ludens: A Study of the Play-Element in Culture* (Boston: Beacon Press, 1950), p. 101.

43 All humans need meaning, and meaning must be constructed socially and historically. See Peter L. Berger and Thomas Luckmann, *The Social Construction of Reality* (New York: Anchor Books, 1966).

44 For more evidence of how values and community figured in antiwar veterans' politics, see Mark Hartford's oral history in Lauren Kessler, *After All These Years: Sixties Ideals in a Different World* (New York: Thunder's Mouth Press, 1990), pp. 40–43.

45 Jim Pechin, interview by author, South Bend, Ind., Dec. 3, 1993.

46 Jackson Lears, interview by author, New Brunswick, N.J., Sept. 14, 1988.

47 Mike Heaney, interview by author, New Brunswick, N.J., Oct. 5, 1988.

48 Dennis Kroll, interview by author, Madison, Wis., Mar. 25, 1990.

49 Ibid.

50 Jesse Torres, interview by author, Milwaukee, Wis., Nov. 12, 1993.

51 Ed Sowders, interview.

52 Ann Hirschman, interview.

53 Ben Chitty, interview by author, New York, N.Y., Jan. 5, 1994.

54 For other expressions of this alternative patriotism, see Gioglio, *Days of Decision*, pp. 3, 265, 270, 318–19; Steve Mason, *Warrior for Peace* (New York: Simon and Schuster, 1988), pp. 30, 43; "To Die for a Difference," *Gigline* 1, no. 4 (no date), TL; Daniel Lang, *Patriotism without Flags* (New York: Norton, 1974), p. 59; and Williams *New Exiles*, p. 287.

55 Gibson, "Paramilitary Fantasy Culture," pp. 29–31. See also Slotkin, *Gunfighter Nation*, p. 606.

56 Jesse Torres, interview.

57 Dave Cline, interview by author, Jersey City, N.J., Mar. 1, 1988.

58 Joel Greenberg, interview by author, Chicago, Ill., Mar. 18, 1990.

59 The quote is from Steve Tice, "A Program for Vietnam Vets and Everyone Else Who Cares" (Chicago: WTTW Chicago in association with the Office of the Dean of Students, University of Wisconsin at Madison). Video. For more on the link between peacemaker, citizen, and earthsaver, see Gioglio, *Days of Decision*, pp. 273–75.

60 William Davis, interview by author, Chicago, Ill., Mar. 18, 1990.

61 Joe Cross, interview by author, New York, N.Y., Jan. 18, 1994. Cross served in Vietnam from 1968 to 1969 in Battery A, 1st LAAM Battalion, MAG 18, 1st Marine Air Wing.

62 William Davis, interview.

63 Lamont Steptoe, interview by author, Philadelphia, Pa., Nov. 13, 1989, and Feb. 23, 1989.

64 Joe Cross, interview.

65 Kerry and the VVAW, *New Soldier*, p. 150. For other examples of divided consciousness in antiwar veterans, see Gerald Gioglio, *Days of Decision*, pp. 21, 28–29, 42–43, 268; and Lifton, *Home from the War*, pp. 69, 104.

66 W.E.B. DuBois, *The Souls of Black Folk* (New York: Dover, 1993), pp. 2–3.

67 For a discussion of memory and the Vietnam War, see Richard Moser, "Talking the Vietnam Blues: Oral History and Our Popular Memory of War," in *The Legacy: Vietnam in the American Imagination*, ed. Michael Shafer (Boston: Beacon Press, 1990).

68 *The Veteran 7, no. 3* (June 1977), DCPC.

69 Charles Shaughnessy, interview by author, Washington, D.C., Apr. 25, 1991.

70 This letter was read at the VVAW's twentieth commemoration of Dewey Canyon III, Washington, D.C., Apr. 1991.

71 For Bonus March, see *Winter Soldier* 4, no. 12, (Dec. 1974), DCPC: *Winter Soldier* 5, no. 2 (Feb. 1975), DCPC: *Winter Soldier* 5, no. 3 (Mar. 1975), DCPC; and *The Veteran* 6, no. 4 (Aug.–Sept. 1976), DCPC. For Shays's Rebellion, see *The Veteran* 6, no. 1 (Mar.–Apr. 1976), DCPC. For a general history of the role of the army and veterans, see *Last Harass*, no. 3 (Mar. 1969), TL.

72 See *Winter Soldier* 3, no. 7 (Sept. 1973), DCPC. See also *Fatigue Press*, no. 32 (Aug. 1971), DCPC; and *Gigline* 1, no. 3 (Oct. 1969), TL.

73 See *GI News and Discussion Bulletin*, no. 8 (Aug. 1971), USSF, Box 3, State Historical Society of Wisconsin, Social Actions Collections (hereafter cited as SHSW). In preparation for a GI convention, *GI News* ran a full-page photo of a mass meeting of a soldiers' and sailors' soviet. An underground newspaper written by sailors was called the *Potemkin*. Similarly, a navy paper called *All Hands Abandon Ship* was organized by a group calling itself the Potemkin Collective.

74 VVAW, *The Winter Soldier Investigation: An Inquiry into American War Crimes* (Boston: Beacon Press, 1972) pp. 3–4.

75 See Jan Barry, ed., *Peace Is Our Profession: Poems and Passages of War Protest* (Montclair, N.J.: East River Anthology, 1981); Pilger, "Gook Hunter," in Barry, in *Peace Is Our Profession*, p. 286; Platke, "Shoot out at Planet Earth," in Barry, *Peace Is Our Profession*, p. 291; and Holm, "Forgotten Warriors, *Vietnam Generation* 1, no. 2 (Spring 1989): 65.

76 Steve Shuey, interview. See also *Omega Press* 4, no. 8, (Dec. 1973), TL.

77 VVAW, *Winter Soldier Investigation*, p. 156.

78 *Black Unity* 1, no. 2 (Sept. 1970), TL.

79 *Last Harass*, no. 3 (Mar. 1969), TL. This quote was also used in *Gigline* 1, no. 4 (Nov. 1969), TL; and *Graffiti* (Moratorium Issue, 1969), TL.

80 Jim Pechin, interview.

81 OM (Jan. 1970), TL.

82 VVAW leaflet, Box 10, SHSW.

83 Ibid.

84 William Davis, interview.

85 Robert Townsend, interview.

86 *Vietnam GI* (Apr. 1968), TL.

87 Corporal Toby Hoffler, an African American marine from Brooklyn, is cited by Wallace Terry, "Bringing the War Home," *Black Scholar*, 2, no. 3 (Nov. 1970): 6–16.

88 Barry Romo, interview.

89 Lamont Steptoe, interview.

90 Richard Perrin, quoted in Williams, *New Exiles*, p. 169.

91 DeCamp, "G.I. Movement in Asia," p. 115. For other examples of the American Revolution as metaphor in the GI press, see *Omega Press* 1, no. 6 (Apr. 14, 1972), TL; *OM* 1, no. 4 (Oct. 1969), TL; *The Paper* 1, no. 2 (Sept. 28, 1971), TL; *Offul Times*, no. 3 (July 4, 1972), TL; and Williams, *New Exiles*, p. 266.

92 *Fatigue Press*, no. 28 (Feb. 1971), DCPC.

93 James Credel, interview by author, Newark, N.J., July 9, 1992.

94 *Where It's At* 2, no. 2 (undated), TL.

95 *Bragg Briefs*, 2, no. 2 (Sept. 1969), TL.

96 "An Army of People," *The Ally*, no. 21, (Nov. 1969), TL. See also "Hair," *The Ally*, no. 23 (Jan.–Feb 1970), TL. For similar usage of Madison, see *Anchorage Troop* 1, (Jan. 1970), TL.

97 Printed in *Shakedown* 1, no. 8 (Sept. 12. 1969), Rutgers University Special Collections, New Brunswick, N.J.

98 The quote is from Huey Newton, "Towards a New Constitution," *Black Unity* 1, no. 2 (Sept. 1970), TL.

99 *Aboveground* Final Issue (May 1970), TL. For other references to the discourse of the American Revolution in the GI press, see "Democracy in the Military," *Fatigue Press*, no., 29 (May 1971), DCPC; and "Stuck Inside the Stockade," *Fatigue Press*, no. 40 (May 1972), TL; *The Veteran* 11, no. 2 (Spring 1981), DCPC; "Subversive Literature," *Graffiti* (Moratorium Issue 1969), TL. See also "Readers Rap" and "True or False," *Gigline* 1, no. 4 (Nov. 1969), TL; and "The Army and the Bill of Rights," *Left Face 1, no. 4 (1969), TL. Among the numerous literary expressions, see W. D. Ehrhart, "An Address to Middle America," in In the Shadow of Vietnam, pp. 17–20;* and Berenbak, "When Peace Becomes Reality," in Barry, *Peace Is Our Profession*, pp. 195–96.

100 Seidenberg and Short, *A Matter of Conscience*, p. 44.

101 *Winter Soldier* 3, no. 6 (Aug. 1973), DCPC. Also at Fort Bragg, Private Joe Miles was arrested for distributing copies of the Bill of Rights. See Fred Halstead, *GIs Speak Out against the War: The Case of the Ft. Jackson 8* (New York: Pathfinder Press, 1970), p. 7.

102 DeCamp, "GI Movement in Asia," p. 111.

103 *Gigline*, no. 5 (June–July 1970), TL.

104 For other evidence of historically minded actions, see "March to Celebrate Independence," undated MDM leaflet, USSF, Box 5, SHSW; and Servicemen's Liberation Front, leaflet, Mar. 1970, listing ten demands and the Declaration of Independence. Copy in possession of author.

105 David Carter, interview by author, South Bend, Ind., Dec. 3, 1993.

106 "An Army of the People," *The Ally*, no. 21 (Nov. 1969), TL.

107 DuBois, *Souls of Black Folk*, p. 7. See also Harold Cruse, *The Crisis of the Negro Intellectual* (New York: Morrow, 1967), pp. 12ff. 454ff.

108 The historical development of the new soldier is deeply traditional and represents the real development of new social forms. Just as myth cannot renew itself without ritual enactment, history cannot be remade without tradition. Ritual and tradition are the categories of experience in which lived moments and myth or history interact. That is to say that just as ritual is the experience and expression of mythical consciousness, tradition may be understood as the articu-

lation or mobilization of historical consciousness. This tension between new and old orders the dynamic historical power of the soldier ideal. For a discussion of the relative equivalence of myth and history, see Claude Levi-Strauss, *The Savage Mind* (Chicago: University of Chicago Press, 1966), esp. chap. 9. See also Mircea Eliade, *Cosmos and History: The Myth of the Eternal Return* (New York: Harper and Row, 1959), esp. chap. 1. Max Horkhiener and Theodore W. Adorno also present the case for a collapse of the difference between myth and history (*The Dialectic of Enlightenment* [New York: Herder and Herder, 1972]).

109. Among many Vietnam veterans there is a parallel to the new ideals suggested by the military antiwar movement. In a sense the new universals recontextualized the life choices of many veterans who would never call themselves antiwar. Despite a wide difference of opinion on the war itself, Vietnam veterans as a group are highly represented in socially redeeming behavior. Teaching, youth and drug counseling, community work, charitable and volunteer work, health care, and veteran counseling, thousands contribute to heal, nurture, and educate their communities and nation. In most cases these choices and actions reflect the same sort of commitment to community and values typical of the new winter soldiers.

For many soldiers Vietnam reinforced community values in their preexisting, untransformed condition. For elite soldiers who worked as advisers with Vietnamese troops or in small counterinsurgency units, and for some soldiers who fought relatively conventional warfare against North Vietnamese Army NVA regulars, the combat experience approximated their cultural expectations. Even for many other soldiers exposed to the chaos of the war the transformations did not occur. The awareness of divided consciousness or betrayal was not experienced in the same way. Yet this kinship between dissident and more politically conventional veterans is possible because the dynamic of transformation that created soldier and veteran dissent depended upon a strong sense of continuity with earlier-held values. In *Bringing the War Home*, especially chap. 6, John Helmer uses an intensive sociological approach to the study of this question.

Sources

Published sources are cited in full in the Notes.

GI and Veteran Newspapers

GI newspapers were a pervasive but ephemeral media for soldier dissent. Precise dates of publication are often unavailable. The most complete listings, and primary sources for this bibliography, are David Cortright *Soldiers in Revolt: The American Military Today* (Garden City, N.Y.: Anchor Press, Doubleday, 1975). app. B, pp. 283–302; and Harry W..Haines, "Soldiers against the War in Vietnam: The Story of *Aboveground*," *Serials Review* 17, no. 1 (Spring 1991): 85–93.

The following listing contains the name, location, organizational or coffeehouse affiliation (if any), approximate dates of publication, and archive. In addition to the Tamiment Library at New York University (TL), the State Historical Society of Wisconsin in Madison (SHSW), and the Underground Newspaper Collection at Indiana University, Bloomington (UNCUIB), copies of all materials from private collections are in the possession of the author.

About Face. Camp Pendleton and Los Angeles, Calif., GIs and Vietnam Veterans against the War, 1969 to mid 1972, TL.

Aboveground. Fort Carson, Home Front coffeehouse, Colorado Springs, Colo. Aug. 1969 to May 1970, TL.

Act. Paris, France, Resisters inside the Army, Jan. 1968 to 1974, TL.

Aero-spaced. Grissom Air Force Base and Kokomo, Ind., GIs against the War, late 1969 to late 1970, TL.

All Hands Abandon Ship. Newport Naval Base, R.I., Potemkin bookshop, mid 1970 to Nov. 1976, TL.

All Ready on the Left. Camp Pendleton and Oceanside-Vista, Calif. MDM, Aug. 1970 to early 1971, TL.

The Ally. Berkeley, Calif., Spring 1968 to Spring 1972, national and international distribution, TL.

Amex-Canada. Canada, Mar. 1969 to Nov. 1976, WSHS.

Anchorage Troop. Fort Richardson, Elemendorf Air Force Base, and Anchorage, Alas., Jan. 1970 to early 1971, TL.

As You Were. Fort Ord and Monterey, Calif., late 1968 to Apr. 1970, TL.

Attitude Check. Camp Pendleton and Oceanside-Vista, Calif., Mar. 1969, Nov. 1969, Mar. 1970, TL.

The Black Vet. Brooklyn, N.Y., Black Veterans for Social Justice, 1991 to present. Black veterans for Social Justice, 686 Fulton St., Brooklyn, N.Y. 11217.

Black Unity. Camp Pendleton, Calif, Sept. 1970 to mid 1971, TL.

The Bond. New York, N.Y., American Servicemen's Union, June 1967 to 1975, TL.

Bragg Briefs. Fort Bragg, Fayetteville and Spring Lake, N.C., GIs United to End the War: Haymarket Square, Quaker House, Mbari Cultural Center coffeehouses, Spring 1969 to at least late 1974, TL.

Camp News. Chicago, Ill., Chicago Area Military Project, early 1970 to August 1973, national and international distribution, UNCIUB.

Fatigue Press. Fort Hood, Killien, Tex., Oleo Strut coffeehouse, mid 1968 to May 1972. TL and private collection of Dave Cline.

FED-UP. Fort Lewis and Tacoma, Wash., Shelter Half coffeehouse, late 1969 to at least late 1974, TL.

Gigline. Fort Bliss and El Paso, Tex., GIs for Peace, GIs for Peace House coffeehouse, mid 1969 to mid 1972, TL.

GI News and Discussion Bulletin. New York, N.Y., and San Diego, Calif., USSF and GI Project Alliance, Jan. 1971 to at least late 1974, SHSW.

Graffiti. Heidelberg, Germany, 1969 and 1970, TL.

Hansen Free Press. Camp Hansen and Camp Schwab, Kin-Son, Okinawa, Peoples House and United Front coffeehouses, 1972 and 1973, TL.

Last Harass. Fort Gordon and Augusta, Ga., Home in the South coffeehouse, late 1969 to late 1971, TL.

Left Face. Fort McClellan and Anniston, Ala., GIs United against the War, GIs and WACs United coffeehouse, late 1969 to Summer 1972, TL.

Lewis McChord Free Press. Fort Lewis, McChord Air Force Base and Tacoma, Wash., Shelter Half coffeehouse, Aug. 1970 to 1974, TL.

Navy Times Are a Changin'. Great Lakes, Ill., MDM, Feb. 1970 to 1973, TL.

New Army. New York, N.Y., USSF, 1971, SHSW.

Offul Times. Offutt Air Force Base and Omaha, Neb., Omaha Military Project, Apr. 1972 to 1973, TL.

OM. The Pentagon and Washington, D.C., Apr. 1968 to 1970, TL.

Omega Press. Koza, Okinawa, Omega House and People's House coffeehouses, Pacific Counseling Services, 1973, TL.

The Paper. Cherry Point Marine Corps Air Station and Cherry Point, N.C., Aug. 1971 to Fall 1972, TL.

People's Press. Fort Campbell and Clarksville, Tenn., People's House coffeehouse, early 1971 to Fall 1972, TL.

Rage. Camp Lejeune, New River Marine Corps Air Station, N.C., Jacksonville Defense Committee, Fall 1971 to at least late 1974, TL.

Right-on Post. Fort Ord, Seaside, Calif., MDM, 1970, Reproduced in House Committee on Internal Security, *Hearings before the Committee on Internal Security*, 92d Cong., 2d sess., part 3, 1972.

Shakedown. Fort Dix, N.J., Coffeehouse coffeehouse, Mar. 1969 to Apr. 1970, Alexander Library, Rutgers University, New Brunswick, N.J., and TL.

Short Times. Fort Jackson and Columbia, S.C., The UFO coffeehouse, 1968 to Spring 1972, TL.

Task Force. San Francisco, Aug. 1968 to 1969, WSHS.

Travisty. Travis Air Force Base and Suisun City, Calif., Summer 1971 to Fall, 1973, TL.

Up against the Bulkhead. San Francisco, Calif., MDM, early 1970 to at least late 1974, TL.

Up from the Bottom. San Diego, Calif., Concerned Military and Center for Servicemen's Rights, Sept. 1971 to at least late 1974, TL.

The Veteran. Chicago, VVAW, Mar. 1976 to present, national distribution, VVAW national office, Chicago, Ill.

Veterans Stars and Stripes for Peace. Chicago, Veterans for Peace, Sept. 1967 to 1972, national distribution, TL.

Vietnam GI. Chicago, Ill., late 1967 to June 1969, international distribution, TL.

Where Are We? Fort Huachuca and Davis Monthan Air Force Base, Ariz., May 1971 to mid 1972, TL.

Where It's At. West Berlin, Germany, Apr. 1968 to 1970, TL.

Winter Soldier. Chicago, VVAW, 1970 to 1976, national distribution, VVAW national office, Chicago Ill.

Womens' Newsletter. New York, N.Y., USSF, Aug. 1970, WSHS.

Interviews

Arm, Ron. Madison, Wisc. Nov. 13, 1993. Vietnam veteran, member of the VVAW.

Bailey, Annie, Milwaukee, Wis. Mar, 21, 1990. Member and past Midwest coordinator of the VVAW.

Barry, Jan. Montclair, N.J. June 5, 1985. Vietnam veteran, cofounder and founding president of the VVAW.

Bradley, Thomas. Asbury Park, N.J. May 24, 1985. Vietnam veteran.

Brown, John. Lakewood, N.J. Feb. 1, 1990. Vietnam veteran, veteran counselor.

Carter, David. South Bend, Ind. Dec. 3, 1993. Vietnam veteran, Agent Orange activist.

Chitty, Ben. New York, N.Y. Jan. 5, 1994. Vietnam veteran, member and current East Coast coordinator of the VVAW.

Chomsky, Judith. Philadelphia, PA. Dec. 20, 1989. Lawyer, antiwar activist, and GI counselor.

Cline, David. Jersey City, N.J. Mar. 1, 1988. Vietnam veteran, member and national coordinator of the VVAW, member of the VFP.

Cline, David. Correspondence to his parents dated Aug. 17, 1967. Letter was donated to the author by the writer.

Credel, James. Newark, N.J. July 9, 1992. Vietnam veteran, past president of the National Association of Black Veterans.

Cross, Joe. New York, N.Y. Jan. 18, 1994. Vietnam veteran, member VVAW.

Curry, David. Speech at twentieth anniversary of Dewey Canyon III, Washington, D.C., Apr. 14, 1991 (recorded by author). Vietnam veteran, member and past national office staff of the VVAW.

Davis, William. Chicago, Ill. Mar. 18, 1990. Vietnam veteran, member and past national coordinator of the VVAW.

Greely, Dennis. Newark, N.J. July 12, 1985. Vietnam veteran, veteran counselor.

Greenberg, Joel. Chicago, Ill. Mar. 17, 1990. Vietnam veteran, member of the VVAW.

Heaney, Mike. New Brunswick, N.J. Oct. 5, 1988. Vietnam veteran, American historian.

Hirschmann, Ann. Cranbury, N.J. May 8, 1991. Nurse, member of the VVAW.

Jameson, Linda. Madison, Wis. Nov. 13, 1993. Member of the VVAW.

Jesperson, Jess. Milwaukee, Wis. Mar. 21, 1990. Vietnam veteran, member and current Midwest regional coordinator of the VVAW.

Klein, Jack. Milwaukee, Wis. Mar. 20, 1990. Vietnam veteran, member of the VVAW.

Kroll, Dennis. Madison, Wis. Mar. 25, 1990. Vietnam veteran, member of the VVAW.

Lears, Jackson. New Brunswick, N.J. Sept. 14, 1988. Vietnam-era veteran, American historian.

Leepson, Marc. South Bend, Ind. Dec. 4, 1993. Vietnam veteran, member of the VVA and arts editor for the VVA *Veteran*.

Lindquist, John. Milwaukee, Wis. Mar. 22, 1990. Vietnam veteran, member and past national coordinator of the VVAW.

Muscari, Vince. Interviewed by Pacer Smith. New York, N.Y. June 25, 1994. Vietnam veteran, member of the VVAW and Gay Veterans Association.

Osmer, Guy. Wanaque, N.J. June 21, 1985. Vietnam veteran, past member of the VVAW.

Romo, Barry. Chicago, Ill. Mar. 18, 1990. Vietnam veteran, member and national coordinator of the VVAW.

Payton, Greg. Irvington, N.J. Dec. 1, 1989. Vietnam veteran, member of the VVAW.

Pechin, Jim. South Bend, Ind. Dec. 3, 1993. Vietnam veteran, past member of the VVAW, member of the VVA.

Pinchinson, Lou. Highland Park, N.J. Feb. 4, 1990. Vietnam era veteran, past member of the VVAW.

Schnall, Susan. New York, N.Y. Oct. 25, 1990. Vietnam-era veteran, GI movement leader.

Schultz, Elroy. Two Rivers, Wis. Mar. 21, 1990. Vietnam veteran, member of the VVAW.

Shaughnessy, Charles. Washington, D.C. Apr. 25, 1991. Vietnam veteran, member of the VVAW.

Shuey, Steven. Somerset, N.J. Jan. 14, 1988. Vietnam veteran, veteran advocate, past member VVAW, member VVA.

Sowders, Ed. New Brunswick, N.J. Apr. 4, 1991, and June 1, 1989. Vietnam veteran, past member of the VVAW.

Steptoe, Lamont. Philadelphia, Pa. Feb. 23, 1989. Vietnam veteran, poet.

Sutton, Michael. Chicago, Ill. Mar. 18, 1990. Vietnam veteran, member of the VFP.

Torres, Jose. Milwaukee, Wis. Nov. 12, 1993. Vietnam veteran, advocate for homeless veterans, member of the Oneida Nation Veteran Advisory Council, member of the VVAW.

Townsend, Robert. Highland Park, N.J. July 10, 1985. Vietnam veteran.

Upton, John. Washington, D.C. Apr. 25, 1991. Vietnam veteran, member of the VVAW.

Urgo, Joe. New York, N.Y. July 2, 1985. Vietnam veteran, past member of the VVAW, member of the VVAW-AI.

Whiteagle, Morgan. Madison, Wis. Nov. 11, 1993. Winnebago elder.

Wilders, William. Personal correspondence to James F. Wilders. Copy donated to author by Gabrielle Wilders.

Zastrow, Peter. Chicago, Ill. Mar. 16, 1990. Vietnam veteran, member and national coordinator of the VVAW.

Government Documents

BDM Corporation. *A Study of Strategic Lessons Learned in Vietnam.* 9 vol. Distributed by Defense Technical Information Center, Defense Logistics Agency, Alexandria, Va., 1979. Microfilm published by Scholarly Resources Inc. and Navy Historical Library, Washington, D.C.

House Committee on Internal Security. "Investigations of Attempts to Subvert the United States Armed Forces," 3 vol. 92d Cong., 2d sess., 1972.

National Archives, Suitland Reference Branch, Washington, D.C. "Inspector General Report of Investigation no. 72–11." Records of the United States Forces in Southeast Asia, 1950–75, Record Group 472.

Olson, Howard C., and R. William Rae. *The Determination of the Potential for Dissidence in the U.S. Army,* vol. 1: *Nature of Dissent.* McLean, Va.: Research Analysis Corporation, 1971. Rae, R. William, Stephen B. Forman, and Howard Olson. *Future Impact of Dissident Elements within the Army on the Enforcement of Discipline, Law and Order,* vol. 2, McLean, Va.: Research Analysis Corporation, 1972.

Unpublished Manuscripts

Berg, Manfred. "Soldiers and Citizens: War and Voting Rights in American History." 1993. German Historical Institute, 1607 New Hampshire Ave., N.W., Washington D.C. 20009.

Hayes, James Robert. "The War within a War: Dissent in the Military with an Emphasis on the Vietnam Era." Ph.D diss., University of Connecticut, 1975.

Kaledin, Eugenia. "Lexington, Mass.: Memorial Day 1971." Paper presented at America and Vietnam: From War to Peace, Notre Dame University, Dec. 4, 1993.

Mariscal, George. " 'Our Kids Don't Have Blue Eyes, but They Go Overseas to Die': Chicanos in Vietnam." (Paper presented at America and Vietnam: From War to Peace, Notre Dame University, Dec. 4, 1993.

Mavis, Ralph. " 'I'm Not a Murderer, nor Am I a Hero': Troop Culture among Combat Veterans in Vietnam." Paper presented at the Organization of American Historians annual meeting, Anaheim California, Apr. 1993.

Reiff, John David. "Human Dignity under Attack: The Political and Military Socialization of Vietnam Veterans." Ph.D diss., University of Michigan, 1982.

Retzer, Joseph David. "War and Political Ideology: The Roots of Radicalism among Vietnam Veterans." Ph.D diss., Yale University, 1976.

Wikler, Norma Juliet. "Vietnam and the Veterans' Consciousness: Pre-Political Thinking among American Soldiers." Ph.D diss., University of California, Berkeley.

Archives

Fisk University Library, Fisk Oral History Collection. Fifteen African American Vietnam veterans on tape.

Indiana University, Bloomington, Ind., Underground Press Collection. Underground newspapers on microfilm.

State Historical Society of Wisconsin, Social Action Collections. The papers of the VVAW, VFP, USSF, and underground newspapers.

Tamiment Library, New York University, New York, N.Y. Underground newspapers.

Film

Different Sons. Jack Ofield and Arthur Littman. 1970. Bowling Green Films, 309 5th Ave. #412, Brooklyn, NY 11215.

Invisible Force: Women in the Military. Based on a conference sponsored by the William Joiner Center, Nov. 1985. Video, copyright 1986. William Joiner Center, University of Massachusetts—Boston, 100 Morrissey Blvd., Boston, MA. 02125.

It's Only the Beginning. Vietnam Veterans against the War, 1972. VVAW Inc., National Office, P.O. Box 408594, Chicago, Ill. 60640.

"A Program for Vietnam Vets and Everyone Else Who Cares." Chicago: WTTW Chicago in association with the Office of the Dean of Students, University of Wisconsin at Madison. Video. VVAW Inc., National Office, P.O. Box 408594, Chicago Ill. 60640.

The Winter Soldier. Winterfilm. 1972. 20/20 Productions, P.O. Box 198, Chesterfield, N.H. 03443.

Index

About the Author

RICHARD R. MOSER received his Ph.D. from Rutgers University in 1992. He is assistant professor of history at Middle Tennessee State University and resides in Nashville. Mr. Moser's previously published work, "Vietnam Oral History and Our Popular Memory of War," was included in *The Legacy: The Vietnam War in the American Imagination* edited by D. Michael Shafer (1990).